RE
DON'T MES

"Courage, above all things, is the first quality of a warrior."—Carl von Clausewitz. *Don't Mess with This Mama,* is an inspiring story of how one family showed warrior-like courage through the challenge of international adoption. As a person involved in caring for the orphans in Haiti since 2003, I believe that all children need a warrior to advocate for them. This story challenges readers to ask themselves: "Whose hero am I?".

Andrea P. McGinniss, executive director,
Hands and Feet Project, Inc.

Don't Mess with This Mama is a compelling, real-life story that I couldn't put down. It reveals the nature of our Father as one who contends against Hell or high water for us to be *His*—gathered from across the world into our identity as sons and daughters.

My eyes welled up with tears, my heart was full, and my hope was on the edge of its seat. Missy has beautifully interwoven their tumultuous family story with realities of fear, faith, and love that we all encounter when God calls us out on the waters. Grow with them on their adventure while continuing to believe God for your own!

Joey LeTourneau, author of *If God Had a House* and
director of ACTS Family: World

Don't Mess with This Mama is an honest and transparent telling of a heart-journey...one of a life-saving pursuit, no matter the inconvenience, obstacles, danger, or cost involved.

I highly recommend this book. *Don't Mess with This Mama* will touch your heart and open your eyes to those in need of love around you and provoke you to action.

Rebecca Nichols Alonzo, *New York Times* bestselling author of *The Devil in Pew Number Seven*

Missy beautifully captures the heart of a mother struck with compassion and a will to fight for a child she loved before she ever saw her face. It is a love that few can understand unless you have had your heart pierced to the core through adoption. These kids pull love out of us that we never knew we had. Thank you, Missy, for capturing this story in a way that beautifully challenges everyone who reads it to stand stronger in their faith, no matter what their battle may be. God is faithful.

Kelly Putty, founder of Ordinary Hero

The story of FAVOR is an incredible story of FAITH! I personally walked through this journey with the Worton Family in friendship, prayer, emails, texts, and FaceTime. Missy did such an excellent job in vividly recalling every detail. You will be uplifted, inspired, and blessed by *Don't Mess with This Mama*!

Angie DeBlieux-Bryan, entertainment executive consultant, producer, and friend

Missy Worton's book *Don't Mess with This Mama* is riveting! I could not put it down as each chapter pulls you into the next. Missy has written it so masterfully that you ride the crazy rollercoaster of adoption in Ethiopia with them, feeling the emotions and experiencing the drama as it plays out. *Don't Mess with This Mama* tells the story of a real family, real fears, real danger and real love. In its pages, Missy inspires hope and pours courage into the reader to live out their own story with faith.

This page-turner is also so pertinent given the challenging global issues with adoption and human trafficking.

Denise Padayachee, Wells Training and Missions NPC founder, author of *The Book of Acts, Practical Guide to accessing the miracle power of God.*

Don't Mess with This Mama is a truly inspirational story of a fearless mama that rescued her daughter from the enemy's clutches in Ethiopia! This story releases the very overcoming spirit we are destined to walk in as sons and daughters of a supernatural God. You will see how, through divine intervention and angelic protection, this mama, Missy, and her husband, Mark, were able to leap over every obstacle to bring their daughter home. This family's journey brings hope for promises fulfilled and joy in the fulfillment! Missy is my hero and I am so honored to be her friend. She has taught me so much about the Father's love from living in a place of being "seated" inside His heart.

This book is a testimony of triumph against all odds and it will leave you expectant for more.

Kimberly Rivera,
Christian Recording Artist, and friend

Don't Mess with This Mama
Risking Everything to Rescue Our Daughter

Paperback ISBN: 978-1-64746-124-9
Hardback ISBN: 978-1-64746-125-6
Ebook ISBN: 978-1-64746-126-3

Library of Congress Control Number: 2020901114

Printed in The United States of America
Published by Author Academy Elite
P.O. Box 43, Powell, OH 43035
www.AuthorAcademyElite.com

Editor: Loral Pepoon, cowriterpro.com
Cover Art: © 2020
Cover Design: Debbie O'Byrne
Photos used in this book are the Worton's family photographs.

Missy Worton's book *Don't Mess with This Mama* is riveting! I could not put it down as each chapter pulls you into the next. Missy has written it so masterfully that you ride the crazy rollercoaster of adoption in Ethiopia with them, feeling the emotions and experiencing the drama as it plays out. *Don't Mess with This Mama* tells the story of a real family, real fears, real danger and real love. In its pages, Missy inspires hope and pours courage into the reader to live out their own story with faith.

This page-turner is also so pertinent given the challenging global issues with adoption and human trafficking.

Denise Padayachee, Wells Training and Missions NPC founder, author of *The Book of Acts, Practical Guide to accessing the miracle power of God.*

Don't Mess with This Mama is a truly inspirational story of a fearless mama that rescued her daughter from the enemy's clutches in Ethiopia! This story releases the very overcoming spirit we are destined to walk in as sons and daughters of a supernatural God. You will see how, through divine intervention and angelic protection, this mama, Missy, and her husband, Mark, were able to leap over every obstacle to bring their daughter home. This family's journey brings hope for promises fulfilled and joy in the fulfillment! Missy is my hero and I am so honored to be her friend. She has taught me so much about the Father's love from living in a place of being "seated" inside His heart.

This book is a testimony of triumph against all odds and it will leave you expectant for more.

Kimberly Rivera,
Christian Recording Artist, and friend

Don't Mess with This Mama
Risking Everything to Rescue Our Daughter

Paperback ISBN: 978-1-64746-124-9
Hardback ISBN: 978-1-64746-125-6
Ebook ISBN: 978-1-64746-126-3

Library of Congress Control Number: 2020901114

Printed in The United States of America
Published by Author Academy Elite
P.O. Box 43, Powell, OH 43035
www.AuthorAcademyElite.com

Editor: Loral Pepoon, cowriterpro.com
Cover Art: © 2020
Cover Design: Debbie O'Byrne
Photos used in this book are the Worton's family photographs.

Editorial liberties: Names of God and references to Him are capitalized, and satan and the enemy are lowercased. For security reasons, names of selected individuals as well as the name of the place where Missy and Mark's apartment (referred to The Academy in the book) has been changed.

Disclaimer:

The conversations in this book all come from the author's recollections, as well as, several of the individuals featured in this book. They are not written to represent word-for-word transcripts. Rather the author has re-told them in a way that evokes the feeling and meaning of what was said. In all instances, the essence of the dialogue is a close and accurate account of what took place. The author has changed the names of several individuals and places, and may have changed some identifying characteristics and details for the protection of many in this book.

DON'T MESS *With This* MAMA

Risking It All to Rescue Our Daughter

A TRUE STORY

MISSY MAXWELL WORTON

FOREWORD BY CHRIS OVERSTREET

Dedicated to

my Amazing and Loving

Father

Curtis Lile Maxwell Jr.

(July 11, 1924–September 13, 2016)

You gave me the courage to always

choose what was right—not easy.

You taught me to give generously, love deeply,

and speak for those who have no voice.

I learned to value all individuals,

not by what they could

add to my life, but because they were God's creation.

I learned to love unconditionally by watching you.

FOREWORD

It was October of 2012, when my wife, Stefanie, and I (Chris Overstreet) were unexpectedly redirected to Addis Ababa, Ethiopia, where we would meet Missy Worton in a hotel lobby. Later I would find out that God had strategically designed that meeting—one of His many divine appointments in the gripping story told in the pages ahead of *Don't Mess with This Mama.*

The circumstances felt like we were in a movie. Halfway into our connecting flight from Uganda, where we had been working with a mission's outreach, to Rome on our way home to America, the pilot came over the speaker announcing that our flight had been redirected to Ethiopia due to Hurricane Sandy. Ethiopia! My wife and I were exhausted as we went to retrieve our bags. The airline had promised us a nice hotel to sleep in and a ride to and from the airport for our trouble. We were looking forward to a good night sleep after being on an airplane most of the day.

When we arrived at our hotel, I looked at Stefanie and said, "This doesn't feel right. The guy standing outside is a pimp." That was just the beginning, as we walked into our hotel room Stefanie screamed as we both watched a cockroach crawling across the bed. "Okay, we are not staying here," I said. We walked down the steps and got a ride back to the airport. Where we hoped to find another hotel, preferably without bugs joining us. The hotels were booked around the city, but miraculously, at the last minute, we got the last available room at the Addis Ababa Hilton. Praise God! I felt like the Lord had specifically reserved that room for us. We were so thankful and happy to have a nice clean bed to catch up on some needed rest.

The following day we decided to make the most of being in Ethiopia and adventured around the city near the hotel where we were staying. As we walked, I began to think about the deep biblical history in Ethiopia. I thought about Philip and how thankful I was that he said yes to obey the Lord. I want to specifically share this story because it demonstrates how God knows how to get us to the right place to make an impact on others around us. The Ethiopian man was near Philip, and Philip was used by God to impact all of Ethiopia with the gospel.

> Acts 8:26–40, NIV, says: "Now an angel of the Lord said to Philip, "Go south to the road—the desert road—that goes down from Jerusalem to Gaza." So, he started out, and on his way he met an Ethiopian eunuch, an important official in charge of all the treasury of the Kandake (which means "queen of the Ethiopians"). This man had gone to Jerusalem to worship, and on his way home was sitting in his chariot reading the Book of Isaiah the prophet. The Spirit told Philip, "Go to that chariot and stay near it."
>
> Then Philip ran up to the chariot and heard the man reading Isaiah the prophet. "Do you understand what you are reading?" Philip asked.
>
> "How can I," he said, "unless someone explains it to me?" So he invited Philip to come up and sit with him.
>
> This is the passage of Scripture the eunuch was reading:
>
> *"He was led like a sheep to the slaughter.*
> *And as a lamb before its shearer is silent,*
> *So he did not open his mouth.*
> *In his humiliation he was deprived of justice.*

> *Who can speak of his descendants?*
> *For his life was taken from the earth."*
>
> The eunuch asked Philip, "Tell me, please, who is the prophet talking about, himself or someone else?" Then Philip began with that very passage of Scripture and told him the good news about Jesus.
>
> As they traveled along the road, they came to some water and the eunuch said, "Look, here is water. What can stand in the way of my being baptized?" And he gave orders to stop the chariot. Then both Philip and the eunuch went down into the water and Philip baptized him. When they came up out of the water, the Spirit of the Lord suddenly took Philip away, and the eunuch did not see him again, but went on his way rejoicing. Philip, however, appeared at Azotus and traveled about, preaching the gospel in all the towns until he reached Caesarea."

After spending a few hours in the city, we returned to the hotel to pack and return to the airport. We were hoping to find a flight back to America. Little did I know then that a "God appointment" was about to happen. He was going to put two people in the right place at the right time for His purposes—just as He had done in Philip's story. As we walked out of the elevator, I saw a woman with her daughter sitting on a nearby couch. That woman was Missy Worton.

I thought she and her family had possibly been on the same flight as my wife and I, so I asked if they were also stranded from the storm. I found out their plane had just landed, and they were about to adopt their second child from Ethiopia. Missy began to share the difficulties they had run into trying to adopt their little girl. She and her husband were preparing for a rescue mission with others to deliver their daughter from a bad situation.

As Missy began to talk about their situation, I felt the heart of God for this family and my utmost respect went out to them. *Wow*, I thought, *here is a family that loves Jesus and His children so much.* Missy pointed at her husband, Mark, who was checking the family in at the hotel counter, and to her daughter, McKenzie, who momentarily looked up and gave us a smile then returned to her nap. As I listened to Missy tell me about what they had gone through to adopt this child and how they were planning a rescue mission the next morning, the only word that came to my mind was "favor." *Lord, give them favor*! I thought. I knew God had given this family favor in this situation. I felt the unction of the Holy Spirit lead me to pray with her and declare ***the Lord is giving you favor. He is with you***. I strongly felt that God was with them and they would find favor in the journey. When we finished praying, Missy was grinning and began to laugh. "Did I tell you her name was Favor?" she said. Little did I know that the little girl she was rescuing was named Favor. Missy hadn't told me, but God in His goodness had declared He was giving them "Favor."

I walked away from that conversation and told Stefanie how strongly I had felt God with them and what they were getting ready to do. I had no idea if my path would ever again cross with Mark and Missy.

Sometime later, I was at Bethel in Redding, California, when a woman approached me who was good friends with Missy. She told me part of the outcome and asked if she could put me in contact with the Wortons, so that I could hear their story firsthand. Missy contacted me a few days later and shared how they rescued their daughter, Favor. She told me how much she and her husband had been encouraged by a prophecy I had spoken over her at an event in Tennessee months before we ever met in Addis Ababa, and then by the prayer I had declared over their situation in Ethiopia. God strategically put me where they were in Ethiopia at the time when they were there to strengthen their faith and brought hope.

As you read this powerful and compelling real-life story, you will discover that God's love will lead you to places that you never thought you would ever go to bring hope and healing to others. I believe that this book will inspire many people to hope again, trust again, and to never give up no matter how tough things may get.

Be prepared as you read *Don't Mess with This Mama* to go on a journey as if you are with the Worton family, as they do their part to rescue Favor. My prayer is that God would not only reveal to you how much He loves you and how much he loves others but also that you will see how He equips willing people to participate in His amazing work as He fights the battles.

With Love and Great Respect,
Chris Overstreet

Evangelist
President & Founder of Compassion to Action
www.compassiontoaction.com

OUR JOURNEY INTO ADOPTION AND INTO DON'T MESS WITH THIS MAMA

If you had told me that we would adopt 10 years ago—and that I would write a book about part of our experience—I would have not believed you. Don't get me wrong, we supported adoption, and we helped others raise support to bring home their adopted children. We just never saw ourselves called to it. My husband Mark and I were totally content with the two beautiful children God had blessed us with in our comfortable middle Tennessee home.

Then, suddenly, everything changed.

I received an email forwarded from a friend, who had adopted internationally, about some "waiting children" in desperate need of a forever family. Waiting Children are orphans who are in one of three categories: they are usually past the age of five, are a sibling group, or are special needs.

I remember opening that email—it's when time stopped, and it was the catalyst for our world changing forever. It was also the first time I saw Shewit, our first adopted child. I gazed at a little mischievous boy with a grin that would brighten up any day, holding a pink soccer ball.

Something happened. I mean really happened deep inside my soul—I immediately loved him. My eyes quickly filled with tears as if I were seeing a piece of me that had been missing from my life. I had an overwhelming desire to help him. I wanted the best for his life. I wanted this little boy to achieve all God had destined him for. What I didn't realize then is that I was tapping into the heart of God. The call of adoption...loving another as your own, wanting the best for his or her life... mirrors how our Heavenly Father adopted us as His own and has great plans for us. That call is valuing another no matter the personal cost.

It took much courage to move forward into adoption, and we didn't take it lightly. We knew this was another child to raise up and provide for. Mark especially battled with the idea until he had an "aha" moment—a revelation hit him that Joseph acted as an adoptive father to Jesus. *If God chose Joseph, an ordinary man, to raise the son of God in his most formative years, why wouldn't he use me to raise an orphan to be a son?* The Bible may not say that Jesus was adopted, but we do know that Joseph had a big part in Jesus's developing years, serving as a father figure. Raising a child that He puts in our lives is clearly part of God's plan—and we felt compelled to answer the call.

Some people ask us why we adopted from Ethiopia and not from America. My answer is simple. God chose the children we would adopt—we didn't go shopping. The email had been a divine appointment about that particular child. Shewit's adoption was flawless and simple from the word go.

Adopting Favor, our second adopted child and the journey described in this book, was an extraordinarily challenging, almost unbelievable experience.

I don't want readers to think most adoptions are as complicated as the story represented in this book—they aren't.

I believe that our unusual, rare story happened for God's purposes—to radically grow our faith, our marriage, our willingness to sacrifice our lives for His purposes, and our ability to affect others beyond our family.

Through our journey, we found that sometimes life looks like an obstacle course with seemingly impossible circumstances that block our path to fulfill those God-given purposes. In reality those "impossible" blocks are the fortifiers of our faith that we need to see Him overcome to prepare us for the next steps in His purposes for us.

Our story is a journey about receiving the love and favor that God has placed on our lives as His sons and daughters. It's about finding the warrior-like courage to do something way beyond our comfort zone and discovering the value of life in the most unlikely places. It's also about believing that God really does have great plans for each of us—just as Jeremiah 29:11 tells us—despite what our circumstances look like.

In every step of our journey, remembering what God had promised us and what He had done previously enabled us to tune out the voices of doubt, fear, and failure. We pushed forward knowing life had more for us. We continue to believe the cry of every human heart that says: "I was made for something more. I was made for greatness. I was made to be courageous. I was made to impact others to be more." And, by God's grace, our story did and is affecting others.

An Invitation for You to Receive God's Love and Love Others Like a Warrior "Mama"

Mark and I want to invite you on a journey of radical faith. As you read our story, *Don't Mess with This Mama,* we hope you will discover or rediscover that you are highly favored by a God who cares about you—a God who is bigger than any of your difficult circumstances. May you always choose to love, overcome, and be courageous in every challenging situation you encounter.

I wrote this book to invite all of you to rise up and hear the "mama" call beating in your heart. You don't have to be a biological or adoptive mama, or even a woman to know the calling of a warrior spirit that rises up on behalf of another. It seeks out justice for those who are set for destruction and have no voice of their own. It guards, protects, and fights for the good of another no matter the personal cost.

We pray that God will not only encourage you with His love but that He will also grow the warrior "mama" in you to help whomever He may put in your path. Some of you, as have many who have heard our story, may be led to join the fight to help orphans and those in human trafficking situations. If that happens to you as you read, I encourage you to pray, and to see the section at the end of the book called "How You Can Help."

May God bless each of you.
Mark and Missy Worton

PROLOGUE

Daniel's Dream

TWO YEARS EARLIER—Debre Birhan, Ethiopia

The tall African grass swayed back and forth.
Left to right, right to left.
Hidden within was something evil, steadily moving forward.
Left to right, right to left.
Systematically stalking its prey.

We start a soccer game on the courtyard in the small orphanage we call home, until our forever families come and take us to America. Soccer is the best way to spend the day for most of us, especially a nine-year-old boy like me.

With just one glance, you can see that our orphanage is in drastic need of repairs. The smell of poverty surrounds us, but we don't notice. Dust kicks up as we race after the ball, yelling directions as if we are playing the World Cup Championship. I aim at our makeshift goal, and I kick the ball right between my two friends into the grassy area.

"Goal!" I yell, as my arms shoot up and my teammates gather around me in triumph. It doesn't matter that we don't have a fancy ball or a big goal—this is soccer at its best. I run to retrieve the ball now resting next to the tall tin fence that protects the orphanage.

As I step into the tall grass, I stop abruptly. I can still hear my mother's voice warning me to be careful when walking into grassy areas. But there, next to the fence, is our most valued possession. I forget my mother's warnings and run through the grass, picking up our ball and brushing it off.

Suddenly, I feel something move behind me.

I turn to look in the direction of the movement. I can feel my eyes widening with fear. I know the pattern well and it is coming directly at me.

Left to right, right to left.

There is no escape.

"What's wrong with you? Throw the ball in," one of my friends yells.

I can't move.

I know I need to warn my friends, but when I open my mouth, no words come. Paralyzed, I watch the nightmare unfold. My heart is beating louder than my thoughts. I can feel my breath struggling to get out.

"Daniel, throw the ball in," my friends yell again. They are unaware of the horror that is beginning to happen.

I slowly start backing up toward my friends, gripping the ball in my hands, with my eyes firmly fixed on the moving grass.

Left to right, right to left.

I try to swallow, but my mouth is dry. Something huge is coming directly toward me.

Left to right, right to left.

Now, only a few tall blades of grass are left between this giant stalker and me.

A loud car horn blows. I scream and run towards the courtyard, dropping the ball in my panic.

A huge python breaks through the bushes behind me, slithering toward us. We all scream in horror, not knowing where to run. The snake's tail whips around our feet and wraps itself around a few of our bodies, squeezing us together.

The nurse runs out as she hears our blood-curdling cries. She sees the python and starts screaming for help. I can see the workers running from every direction.

We are now trapped in a corner near the far side of the fence, looking at the piercing gaze of a terrifying enemy.

The python's tail squeezes us closer together as it draws near. We are all trembling as his eyes begin to study his prey.

The families and workers watch from a distance in disbelief—helpless.

One of the groundsmen grabs a large shovel and runs toward the python in a desperate attempt to help us. The python whips around and strikes at him. He stumbles back a few steps and falls to the ground, completely vulnerable as the python rises above him.

I can feel that the python has loosened its hold on us. We squeeze out and run toward the van as fast as we can. Our movement catches the python's attention and it tightens around those still trying to escape. Several of my friends—other children who were also trapped—jump over the creature and run into the arms of the waiting family members, who pull them into the van and shut the door.

I run the other way, through the grass and into my family's arms, relieved to be safe. I turn to see if all my friends have escaped to safety, but four children are still trapped by the python. I don't recognize any of them. I watch as they stand paralyzed, suffocating under the stare of a threatening hunter who is moving in for the kill.

* * * * *

Daniel bolted up from his bed, covered in sweat and gasping for air. The nightmare was too real to dismiss.

Who are these four children?

He knew God was warning of an unseen danger coming to keep the children at the orphanage from their forever families...A "python" spirit.

"The enemy comes to steal, kill and destroy," Daniel whispered to himself. He pulled back the covers, knelt beside his bed and began to pray.

CHAPTER 1
FINDING FAVOR

"As the world slips into the deepest darkness, the greatest lights will emerge... Warriors who have not come to kill and destroy, but to heal and set the captives free."

—Rick Joyner, author of *The Final Quest*

July 1, 2011 was a beautiful summer morning in Tennessee. My husband Mark and I stood on our dilapidated back deck, looking over some plans that I had drawn for a backyard makeover. We had that one yard in the neighborhood that was always mowed but badly needed a landscaper and some personality. Mark had received a big bonus from his company, and I was anxious to make our backyard more enjoyable for the whole family. As I pulled off a rotting piece of wood from our railing, I looked around and noticed weeds growing out of what once was my failed attempt to grow a container garden. It's safe to say that with my brown thumb, we would be in serious trouble if my family had to rely on me to grow our food.

"I wish it could be done right now," I joked. "Tomorrow would be great—like how they do it on HGTV."

"We've waited seven years," Mark said. "What's another few months?"

In our family, Mark is the one who is patient—a wonderful quality for raising kids or bringing some balance and boundaries in a hectic world—but it also means he's not going to jump into anything very quickly, especially if it costs much money. He also stands six feet tall next to my *almost* five-foot frame, which makes him extremely hard to argue with, especially since I have to look up to him to make my point.

"True, but it would be nice to enjoy it before it gets cold!" I said with a raised voice, as Mark walked into the house. Mr. Wisdom had already spoken and left the scene.

My phone rang. It was my friend and neighbor, Cindy. Cindy and her husband had adopted five children from Ethiopia, and she was a vocal advocate for the millions of orphans around the world. Her teenage daughter, Hope, had inherited that same spirit and was spending her summer in Ethiopia, interning for Covenant Orphanages.

"Did you see the email I sent you?" she asked.

"No, not yet," I answered. "Did you send something good?"

"Well, yes! Hope emailed me last night from the orphanage in Ethiopia. She's met a little girl who she says fits perfectly into your family. Hope says that she's a definite Worton."

"What do you mean, she's a definite Worton?" I asked. *She must be really loud and obnoxious to fit into this family!* I thought.

"She's just full of life and sweet and you're not going to believe what her name is..." Cindy paused dramatically. "Her name is Favor!"

My heart leapt and my eyes immediately started to water. "Did you say...Favor?" I asked. "As in God's favor?"

"Yes...Favor!" Cindy answered. "I knew you would just love that. You're always praying for favor."

She was right. As long as I could remember, I was always praying for the blessing of favor, talking about the love of God's favor, and praying God's favor over others. Favor was one of the best descriptions of God's unmerited grace. I had heard Graham Cooke, a Christian speaker, say, "Favor is a divine advantage at work in someone. We're not given favor because of who we are, or what we've done, but who Jesus is in us."[1] Favor was definitely one of my "go-to" favorite words.

Tears filled my eyes as I listened to Cindy tell me what Hope had seen at the orphanage where she was interning.

"Hope said that Favor just came into the orphanage. She is an older child, around five or six years old. She's precious."

Favor's name called out and grabbed me by the heart with a familiar sound. I knew that God had sent Hope to this orphanage to meet Favor. I had prayed for favor my whole life, but now it was connected to a little orphan girl who I knew needed us.

"Email Hope, and she'll tell you all about her," Cindy said. "Let me know what you find out. I am so excited!"

I hung up the phone. My heart was pounding out of my chest, and I knew I was pregnant with the thought of adding a sweet—and possibly loud—little girl to our family. I immediately hunted down Mark, who was busy working in the office.

"Hey, you got a moment? I just talked to Cindy and she's got some exciting news from Hope in Ethiopia."

Mark looked up at me with a *I'm not sure I want to hear this*, mixed with a *What is my wife getting us into now?* look.

"So, what has Hope been up to in Ethiopia?" he asked.

I paused, wanting to choose my words wisely, then threw all caution to the wind. "She met a little girl who needs a family," I blurted out.

He looked at me, not saying a word, then took a deep breath. "Well, then tell Hope to adopt her."

"Mark! Her name is Favor, and Hope says she's a definite Worton," I said.

"Why is she always trying to add children to our family?" Mark asked. "Did you ask her to be looking while she was there?"

"Mark, I have always told you that I knew there was another child out there for us, and I have always known that it was a girl," I said, as my mind suddenly went back to a reoccurring dream that I'd been having since we'd found out that our first adopted son, Shewit, had a sister. She would've been about the same age that Favor was now. We had such high hopes to adopt her until we were told that she had passed away, but a little girl would continue to visit me in my dreams. She was beautiful. She was dressed in a pink frilly dress, had eyes I could never forget, and wore a smile that would brighten up any room. I didn't know who she was, but I somehow knew that this little girl was supposed to be part of my life. My heart knew it, and I felt a hole where she was missing.

"And?" Mark said, pulling me back into the conversation

"And, I believe Hope has a very sensitive spirit. She doesn't just try to add kids to our family. She knows who will be perfect for us. She said Favor is a Worton. She's never said that about any child before."

"Well," Mark said, "is she LOUD?" We were both aware that with each child, our family was getting progressively louder. When we picked up Shewit, our third child and first adoption from Ethiopia, the orphanage director told us that they had been praying for us, knowing that we had to be a very "special" family. He was tons of fun, *extremely* active, and a bit mischievous.

"Well, it isn't good timing for us," he continued. "You know we can barely handle the kids we have. I thought you wanted a new backyard. We can't do both! Can we just talk about this later?" I could see Mark was frustrated. He abruptly stopped the conversation and went back to work, but I knew it wasn't over, and so did he.

I went to my room and emailed Hope. On one side, I knew that this little girl was our daughter. On the other side, I had a husband who had just told me that he wasn't ready for another child. And the last time I was ready to adopt, it took more than three years for him to take the plunge. I also respected my husband and didn't want to force anything on him—especially a child.

I decided to find out more about this little girl taking over my thought life. *Was she healthy? Was she abandoned? How old was she? Did she already have a family working toward adopting her?* There was so much about her that I wanted to know. I sent the email, and I prayed some kind of reply would quickly come.

* * * * *

A few nights later, Mark walked into our bedroom. I could tell he was deep in thought. I had been careful not to say anything else about adoption, but I had spent many hours praying that if it was God's will for us to have this little girl, that He would make a way. Mark's heart would have to be changed. Two facets I know about my husband: he is open to hearing from God and he is quick to seek His face on major matters. As I looked at him, wondering what was going on, he seemed to be searching for the right words to say.

"Have you heard from Hope yet?" he asked.

"Yes," I said, still trying to read his face. "Are you really interested in knowing what she said?" Without a sound, he gave me the go-ahead to tell him.

"Favor is beautiful," I started. "She's healthy, she's lost both her mom and dad, and she needs a family. Hope is checking with Pochi to see if Favor is available for adoption." *Why is he asking if he isn't ready? Is this a sign that things are changing?*

Mark stood silent.

"Mark, do you remember when I met Pochi the first time?" I asked. Pochi was the director at Covenant Orphanage where

Favor was living. Pochi was a beautiful African woman who presented herself with a spunky confidence, and had a kind, but matter-of-fact way about her. She had visited America about a year and a half ago, and stayed with Cindy to visit four of the children Cindy had adopted from Covenant Orphanage.

"Wasn't it right before we got Shewit from Ethiopia?" he asked. I could tell he was clueless beyond that, but I would never forget my first conversation with Pochi. Her words stirred my compassion and sprouted a seed within my heart for a little girl.

"She told me that someday I would be coming to Ethiopia and adopting a little girl from her," I said. "I've never forgotten that. I've been praying for favor my whole life. It will be exciting to see a picture of her." I couldn't hide my joy as I began to break into a smile.

Mark smiled. He knew it was true, but a struggle was going on inside of him. He was interested in Favor, but he wasn't totally convinced that he was ready to go through the adoption process again. Transitioning another child into our family would change the dynamics again, and older-child adoptions come with challenges. "So, when is Hope supposed to be sending a picture?"

"I guess when she takes one," I told him.

* * * * *

In Ethiopia, Hope—who had come all the way from our neighborhood in Franklin, Tennessee—was helping the older children get ready for pictures. They loved the attention and the new clothes. Favor especially loved having her hair done. Hope straightened Favor's tight curls and pulled them back in a neat ponytail. Favor looked at her blonde Barbie doll with a ponytail and pointed out that she and the doll had the same hair now. Hope took the pink dress off the bed and handed it to Favor. Her eyes widened with excitement as she squealed with joy. Pink was her favorite color, and she loved wearing frilly dresses!

Favor felt like a princess in her new dress and fixed hair. Hope pulled her camera from her satchel and took the kids into the front yard of the orphanage. Favor couldn't stand still as Hope captured her on film. Her little fingers excitedly played in front of her and her eyes sparkled. In each shot, she radiated beauty and confidence. Without a doubt, there was something very special about this little girl. She had God's favor all over her.

* * * * *

The next morning Mark and I woke up early. Mark started checking email as I laid in bed, deciding if I wanted to get up yet.

"There's an email from Hope," he said. "It came with an attachment."

I bolted up like a shot of caffeine had hit my heart.

Mark looked at me before he clicked on Hope's email. "Are you ready to see what Favor looks like?" he asked. I nodded yes, but I could barely breathe. Mark took a deep breath, then clicked the attachment.

What happened in the next few moments felt like a dream. There she was—in her little pink, frilly dress—arms out in front of her, and oh, that smile! It immediately captured my heart. I looked at Mark, whose eyes were fixed on her. He didn't say a word. As I looked at this sweet little girl, I knew without a doubt that I already loved her. It wasn't her beauty that drew me...but something far stronger.

I already knew her.

"That's her!" I whispered in amazement.

Mark looked at me for a moment. "Yes, it is." Then he realized it was deeper. "Wait, what do you mean?"

"That's her!" I said again. "That's the little girl who's been coming to me in my dreams for the past two years!"

Mark took a closer look at the picture.

Incredibly, God had been preparing me to recognize Favor two years before I would ever lay eyes on her. His goodness rocked my world in that moment. Tears of thankfulness streamed down my face. My joy was uncontainable as I realized what God had done.

Now I just had to wait for Mark to be on board.

Our first glance at Favor. Could my dream of adopting a little girl become a reality?

CHAPTER 2
THE BATTLE BEGINS

"Faith is the art of holding on to things in spite of Your changing moods and circumstances."

—C. S. Lewis

Adoption agencies in Ethiopia were busy scheduling court and embassy dates to avoid delays during the upcoming rainy season that would shut government offices down for about three months.

Recently, there had been an issue rocking the adoption world that made international news. The media was saying that not all of the declared orphans were actually orphans—meaning that the children's parents had died or abandoned them. According to the circulating story, some of these Ethiopian children, who were being portrayed as orphans, had been given up for adoption by their parents, in hopes that the children would be given a better life. The media made it look like the adoption agencies had manipulated these families by telling the parents that their kids would be raised in another country, receive an education, and then be sent back to help their families in Ethiopia. The media story was making it appear that the orphan situation in Ethiopia wasn't as severe as it previously seemed.

The problem with that story is that as of the year 2007, approximations estimated that Ethiopia had more than 5 million orphans, including 1.5 AIDS orphans.[1] Not only was it unethical to try to convince potential future adoptive parents that forever families weren't necessary but also the information about the possibility of the children returning to their home country was also inaccurate. When you adopt a child, that child is declared irrevocably yours. In Tennessee, an adoptive family can disinherit their biological children but cannot disinherit an adopted child. When Americans adopt, they adopt for forever, thus the term "forever-family." That child, by law, is as much a part of the family as the biological children.

* * * * *

Hope was excited to tell Pochi that she thought she had a forever-family for Favor. She knew we belonged together, but she had yet to receive a definite "yes" from the Wortons.

Pochi made her point strong and clear to Hope. "Tell Missy that if she and her husband are serious about Favor then she needs to email me as soon as possible, telling me they are moving forward, or I will refer Favor to another family this week."

"Okay, I'll let her know that you need a definite answer," Hope said. "I think Favor would be perfect for them."

"Well," Pochi declared, "if it is to be, God will make a way for them to be together. God chooses the families for these children."

* * * * *

My heart grew anxious when I read Hope's email relaying that Pochi needed an answer. I knew I couldn't push Mark into an adoption, but it had almost been a week since we had learned about Favor. A decision had to be made soon, or we would lose her. I asked God how I might approach Mark. All that came to me clearly, however, was that I should not speak to him about the matter—I would give it to God instead. If adopting Favor was the path we should be taking, God would make a way. Not talking with Mark about Favor was a leap of faith, but I didn't want to push my husband into something he wasn't ready for. My heart ached. I wanted Favor so badly that my mind kept trying to figure a way to make the adoption happen, but then I would calmly lay it back down at Jesus' feet.

The next couple of days felt like months. I had to leave the room on several occasions to keep from saying something about Favor. It was like being on a diet and having the best bakery in town in your kitchen. I could see it and smell it, but I couldn't taste it. Favor was all I could think about, and to not speak about her with the most important person in my life felt downright miserable.

Three days had passed since God told me not to say anything else to Mark. Mark walked in as I was getting ready for bed and leaned up against his sink. He looked at the floor, then at me, then back at the floor.

"Are you okay?" I asked.

"I've been thinking..." Mark nonchalantly said.

"Oh, living on the edge," I joked. Mark gave me "the look" and rolled his eyes.

There was a long, silent pause.

"I was thinking about a future discussion I didn't want to have when I got to Heaven." He paused and looked at me. "I can't imagine getting to Heaven and hearing my Heavenly Father say, 'Well Son, you totally missed it on saving the orphan, but hey, great job on that new backyard!'"

My eyes teared up and my chest heaved with emotion. I was watching a miracle unfold before my eyes.

"Let's go and give a little girl a family!" Mark said with a smile. "I'm all-in on moving forward with this adoption."

I couldn't wait to put my arms around him. I was so thankful that God had chosen us for her, and I was so grateful that I had stayed out of the way—for once in my life. I was happy that I had waited for Mark's decision. I was also grateful to be married to a man who cared enough to stop and pray about things that he was uncomfortable doing. He moved forward in obedience because his first desire was to please his Heavenly Father.

* * * * *

It was now July 9, I didn't have any time to waste—we wanted to proceed with our application before anyone else did. I contacted the necessary people to move forward with our adoption. First, I talked to Pochi, who reminded me that we would need to get a referral from Ethiopian Adoption International (EAI), the accredited international adoption agency that represented Covenant Orphanage. Accredited international agencies guide the family through the process of obtaining an adopted child's visa following the rules of the Hague Convention on Protection of Children and Co-operation in Respect of Intercountry Adoption.

So, my next move was to call EAI. Because I thought EAI's role was to guide us, I was surprised by the conversation that followed. Instead of a warm voice on the other end of the line providing useful information, the lady that answered began the conversation with silence, leaving me wondering what to do. After what seemed like a long time, she spoke up.

"Are you requesting a specific child?" Her voice was gruff.

"I'm requesting a specific orphanage," I said. "I was told that you refer for that orphanage."

I understood that the reason why adoptive families have to get referrals is to make sure the best interest of the child is protected. A referral from a credible organization is seen as a way to prevent a child from ending up with people who may not have good motives for adopting the child. However,

I also knew that our intentions were nothing but pure, and based on our last experience adopting, I thought that an adoption agency would strike a balance between protecting the child and welcoming a potentially strong adoptive family to apply.

I was trying very hard to not upset this woman who obviously was having a very bad day.

"Okay," she said. "What age range are you requesting, and do you want a boy or girl? Or does it even matter to you?" I was stunned. I couldn't believe I was speaking with an adoption agency with these questions and their tones. I had spoken with animal pounds that had more compassion for adoption than this woman.

"Do you even know what you want, or does it matter?" she asked again, this time a little more agitated.

"We are wanting to adopt a little girl between five and seven years old," I answered.

"I don't believe they have any that age at this time," she snapped back. I knew they did. I took a breath, trying to hold my attitude in check.

"Could you please check on that for us?" I asked.

"I can refer you to another orphanage. I'm sure we have a boy that age," she said.

"Actually," I said, "we would like a girl, and we would like to stay with the orphanage I requested."

Suddenly her tone changed from harsh and unfeeling to a sweet grandmother trying to help me out. "Well," she said, "is there already a child you know about that you would like us to refer to you?" I could taste the sugar in the air.

"We know Pochi," I answered carefully, "and we feel God has brought us together for this adoption."

As quickly as the sweet grandma came, she vanished. Now I was left on the phone with a creature from the black abyss. "Well," she snapped, "I don't care if God *Himself* told you. I will *NOT* be referring any little girl to you from them."

My mind was spinning. *Did I just hear her say she wouldn't refer a little girl? This made no sense! Everything about this was wrong. How would we adopt Favor if this was the only agency that represented Covenant Orphanage? Did this woman have something against this orphanage? Maybe she didn't like me?*

"Let me ask you," I calmly said. "How many families does your agency have waiting in line requesting a five- to seven-year-old child right now?"

"I don't believe we have any at the moment," she blurted out.

My emotions welled up inside and went beyond my ability to hold back any longer. "Yes, you do." My voice started to break. "I'm right here on the phone asking for a child—and you're refusing my request."

The woman was very quiet on the other end of the phone. Finally she said, "I have a problem with you requesting a certain child or orphanage. We are re-evaluating pre-identified cases and how we handle them. If you want this child, you'll have to find another agency."

That was it.

I was shocked. Pochi had told me I had to call EAI to proceed with adopting Favor. I knew many people who had "pre-identified" cases, meaning that they had picked specific children through specific orphanages—without any problem. I didn't understand what was happening.

I hung up, feeling like I was hanging over the Grand Canyon by a thread. I was unable to control my tears. I called Mark. As I relayed the news, he became more frustrated and angry. He knew if we would face a spiritual battle, then there must be something very special about this adoption for the enemy to step in so quickly to stop it. Mark and I prayed together over the phone. We decided that we should get Pochi involved.

I emailed Pochi, relaying to her what the woman at EAI had said. I had signed the email "Brokenhearted." Pochi quickly responded with encouragement that lifted my spirit and strengthened my soul:

> I don't understand why she (the woman at EAI) has a problem with that. This is the fourth child we have referred this way through their agency. I want to tell you, this is not the agency. This is warfare, and we are used to it. This has happened to almost all our children at some time in their process. Don't lose heart...God is on HIS THRONE! The enemy will always try to stop God's purpose in each child but the good news is that he never was the winner—OUR GOD IS THE WINNER, ALWAYS! As it says in the Bible, "We are more than conquerors through Him that loved you." That is what we know. If God speaks, be sure He will complete it. Missy, don't lose heart and don't give up. God is in control.

"Okay, God," I prayed, "I find myself in another war. How do I win this battle?"

Prayer.

Prayer—the duct tape of Heaven! It's how God worked His will when I prayed for Mark's heart to open up for us to proceed with providing for and adopting Favor, so I began to pray. I prayed that this woman would be removed from her position. Then I got convicted and prayed that I would somehow find it in my heart to forgive her. I wanted to be able to work with her in harmony for the sake of a little girl.

The next step was to stand on His promises and wait.

Finally, on August 11—more than a full month after my inquiry—we received an email from EAI, from the same woman who had left me in tears. It wasn't much, but it held a glimmer of hope:

> We are still working on this, given that he is six and male, his chances of getting a family is not so good. I'd like to proceed but need the go-ahead from our coordinator in Ethiopia. I hope to have an answer soon.

I looked at the tag line after her signature. "One adoption won't change the world, but it will change the world for one child." Was she messing with me? She was still referring to my little girl as a male. After all, it mattered to Favor that we would be adopting HER—not a little boy. I was nervous and a little put off that she couldn't get the boy/girl description right.

I thanked her and clarified that we were still requesting a little girl. A few hours later, our response came:

> I had thought it was a boy, but it doesn't matter. Here is the message from our attorney that came a few minutes ago. He has talked with the director and they are in favor of giving the child to you. So go ahead!! You need to file an application.

I was so excited that I decided to ignore the "it doesn't matter" comment. We had been given the go-ahead, and that night we shared the big news at dinner with our three children: Matt, McKenzie, and Shewit. It was official: the Wortons were adding another child to their family.

Getting this adoption started was tougher than our last adoption, but we knew that, in the end, God would win this battle. This adoption had a divine purpose...it made sense that everything might not be easy. The enemy hates adoption because it is the mirror image and heart of our Heavenly Father. The bigger the battle, the larger the call of purpose and destiny is.

* * * * *

The months flew by, and Christmas was approaching. In record time, I had sent our dossier, which is an application file containing financial records, employment, health, background checks, police reports, and more. Everything that the adoption agency, orphanage, and government agencies needed to move to the next phase of our adoption was done on our end. We all talked about Favor being home in time for summer. After

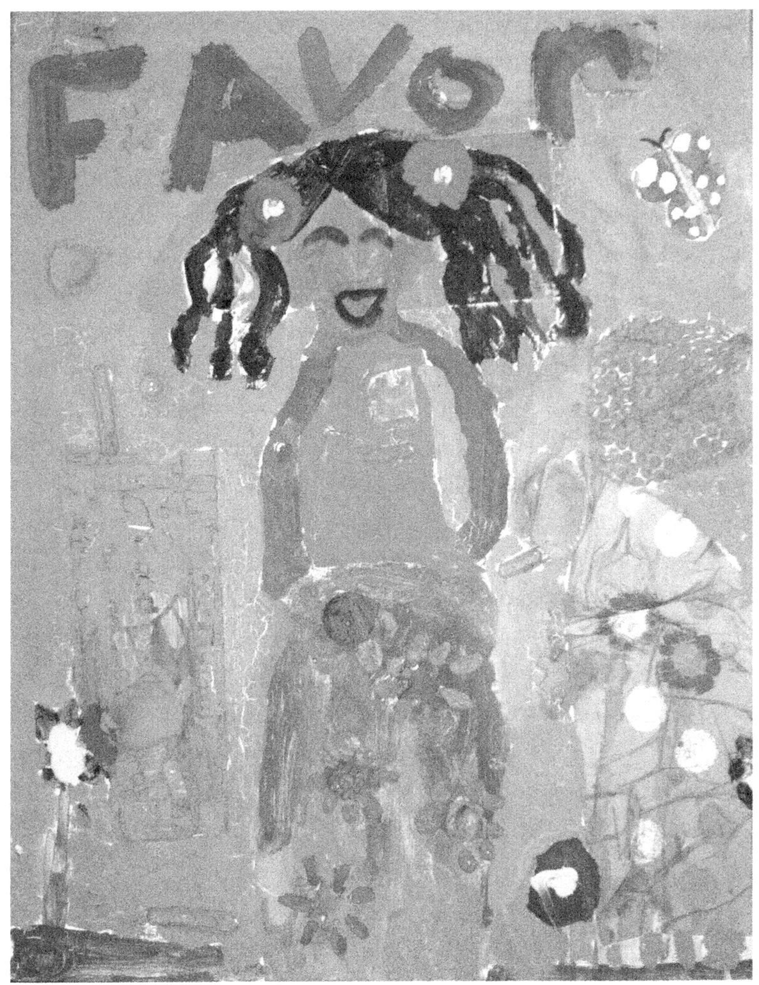

McKenzie, excited about getting a little sister, painted this picture of Favor.

all, when we adopted Shewit, it took a total of six months until we had him home. I knew two trips to Ethiopia might make it a little longer, but not much. I had no idea that Shewit was a miracle adoption because of how smooth it had been.

Seven, then eight months passed, and we still had no word from Ethiopia or our agency. We started feeling like something was wrong. Then suddenly, nine months into this adoption, I started having a physical pain in my body that felt exactly like labor pains.

After two biologically-delivered children and one adopted child, I was well aware that my body had a quirky tendency to physically show symptoms that were happening in the spiritual realm. When I went into labor with my first two children, we realized that the labor produced hypertension, and the doctors worked to keep me from going into cardiac arrest during childbirth. Then, on the day of Shewit's court date, when he officially would be birthed into our family by law, I went into "labor"—complete with the symptoms of hypertension. The moment we heard we had passed court, the hypertension disappeared. I was having "labor pains" again, but the timing was wrong—I knew there was still so much that needed to happen.

I told Mark about the pains, and he said, "We must be getting ready to bring home our little girl."

"No," I said, "it's too early. We haven't been given a court date. Something feels terribly wrong, Mark."

"Don't worry," Mark calmly said, "let's just pray and put it in God's hands. That's what we've done so far and it's worked out alright."

Mark was right. How could I worry about this?

* * * * *

The following afternoon, I got a call from Cindy. She had received an urgent prayer request from Pochi.

"Missy," her voice broke, "it's about the orphanage. I fell to my knees when I read it. It's awful!"

My heart was in my throat the moment she had mentioned the orphanage. I don't remember hanging up the phone or even bolting out of the front door. All I knew was my feet couldn't move fast enough as I ran across my lawn to Cindy's home. Something horrible had happened—and I prayed that it didn't involve Favor.

CHAPTER 3
THE ENEMY COMES TO STEAL

"The thief cometh not, but for
to steal, and to kill, and to destroy:
I am come that they might have life,
and that they might have it
more abundantly."

—John 10:10, KJV

When I opened the door to Cindy's home, I could see that she had been crying and was very emotional. I asked God for the grace to face whatever news she had.

"What's going on?" I asked. "Is Favor okay?" Cindy pulled up the email and turned it for me to read. The email started with "URGENT PRAYER REQUEST!" I swallowed hard and began to read, trying not to miss anything, looking for Favor's name—anything—to let me know she was okay.

> Please pray for our older children at the orphanage. There is a new policy that says older children should be placed in a foster care home. Since our home is the only one with older

> children, the policy affects us. There are people here in Ethiopia who are willing to take care of the children, but they only want them as servants. They don't care about the babies... isn't that weird?
>
> I have been crying since I heard from our coordinator. You know how much we love our children. We are fasting and praying the next three days. Pray that they will allow us to be the foster parents of the children and they will not take them. We desperately need your prayers! This is what Daniel (who is now adopted), told us that he had dreamt about. There are four children they are taking for foster care. It feels like they are stealing them. I'm sure you understand how we feel. Pray!
> God Bless You,
> Pochi

I felt completely numb.

"Do you know what four children they are taking out?" I asked.

"I'm not sure," Cindy answered, "but Favor could be one of them. They only had four older children there. The rest are babies." The noise in my head was deafening, and I couldn't get my mind wrapped around what was happening.

"What does this mean?" I asked. "We can still adopt her, right? It's just foster care." I was doing my best to understand the seriousness of what I was hearing.

"These children will be put in homes to be someone's servant...or worse," she said. "We'll never see them again. So, no—you wouldn't be able to adopt her."

The last statement felt like a tornado passing through my senses. Cindy's eyes began filling with tears as she buried her face in her hands. I stood beside the table, unable to respond.

From the moment I had heard Favor's name, I had bound myself to her. I knew God had brought me a gift of a daughter from another country. All my plans for the days ahead included her. *Now someone was trying to take her away from us and make her a servant? How could this be right?* I felt completely helpless and vulnerable in that moment. *What could I possibly do to stop this?* She was halfway across the world, and all I wanted to do was hold her. Even if I could hop on a plane and be there, I was dealing with a world I didn't know. *Where would I begin?*

Cindy and I grabbed hands and began praying into the situation. I suddenly felt my spirit still and come to a place of peace. I took a deep breath, and before I realized it, I was speaking. "I trust Him," I said. "I trust Him." It came from the depths of my soul. I said it again. I had no other words. "I trust Him. He has never failed me. I trust Him." I stood there knowing that all I could do was *trust Him*. He was the one holding her safe in His arms, He would make a way for her to be kept in the orphanage, and He would keep her from the bondage of slavery.

* * * * *

Later that day in Ethiopia, chaos erupted at Covenant Orphanage. Officials from the local government office had arrived to take the four children away. Favor was terrified because she didn't understand what the men were saying or where the men wanted her to go. She ran and hid. She didn't know these men, and she feared that they would give her away to a bad person or to someone who would do something horrible to her. She felt safe at the orphanage, and she liked the orphanage nurses who took care of her.

The children were crying. The orphanage workers were crying as they were trying to comfort the children. Pochi begged the officials to leave the four children at the orphanage so they would not be frightened. She told them that she now had an Ethiopian worker who was willing to provide a temporary home for those children until their forever families arrived. Pochi then proceeded to ask if the orphanage could be allowed to be part of the foster care program because of this worker's willingness. This action was a way to provide what the government was looking for. Thankfully, the officials agreed to the plan.

* * * * *

Back at home, Mark had just hung up the phone with his regional boss of more than 11 years. His company had started a massive downsizing, and more than 60 percent of the employees—from top to bottom—got the news that they had lost their jobs. Mark was one of them.

I walked around the corner as Mark was coming out of the office. The look on his face said it all. I could already see the weight of not having a job resting on his shoulders. I grabbed his hand and led him back into the office where we would have privacy. I knew that he was deeply hurting and was feeling rejected in that moment. I took him in my arms and just held him. Mark losing his job was a slap in the face from a company that Mark had worked hard for and been loyal to beyond his pay. But downsizing was the reality of dealing with corporations and their bottom lines. As his wife, I knew they had just let go of one of the best employees they would ever have.

Mark and I would have to make a decision at some point. We knew that during an adoption, if a parent's job is disrupted, it often stops the adoption process. He was one of the top earners in the company, and his severance package would take care of us for the rest of the year—longer if we would tighten up on our budget. He had plenty of time to find another job before the money would run out. If we had to, we could cash in our stocks and other savings, or pick up side or part-time jobs until he found something else. We made a decision to stay silent about his job loss, believing that a job would come before our adoption was completed.

That night, I realized my instincts concerning something going wrong with the adoption had been correct—the labor pains I was feeling had everything to do with what was taking place in the spiritual realm. The enemy was trying to steal our promises and abort a divine destiny. My prayers increased, and I also had my closest friends and prayer warriors join me in praying for a miracle.

* * * * *

On Sunday morning, the third and final day of the fast that had been taking place at Covenant Orphanage since the officials had threatened to take the children, Pochi stood in Ethiopia at Covenant Church worshiping God, when she felt an overwhelming peace that everything would turn out for the good of the children. God spoke to her. *He had already started a work that could not be reversed.* Pochi knew that the prayers and cries of the saints had prompted a miracle.

* * * * *

First thing Monday morning, Pochi received a call from the secretary to the government official in charge of removing the four children from the orphanage and placing them into foster care. She spoke with urgency.

"Ms. Pochi," the secretary started, "your presence has been requested at our offices in Debre Birhan. This morning, if possible."

"It will take me two hours to get there," Pochi replied, "but I will leave now. May I ask, why the rush?"

"We don't know," she said, "we've been asked to get you here as soon as possible. He (the government official) says it's urgent. He seemed very upset when he came in, and asked that we get you here immediately. He will not say why."

Pochi hung up the phone and drove to Debre Birhan. When she arrived, the secretary rushed her back to the official's office.

The official looked up from his desk. His eyes were swollen and he looked disheveled. He obviously had not been sleeping well.

"You asked to see me?" Pochi said. He grabbed a piece of paper from his desk and held it up in Pochi's face, his fingers clenching the paper like it was his adversary.

"This...this has brought me much turmoil. I have lost sleep and been disturbed over this matter. My whole family has been upset!" he yelled. "I don't know the God you serve, but He has tormented me and my family all weekend. Take your paper and let this child be adopted."

At that, he threw the paper at Pochi and lowered his head. She picked the paper up off the floor and walked out of his office without looking back.

The crumpled piece of paper was the last document needed to complete Favor's adoption. Pochi knew a miracle had just happened, and she knew the almighty God she served had made a way for another child.

Around the same time in Franklin, Tennessee, my labor pains suddenly stopped.

* * * * *

Within days, all the necessary papers were handed to the courts, and we thought that soon we would be traveling for our court date in Ethiopia. Again, however, months passed and no word came. We would later find out that EAI and Pochi had miscommunicated several times, resulting in missed and postponed court dates, setting us back.

In Tennessee, Cindy and Hope, who had been back from Ethiopia for nearly a year, were getting ready to throw a shower for our future little Ethiopian princess. We had decided that we would use the shower to bless a new orphanage being built in Ethiopia with needed supplies. The show of love for Favor and the excitement to bring her home warmed my heart. One by one, my friends used Bible verses to declare blessings over her. There wasn't a dry eye among us. It had been a year since I first heard her name and a seed to adopt her had been planted in my heart. I felt like I was ready to pop. We had battled some major roadblocks to get to this point, and I could almost see the finish line. Within two weeks of the prayers spoken at the shower, we were called with a court date!

The Worton Family pose for a picture before heading to Ethiopia. That in itself is an adventure!

The court date, August 15, 2012, was the last one available before the Ethiopian government agency responsible for adoption closed for the rainy season, and it was in five days! Two of those days would be used for travel. Because it was such late notice, I asked our adoption agent if we could have an hour to decide. I quickly made arrangements for our kids. Mark searched for a good deal on airline tickets. With Mark still job hunting, we were on a tight budget, and finding a good price on tickets was a necessity. Because we needed to fly within the next few days, we knew inexpensive tickets would be a miracle. Every ticket we found online was more than $3,500, and only one was available. We would either have to travel separately or on first class, which was almost double the $3,500. We debated if we should postpone the trip and take a later court date, but we couldn't ignore the push to take action and go. So we said a prayer and pulled up the internet to check ticket prices one more time before giving our answer to the adoption agent. At first, we saw a ticket for the same price, but then suddenly the screen flickered, and updated the information. We couldn't believe our eyes—two seats had opened up, and we secured them for $1,400 each! We were going to Ethiopia!

Before we left, Mark's good friend Clay called and told Mark that as he was praying for our trip, he felt two things would happen. First, I would receive additional insight for a book I'd been working on about how third-world countries have different views of both life before birth and abortion. Second, he felt that something wasn't quite right. He said that we needed to be aware of a "sleight of hand" about a hidden agenda, corruption, or something done under the table in Ethiopia. He didn't feel like this action would damage our adoption, but he did sense that God wanted us to be prepared and recognize this "sleight of hand" when it happened.

His insight didn't surprise me. This entire adoption has been one battle after another, I thought to myself. *This child must have an amazing future!*

* * * * *

After the initial scare that arose when our flight to Washington Dulles was cancelled, we found ourselves on the last two seats going to Washington Reagan Airport. The change in airports gave us an opportunity to see our long-time and dear friends, David and Kathleen Estes. They came to our rescue, shuttling us from Reagan International Airport to our hotel near Dulles Airport.

We had walked through life with this couple in so many major events. After 9/11 happened in 2001, they felt God calling them to help plant a church in New York City. After their house sold the day it went on the market, they moved in with us for six months until they had raised their support and moved to New York City. Then in 2009, unbeknownst to any of us, Kathleen and I were separately forwarded an email with pictures of "waiting children" from Ethiopia who needed families. We saw a picture of Shewit, our third child, for the first time, and we knew that we were supposed to adopt him. Kathleen and David saw pictures of their future children, Chernet and Misganaw from the same email. Not knowing Kathleen received the same email, I called to tell her the big news—only to find out that we had both started the adoption process on the same day! In January of 2010, we flew out of the country together to pick up our boys, who also happened to be best friends. Only God could have intertwined our lives so perfectly through the years, and tonight, though our time was brief, we experienced another amazing blessed time with our dear friends. They encouraged us and sent us on our way.

After the long flight to Addis Ababa in Ethiopia, we arrived tired and ready to go to sleep. As we got off the plane, we were warmly greeted by Josiah from our adoption agency, EAI. He was so helpful and friendly. He took us to the Hilton, where we crashed for two hours before Pochi was going to pick us up and take us to meet Favor. I was so happy to see Pochi again—it had been more than two years since I was first introduced to her in Cindy's kitchen. It felt like we had already been through so much together working towards this adoption for so long.

"Favor is so excited to see you," she said. "She is bursting at the seams to meet her forever mommy and daddy. She's so happy to have a family."

We couldn't believe we were finally going to meet this little girl. She had been in our prayers and on our mind for more than a year now. I looked at Mark. He was smiling, ready to meet his fourth child. His birthday had come and gone during our long flight, but there could not have been a better birthday gift for him waiting in Ethiopia.

We loaded up into Pochi's silver Toyota and traveled for an hour through the most beautiful land. Before we came to Ethiopia for our first adoption, I had always envisioned Ethiopia as a dry desert, but the land was lush with greenery. I videoed the scenery and some of our conversations as Pochi drove and told us all about the daughter we had traveled so far to meet. Favor seemed to bring a smile to Pochi's face when she spoke about her.

I looked over at Mark, expecting to see a man excited to meet his new daughter. Instead, I saw a man who was there in body, but in a fog. Later he told me that he was recalling a message he had heard about the two realms we are all a part of. The first one is the heavenly realm—made of perfect love, peace, and faith. The second one is the Earthly realm—filled with doubt, worry, and frustration. As believers, we reflect the realm that we are most aware of. We can reflect Heaven, or we can reflect the worries and concerns of this life. Mark knew that He was not reflecting Heaven as he started descending into an abyss of worry. Instead of celebrating what God was doing in this moment, his mind started to drift to all the challenges ahead. He needed a new job and a new van. He had another trip to Ethiopia to fund, and another child to provide for.

After an hour of driving through lush terrain, we pulled off of the main road in an area known as Holeta that was very poor but surrounded by beauty. The road took us to a large, blue, double gate. Our hearts started to beat faster, because we knew that Favor was waiting on the other side of the gate. I wondered if she was as excited and as nervous as I was. The gate swung wide open as we got out of the car, and the children ran out to greet us. One by one, they hugged and kissed us on both cheeks. My eyes scanned all the little girls around us, but Favor was not among them.

Then I saw her. I could see that she was barely containing her excitement as she made her way to us. She was dressed in a little black-and-pink-checkered skirt with a black vest and a white shirt peeking out. Her hair was braided back, and she was the most beautiful sight that I had ever seen. She reached up to give me a kiss on both cheeks, looked in my eyes, and said my favorite word, "Mommy."

She looked over at Mark, and as they caught eyes, she got the biggest smile on her face. She hugged him and gave him a kiss on each cheek. I could see Mark's heart was officially melted in her embrace. Just like our older three children, we were immediately filled with love for her. Mark was beaming from ear to ear.

"Happy birthday!" I said as I looked at him.

Favor grabbed my hand, and with her other hand, she grabbed Mark's, and led us into the orphanage where they had prepared a coffee ceremony. I kept looking at her. It was surreal holding her in my arms after all the battles and prayer we had gone through to get here. I wanted—more than anything—to take her home and get her as far away from the foster situation that had almost enslaved her. I had so many questions and emotions rolling through me, but for now—I had her in my arms—and I wasn't planning to miss a moment.

CHAPTER 4
TREASURED DAYS

"A child represents the future hope
of their family and country—
no matter how inconvenient the timing might be."

—Missy Worton

During the next four days when Favor was with us, we would enjoy our time together to the fullest, trying to suck every bit of marrow out of the bone of life. Favor was effervescent. A presence radiated from her, expressing that she was made for something great. She was a precious gift that was more than we could've asked or hoped for. She was full of life and expectation. We noticed her confidence and playful personality right away. She rushed to my side at every opportunity just to give me a hug and say, "Mommy," reminding herself that she had a mommy and daddy again.

We celebrated Mark's birthday with a tiramisu cake that Pochi had bought for him, and we watched as Favor opened the gifts we'd brought her.

Mark celebrating a wonderful birthday on the day we met Favor.

Her squeals made us laugh, and we quickly found out pink was her color, especially if the pink item had some bling. One shirt stood out from the rest and was clearly her favorite. It was a turquoise top with a bursting pink flower covered with bling, and the words *Pick Me*.

Sleep was elusive that night, either from the excitement of the day or the espresso flowing through our veins from Mark's tiramisu cake. Half a bottle of melatonin couldn't get us to sleep. I'm sure the room next to us was wondering what we were up to, as giggles rang out in the dark. We were just happy to be together.

The next day we awoke to a bright-eyed and bushy-tailed Favor. She was ready to get up and get going. Mark and I, on the other hand, could barely move—let alone operate—from lack of sleep. We needed to get some strong Ethiopian coffee into our bodies before Josiah picked us up for our court appointment.

Favor looked through her drawer of new clothes and picked her favorite *Pick Me* shirt, some black leggings with a skirt, and her sparkly pink boots with matching hair flower. She was a sight for sore eyes.

We ate breakfast at a small bakery on the Hilton premises, then went to wait for Josiah. Mark and I were a little nervous about court because of all the misunderstandings that had taken place with the orphanage and our agency, EAI. Neither organization wanted to take blame for delaying our adoption, so they blamed each other. Josiah drove up 15 minutes late, which set Mark on edge. We had adopted before, and we knew that promptness was key.

"Are you going straight to court?" Mark asked.

"I first must stop by EAI, then we go," Josiah responded, like it was no big deal.

"Our court appointment was at 9 a.m.," Mark said. "It's already 15 minutes past that. We came a long way and don't want to miss it."

"Ethiopian courts are never on time. We are okay for time," Josiah said. Mark looked at me, and I could tell this statement didn't comfort him in the least. We arrived at the EAI complex and were told to get out of the van and "hang out." We were now more than 30 minutes late for our court date.

* * * * *

At the Court of Adoptions, DJ, who often helped the orphanage with the adoption process, waited with Favor's aunt. DJ was a tall, kind man, in his early-to-mid 30s, with a gentle demeanor. The secretary came out of the judge's office and walked briskly down the long hallway toward them. They could tell by her walk that the judge was getting tired of waiting for her last court appointment before they would close for the rainy season.

"Where is your family?" the secretary asked. "The judge is ready for them."

"They are on their way," DJ said.

"Why are they so late?" the secretary asked.

"Maybe traffic is very bad today?" DJ offered. "They are coming, I promise you."

"She will only wait so long," the secretary stated. "If they are not here soon, we will reschedule them in three months to come back."

"Yes, please forgive, they are on their way—many apologies," DJ said, trying to keep a bad situation from quickly getting worse.

"She is not pleased!" the secretary said. She looked DJ in the eyes as if to put an exclamation point on it, then turned around and made her way back down the long hallway. The judge had been newly appointed, and no one really knew what she was like—or what would set her off. One thing was certain—she didn't like to be kept waiting.

DJ dialed up Pochi and told her the situation.

"I was afraid of this," Pochi said. "I will call EAI right now and get them there quickly." Pochi was upset as she dialed the number to EAI. Not showing up was a bad way to treat the courts and she knew this circumstance could again push back Favor's adoption. Why would an agency try to sabotage a family's adoption?

When the agency answered the phone, Pochi was ready to unload on them.

"Why are the Wortons not at their court appointment?" Pochi asked. "If they miss this appointment because of you, you will pay their way to come back in three months!"

"Oh, are they not there yet?" the agent asked.

"You know they are not there!" Pochi snapped at her. "You should've had them there over 50 minutes ago. The judge is tired of waiting on you, and I will let them know it was you that made them late!"

* * * * *

The EAI complex used to be an orphanage. Colorful paintings decorated the outside walls of the building, but there was a sad feeling that hung in the air. I saw a beautiful bush of blossoming pink flowers off to my right side. The bush looked out of place among the deteriorating buildings and unkempt surroundings. I gave Mark the camera and drew Favor close to me for the picture. She felt nervous as she looked around. Suddenly, Jamila, the office manager of the orphanage, ran around the corner.

"Hurry, we must go now!" she said with urgency.

Great! Now, they were in a rush. Mark snapped the picture, and within moments, we were in the van. I looked at my watch—9:58 a.m. We were almost one hour late at this point. My stomach started to turn into knots. I hoped we hadn't made a huge mistake going with this agency, but they were our only choice, and now it was too late.

The elevator door opened to the third floor of the court building. DJ was waiting for us with a big smile, but with a hurried expression. Next to him was a beautiful woman in her early 30s. She smiled when she saw Favor and reached out for a huge hug. Favor nervously smiled and hugged the woman, then looked up at me, and ran back to my side. DJ introduced the woman as Favor's Aunt, Emebet. I ran over to hug her. I knew this had to be hard, and the court date would be one of the last times Emebet would see Favor before she was officially adopted.

"We must go now," Jamila instructed, waving us to follow her down the hallway. The adoption court waiting room, usually full with forever families, was empty. We were whisked directly into the judge's courtroom. We all knew that entering this late was not in our best interest.

The courtroom was small with three desks formed in an "L" shape. The judge sat in the most prominent spot, with the two court reporters seated to her front and left side. A table, overflowing with files, was to the judge's right. A perfect 'U' was created with the table and two desks. Tall windows were in the back, looking out over the city and the surrounding mountains.

The judge glanced up and scanned us from head to toe. She didn't look happy, and you could feel it in her glare. She didn't like her time being disrespected. She looked at Favor, then down to her glittery pink boots. I saw her crack a smile.

"Are you Favor?" she asked with a smile. Favor nodded her head yes, then grabbed me around the waist. The judge looked at me with no expression then back down to her paperwork.

"You can sit down," the judge said, not taking time to look up from her desk. We found a seat and waited quietly for her to speak. During the next few minutes, the judge spoke to Jamila from EAI in Amharic. She sounded perturbed. We hoped it wasn't about our being almost an hour and 15 minutes late.

She turned and directed her next few questions at Mark and me.

"You do know that once you adopt this child, she is yours," the judge stated. "There are no returns. You are responsible for her well-being. Are you able to provide for this child?"

"Yes!" Mark and I answered.

After we answered several more questions, she said, "As of today, you are irrevocably declared her mother and father. Congratulations on the adoption of your little girl. She is your daughter!" Favor squeezed me tightly, as if she understood the last four words. I glanced at the judge, who for the first time gave me a reassuring smile of approval. I couldn't hold back the tears. We hugged Favor tightly, celebrating this amazing moment. We thanked the judge and headed out the door.

* * * * *

We walked out and were greeted by Emebet and DJ. We noticed that Jamila and Emebet were discussing something between each other, and then Jamila left for a while. We had time before Josiah would be picking us up, so I decided to ask Emebet, as many questions as I could. I turned on my video camera to catch the answers for Favor's memory video.

I started with the most obvious question, "What is the one thing you would like to see for Favor? What hopes do you have for her?"

Emebet paused and looked at DJ, who was serving as an interpreter. "For her to be famous," she answered.

Did I hear her right? I asked to make sure my ears weren't tricking me, "Did you say, you hope she is famous?"

"Yes!" She answered back. "Her mother was very beautiful and always had dreams of being a movie star. I want that for her."

I wasn't sure how to respond so I continued with more questions. "Anything else you hope for her?"

"That she is healthy—happy," she said.

"Can you tell me anything about her mother and father?" I asked.

"Her mother and father ran off very young and got married," she said. "Nobody knew that Favor had been born until my sister was sick, and they brought Favor to me when she was four. That was the last time she saw her mom alive. She was very sick and was dying."

"Do you know what happened to her father?" I asked.

"No, only that he had died," she said. I continued to learn about my daughter's past. It made me very sad that such poverty and sickness took so many lives and left so many orphans. I was thankful for this young mother, who gave life to such a special girl, but saddened that she would never see her grow up and become a beautiful woman. That privilege was given to a stranger—me. I was determined to love this child with the love of two moms.

* * * * *

Josiah arrived to pick us up. I think he was surprised that the court appointment went so quickly. Like him, we also were wondering about what was happening. We found it suspicious that Josiah had also picked up Favor's aunt and brought her back to the agency to fill out some paperwork and interview her. This procedure wasn't normal, and we wondered if this was the "sleight of hand" that Clay had warned us about.

The agency had some additional paperwork for us to fill out once we returned to their offices. Then, in the agency courtyard, we were introduced to Adeferese, the president of EAI Ethiopia. He was a professional looking man in his 60s, and he was the man who had cleared the way for us to adopt Favor. I was thrilled to meet him, and especially to thank him for what he had done for us.

"So, this is the little girl?" he said, looking at Favor standing between Mark and me. My excitement and thankfulness to meet him turned to uneasiness. I knew something wasn't right by the way he looked at her. I questioned my feelings. I was judging him on one look, but I sensed that something more was coming through that look. How could this be? This man had helped us to move forward in our adoption. Why did I feel such a strong sense of danger? He walked up to Favor, patted her on the head, and moved on with his day. I had a growing uneasiness and couldn't wait to leave.

As we waited, we met a young woman who had returned to visit this place, which had formerly been the Happy Home orphanage, where she had been adopted 12 years ago. The building now housed EAI, the adoption agency. The young woman asked to take our picture to capture our "gotcha day." She was a view into the future of how successful adoptions looked. I knew that in this orphanage's glory days, many children were helped and adopted. At that moment, however, I could tell that this place was a shadow of what it used to be, both in its spirit and physical representation.

Favor continues to grab our hearts on her "gotcha day."

* * * * *

That afternoon, Pochi had a boy from Covenant Church pick us up to go shopping. We laughed as we recognized that all the tourists were taken to the same cultural market. We realized the local vendors must have a common route for Americans, because we saw more Americans and Europeans than Ethiopians. In this same place where we'd been taken when we came to pick up Shewit three years earlier, we bought beautiful scarves, coffee, and gifts for all our friends and family back home. We enjoyed watching Favor pick out a stunning Ethiopian dress for herself. Seeing her shop for her friends at the orphanage was one of our sweetest experiences with her during those first few days. We soon realized her amazing inner beauty far outweighed her lovely outer beauty.

We returned to the hotel just as a torrential rain, hail, and lightning storm hit the region. Watching the storm from our balcony was thrilling and a little scary, especially when a bolt of lightning hit right outside the hotel grounds—the whole building shook! Mark noticed that everyone stayed in the pool, so being the concerned American that he was, he called down to the front desk to alert the hotel staff that people were in the pool and there was lightning in the area. Nothing changed. We later found out that some people in Ethiopia look at lightning as though it is God saying, "It's your time to go!" If today was their last day, they were determined to go out having the time of their lives.

* * * * *

That night, we enjoyed dinner with Josiah and a woman who was adopting an older child, like we were. We liked Josiah. He had a gentleness about him. At dinner, he shared with us how the government was handling the growing population of orphans. During the previous year, Ethiopia had legalized abortion as a possible way to control the orphan epidemic. But they didn't take into account that families in Ethiopia look at a child as a blessing. A child represents the future hope of their family and country—no matter how inconvenient the timing might be. In a nation where one out of every three children dies, they consider abortion an abomination to survival, life, and hope. Sickness, poverty, and war had made orphans. Abortion was not the answer—it was viewed as a war on children, and the majority of Ethiopians did not agree with this new "right."

As we enjoyed our Ethiopian meal, Mark took his injera bread, a thin pancake Ethiopians use as an eating utensil, and dipped into one of the dishes brought out. He was getting tired of the tibs, a spicy beef sautéed with vegetables that he had been eating since we arrived, and the dish in front of him looked like something new and yummy. Before Josiah could stop him, Mark had taken a huge bite and swallowed.

The expression on his face said it all. "What did I just eat?" Mark nervously asked.

"Raw meat and tomato sauce," the lady with us said.

"Oh, that can't be good," Mark said.

"Most Ethiopians don't eat that because it is very..." Josiah searched for the right word, "easy to get sick with eating this."

That would turn out to be an understatement of the year in Mark's case. That night and during the next 36 hours, he would hover over the porcelain altar at the Addis Ababa Hilton.

CHAPTER 5
SLEIGHT OF HAND

"...if God has called us to this adoption,
He will provide what we need.
Job or no job, what He orders, He pays for."

—Missy Worton

The clock was ticking down—every second inching us closer to saying goodbye to Favor. We cherished every moment. The last night, Favor and I took Pochi out to dinner. Mark was still sick and resting up for our 18-hour flight home the next day.

As Pochi and I talked over our meal, I found out that EAI Ethiopia had blamed us for being late to our court date, telling the judge we were slow filling out paperwork and that was the reason we were so late. That story was another fallacy, and I was getting more and more concerned about our adoption agency telling bold-faced lies! *How many times and ways were they going to sabotage us?* I knew these actions were not normal for an agency, but we had come so far that we couldn't start over with a different agency without losing all the money we'd spent so far. Besides, we were only a few weeks away from being done with this agency.

Favor sat quietly, not touching her food. She looked exhausted, but I could tell that she probably felt the same way I did—we were both dreading the moment that we would have to say goodbye. The new adoption laws, made to protect the children from trafficking, had adoptive families make two trips to Ethiopia—one for the court date and one for the embassy date. When we adopted Shewit, we only had one trip—our embassy date—and then we were able to bring him home with us. This trip was starting to feel like torture to me. We were going to be with Favor long enough to get attached. Then, we would feel the pain of being separated for a few months before we would reunite. They told us it would only be six to eight weeks between the two trips. They might as well have said six to eight years. We didn't want to leave our little girl—and seconds felt like eons.

I asked Pochi about what happened back in April when the men came to take away the four children. I wasn't clear on why they would be able to come in and take children that already had forever families working toward adopting them. I can't say that she made the matter any clearer to me. It sounded like a regional government office decided to bully a local orphanage.

Favor crawled into my lap and fell asleep in my arms as Pochi continued to tell me about the underbelly of the foster care program that almost took my daughter.

"The man that wanted Favor is very powerful and very rich," Pochi said. "Many people say that he is a devil worshiper."

"A devil worshiper?" I asked. "Why would they allow someone like that to be a foster parent?"

"Because he is wealthy, the kids will have a home, and they will be able to stay in Ethiopia," she said.

"Does he have a wife?" I asked.

"No," she answered, "I don't believe he does. The horrible thing about this is that people say he has had foster children before—and they have all died or disappeared mysteriously. Nobody knows why and they cannot find a reason for their death. It's very weird." I couldn't believe what I was hearing. It sounded like a chapter out of a horror book! Yet, I wasn't completely surprised as I had heard and read about how much devil worship and witchcraft existed in Africa. But this time, I was hearing this about the man who was involved in the adoption of MY DAUGHTER!

"Why does he want Favor?" I asked.

"We don't know," Pochi answered. "I can't imagine it is for good reasons. He says he has money to give her a good life and education."

"At what price?" I said, "Her life? She would just be another foster child that died or disappeared."

"This is why we fight so hard for these children," Pochi said. "It is a life and death situation for them."

"Isn't that what adoption is—a life-or-death situation?" I responded. "In some cases, it's a life-or-death situation for their souls."

"Yes, yes," Pochi said. "That is why I pray so hard before referring a child to a family. I care for more than just their lives. I care about where they will be for eternity."

"Pochi," I paused before moving forward with my question, "if this man is so powerful, is Favor safe in Ethiopia? How has he not found her?"

"We moved her to another orphanage in another city," Pochi said.

"Is there any way he can find her?" I asked.

"No," she said, "but it doesn't matter. The paper the regional office gave me released her to the orphanage to be adopted. They gave me their word that she was okay to be adopted. This man is out of it. It would be okay even if we take her back there."

This new information put my mind into a tailspin. Something didn't feel right. I had more unanswered questions than I did before.

"Please tell me she will never be taken back to the other orphanage," I said, looking Pochi in the eyes. She looked away. "Pochi?"

My heart started beating faster. "Pochi, please promise me you will not take her back to the orphanage where she was before—in Debre Birhan," I pleaded.

Pochi looked up at me and took a deep breath. I could tell she was picking her words wisely.

"I think the regional office (in Debre Birhan) wants to see her before she leaves for America," Pochi cautiously spoke. "It's nothing to worry about. I have the paper so they cannot keep her."

My heart felt a sharp pain of imminent danger. "They have no right to see her!" I said. "There is NO reason they need to see her, since that paper is signed! She is now ours, and as her mom, I am telling you that I do not want her to go back to that city. I know it isn't safe for her to be there."

"You do not need to worry," Pochi said, playing with the silverware in front of her to avoid eye contact.

"No," I argued, "I do need to worry. I can't ignore the fact that I feel she'll be in great danger there. Now, I need you to promise me you will not take her back."

"The foster mother will not agree...I'm afraid she will not," she said.

"I don't care," I persisted, "Mark and I don't want her going back."

"Okay, okay," she said, "I will tell her, but the foster mother will not be happy. She thinks she will be in big trouble because they asked her to bring Favor in. She promised them she would. I just don't want to upset her. This is very touchy because she is the foster mother we've put in place to protect Favor from being taken to a place where we couldn't find her. The foster mother works at my orphanage."

"How can she still be a foster mother when I just had a judge tell me Favor is my daughter by law?" I asked. "She can't be an adopted child and a foster child. There is no need for the foster mother now—I am her mother. The papers were signed, weren't they?"

"Yes, they were signed," she said. "She just doesn't want the regional office to be upset with her. She made them a promise."

None of what Pochi was saying made any sense. She wasn't telling me something. I could feel it. I kept asking questions, but I got the same answer, or was encouraged not to worry.

When she dropped Favor and me off at the Hilton, I turned and looked at her.

"I'm begging you not to take her back to that city. I don't know what I'm not being told, but I do know that Favor will be in danger if she's taken back."

"I would never put her in danger," Pochi said. "You do not need to worry."

I shut the car door and watched as she drove out of the complex. My pleas were falling on deaf ears. I looked down at Favor. She was holding my hand and leaning on me, half asleep. I loved her so much, and I couldn't bear the thought of losing her again. Not now. How was I going to leave tomorrow, knowing what I knew?

* * * * *

The next morning I woke up with Favor staring at me. She smiled when she saw that I had caught her. We couldn't understand each other's language, but our eyes and arms spoke beyond words. That morning she was my shadow. I would put on my makeup foundation, and she would grab it and copy me. Then I would take a washcloth and remove it from her beautiful face. I would put my lip gloss on, and she would grab it and apply it to her lips, copying my every move. When I went to flat-iron my hair, Favor took the flat iron from me and wanted to straighten my hair. These were precious moments that I captured for my memories of her, to treasure during our upcoming separation.

Favor and I embracing every moment!

Today was going to be a hard day. I looked over at Mark, who had been up most of the night battling food poisoning. It was obvious that he had lost. He wasn't in any kind of shape to travel in an airplane for 18 hours.

* * * * *

The one-hour trip back to Covenant Orphanage in Holeta was quiet. Favor greeted the children and started handing them the gifts that she had chosen and specially wrapped for them. As she gave these gifts to her friends, Favor had so much pride, which was evident in the way she held herself and watched as each friend reacted to the specially-picked out, unique gift.

Mark planted himself in a chair in the living room of the orphanage. I knew he felt like crawling into a hole, but I watched in admiration as he found strength to entertain the children. They gathered around him as he would try to pronounce some of their words in Amharic. The laughter would explode as he would butcher a phrase. He sat there for more than an hour, with all of them waiting for what he would say and do next. He had them in the palm of his hand, and they loved him.

After dinner with the children, we had to load up and get back to the large city of Addis Ababa, where we would catch our flight back to America. I knelt down to say goodbye to Favor. This moment was the one I had been dreading since before I'd arrived. There she was, the little girl I had dreamt about, fought for, and loved—standing in front of me. If there was any way legally and safely to stuff her into my suitcase and take her home, I would've done it in a second. I fought to stop the tears and show her a happy face that she could remember.

Looking in her eyes, I told her I loved her in Amharic, "Eh-wuh-dih-shah-loh."

She smiled and nodded her head, whispering it back to me.

Mark surrounded by the children at the orphanage.

"I will come back soon and take you to America to live with me," I assured her. "I promise. It won't be long." Then I hugged her and kissed her goodbye, trying to rip off the emotional Band-Aid as quickly as I could. As I turned to go, I felt her arms grab my waist, trying to keep me from leaving. I took a deep breath and grabbed her up in my arms, holding her as tight as I could.

"Father, please protect her," I prayed in a whisper. The nurse came and put her hand on Favor as if to say *it's time*. She turned and hugged the nurse, allowing me to walk to the car. Everyone was seated and waiting as I crawled into the back seat and shut the door. As we drove away, we waved goodbye to all the children standing at the blue gate, but my eyes only went to one. I watched her until I couldn't see her any more. My tears started flowing as if a dam had broken within, and my whole body ached just to hold her one more time. It was almost unbearable. I kept pushing back the feeling that I would never see her again. Mark put his arm around me and, without a word, just let me cry.

* * * * *

Our flight was overbooked so we had to change airlines, and we had an unexpected upgrade to first class. I believe the man at the gate took pity upon Mark, who looked absolutely pathetic by this point. As we waited in the immigration line, Mark suddenly realized he didn't have his jacket with him. It carried all our money in it. He ran toward the security area, hoping he had not left it in the hotel van, or worse. My husband was not himself. Besides not feeling well, he had been way off his game before he ever got sick. When he came back, he had his jacket that had been left in the security area, and thankfully, all the money was still in it.

Once we got to the waiting area, I asked him where his head was. He had been checked out most of the trip, and with some of the comments he was making, I felt like he was slipping into a doubtful and faithless mentality. I had married a man of strong faith, and I was wondering what had happened to him. He had missed the opportunity to enjoy the moments with Favor because his mind had been hijacked by worry of what tomorrow would hold for us financially.

"Mark, who do you think holds our tomorrows?" I asked. He looked at me for a moment and then shook his head, acknowledging the reality called faith. "We both agreed that if God called us to this adoption, He would provide what we needed. Job or no job. What He orders, He pays for, right?" Mark gave me a half-hearted smile.

"I know that," he said. "I just don't feel well."

I started feeling bad for beating him up when he was already down, so I just sat quietly beside him and waited to board.

* * * * *

The Lord gives and the Lord takes away, which explains our second flight—not the same lovely experience as the first. This time, we had the "pleasure" of sitting in the middle seats in the back of the plane. I am a lover of people, but the precious souls that filled those two seats smelled like a bath was on their bucket list of things yet to do.

Halfway through the flight, I opened up my phone to look at the pictures I had taken in Ethiopia. Somehow, the first picture that came up was of my three children waiting for us back in Tennessee. My depression over leaving Favor switched to thankfulness and expectation for the three I had back home. Soon, we were reunited with three very happy kids, holding them in our arms, telling them every moment we could remember about our trip. After all the gifts were handed out and the details shared, we all went to bed. There is something magical about crawling between the sheets of your own bed. It doesn't matter how much hotels try, how amazing or how soft their high-thread-count Egyptian cotton sheets are, they can't compare to the feeling you get at home. I loved being home.

CHAPTER 6
TURMOIL

"Now to Him who is able to do
far more abundantly than all that we ask or think,
according to the power at work within us..."

—Ephesians 3:20, ESV

The next morning, my brother Steve called from New Mexico. He had some bad news about my mother. While I was in Ethiopia, she had fallen and broken her hip, and she needed surgery. The problem is that my mom is highly allergic to anesthesia and has a hard time waking up. I reminded my brother of this issue, and he said it had already been taken care of—she would have a spinal sedative. Her surgery was scheduled for that week. Because everything had been taken care of, the family didn't think it would be necessary for me to go to New Mexico for the surgery since I had just returned from Ethiopia. I was relieved, but felt a little guilty for not being there for my mom.

* * * * *

For the next few days, Mark and I tried to plan out what the following months would look like. We tried to determine what we needed to do before Favor would come home and transition into our family. The first thing on the list was for Mark to continue his job search. Although he had been actively looking, the economy wasn't improving and people were afraid to hire. We were down to one car—a five-seater. With Favor, we would be a six-seat family, so we had no choice but to buy another car.

After the fog I saw come over Mark in Ethiopia, I tried to tread lightly when it came to spending money. After all, we did have another trip to Ethiopia, and Mark still had no job. I really wanted a certain type of van—one that was not only high on the consumer ratings scale but also high in price. Mark set a budget, which was half of the cost of what most of these vans went for—even used.

The van was the least of my battles. After all, this was a "want" not a "need," so I went to the Lord in prayer, and asked if He could find this van for less than $10,000. A video player, leather seats, and compact disc player would be great, but I knew that I was pushing it.

Within a few days, Mark had found the van of my dreams on eBay. It had everything we could've asked or hoped for. I'll admit, we were a little nervous about buying a car on eBay unseen, but we had to try. This was a miracle, and it was a thousand dollars less than our budget. This had to be God! We bid on it...and lost it by a few dollars. We didn't see that coming.

The next day, Mark had bidder's remorse. If only he'd gone up $50 more! He felt the van was ours, so he contacted the business about the van he had bid on. The business informed us that just before he called, the highest bidder backed out. Miraculously, by the end of the day, we were driving our new van home—with everything we asked for and a few extras!

I learned a valuable lesson that week. God is a loving Father, and like most fathers, He loves to give great gifts to His children. He knows the desires of our hearts, and He knows the needs of our day-to-day lives. It never hurts to ask Daddy for what you want. Sometimes His goodness just might surprise you!

* * * * *

When I got home that night, I had another phone call from New Mexico. My mom wasn't waking up from surgery. We all knew the first 24 hours were crucial to her recovery and her ability to ever walk again.

During the next few days, I asked my friends to pray for my mom's healing. Two days passed, then three. Finally, on the fourth day, my mom's eyes opened, but it was clear that she wasn't there. She was unresponsive to her surroundings, looking straight ahead, with no expression and no interaction. Her body was starting to curl up, and her hands drew into her chest. The only things sustaining her were nutrients fed intravenously and her fighting spirit. After a week, the doctors decided an MRI was needed to check her brain activity.

Back in Tennessee, I was being told that there was no reason for me to come because there was nothing I could do, and it looked like my mom was starting to wake up. She would be fine. But I didn't have peace about not being in New Mexico with my mom. That night, I asked God to give me direction. He knows what tomorrow holds, and I'm completely clueless. I'm a dreamer, and I know God speaks to me through my dreams. When I'm dreaming is probably one of the only times that I'm quiet enough to actually listen. That night was no different—and a dream came with God speaking to me.

I found myself walking down a dark tunnel toward a light ahead. As I slowly made my way to the light, I noticed an open door to my right. I peered into the room, only to find another hallway. This one was full of cobwebs and a white substance oozing down the walls. I could smell death, and I could feel the darkness creeping up on me. I shut that door and kept walking toward the light, when I realized that I was in a type of care unit. A man, walking in front of me, stopped at a doorway where the dim light was coming from. He turned and looked at me. It was Jesus. He held out His hand and drew me to His side.

I didn't say a word, but I followed Him into the room. I could barely recognize the person lying in the bed, but as I came closer, I realized it was my mother. Her arms were curled up to her chest, and I could see that her body had no life. Her mind was dark and lifeless, but below her chest, near her stomach, a light shined brightly. I wondered: *Could this light be her spirit?* It seemed that her spirit was alive and well, trapped in a body that was quickly shutting down. Jesus walked over to her bedside, and placed His left hand on her head. The light below her chest started to spread over her body. Then Jesus turned to me.

"Go to New Mexico, and I will do the rest," He said.

I woke up.

* * * * *

Without a doubt, I needed to go to New Mexico, but I was battling this decision. I wasn't ready to leave my kids again. I also knew I didn't have to be there for my mom to get healed. So why did I feel so strongly that I had to go? After all, they had told me she would be okay.

It came down to obedience. Jesus told me to go. Would I obey? Maybe, just maybe, He was going to do something amazing—if I just obeyed.

I sat down with Mark, who was on his laptop. "Mark," I calmly said, "I need to go to New Mexico, and be with my mom." I couldn't believe that I had just opened my mouth and let it come out.

"Okay," he said. "I figured you would." Then I told him about the dream I had.

"I believe her spirit is alive," I explained, "but her brain and body are close to death. I have to speak or sing to her spirit. Only her spirit can hear me now. Jesus will do the rest. He told me He would."

Mark was already looking up flights. "How soon do you want to leave?" He didn't seem worried about the money. At least it came across that way. Somehow, he knew this was a mission from above, and when God directs the path, He makes a way for all the details, including the finances. Exhausted, I pulled the bag that I had just unpacked out of the closet and packed it again.

* * * * *

My brother Steve picked me up at the airport. I found out that the MRI had nothing but bad news concerning my mom's brain, and her body was close to a vegetative state. According to the doctors, we might as well say goodbye, because the mom we all knew and loved wasn't there anymore. In her place lies a shell. As I listened to my brother talk, I knew I had already seen in my dream everything that he was telling me. However, Jesus gave me something the doctors didn't give my mother or family—hope.

The next morning, I couldn't wait to get to my mom's side. My stomach was turning with excitement and anticipation for what Jesus would do. My sweet dad warned me that Mom didn't look like herself. As we walked down the hallway to her room, I recognized everything from my dream. I had already been there, although my physical body had never stepped foot in this building. My dad was surprised when I led the way straight to my mom's room.

I let my dad go in before me. I watched with tears as his feeble body struggled to get up close to his bride of 66 years. He bent down to kiss her still form. There was no movement or sign of life in her.

I looked at her lying there, exactly like she was in my dream. She didn't look like my mom—she only looked like a remnant of her. I didn't see any light, and I felt very cold as

I walked to the side of her bed. I placed my left hand on her head, just like I remembered Jesus had done in my dream. I didn't say any fancy prayer or rebuke death from her body. I just said His name—"Jesus."

My hand immediately became hot and heat started rising from the top of my mother's body. The sensation of heat traveled up my arm. I could feel the most horrible fear, depression, hopelessness, and death move through my body and into my lower chest area. When it came into the place of my spirit, it vanished. I took a breath and opened my eyes, relieved that the horrible feelings had left.

I looked at my mom. Her eyes suddenly opened, and her head turned toward me. She looked directly at me and into my eyes, and smiled.

"Missy, you came!" she said, as clear as a bell. Those were her first words in 10 days, other than a faint "yeah."

My dad, who is practically deaf, shot up out of the chair behind me. "Did she just say something?" he asked in amazement.

"Yes!" I exclaimed through tears. My mom looked at my dad, who had tears coming down his face by then. He had not heard her speak since before her surgery two weeks earlier. He looked her in the eyes and she looked back.

"Did you just speak, Anne?" he asked.

She nodded her head and smiled. "Yes, love you," she said.

My father's face beamed with joy. "I love you," he said. "You scared me! I thought I lost you."

My mom nodded her head, yes. She knew that we had almost lost her. She looked back at me.

"You came," she said, "love you, so much."

"I did!" I smiled. "I love you, Mom." In that moment, I was so thankful that I had obeyed and stepped on that plane. Jesus had visited and healed her, and He had chosen to use me—of all people. My mom and I had always butted heads, but we loved each other. I realized that Jesus had made our bond deeper than the words that had attempted to separate us. We had just experienced the love of God in a very real and magnificent way.

That day, it seemed like the entire care unit had to stop by to see my mom. She would smile at them and nod her head as they would talk about the miracle in front of them.

It was more than just a physical miracle—it was an emotional miracle as well. When several of her kids and grandkids gathered around her, she proclaimed, "I have a beautiful family! Beautiful!"

We all smiled and laughed with thankfulness and joy. The nurses' jaws dropped in amazement. Not only was she speaking—she was speaking in positive sentences—after she had been in a deep depression, saying only negative and hopeless words for nearly a year.

For the next two weeks, I stayed by my mom's side and continued to pray for her to be completely healed. I enjoyed helping my parents—a supernatural strength came into me while I was there. I watched them celebrate each other daily. After 66 years, they were still madly in love. My mom would ask me to sing, and instead of fighting her like I usually did, I brought a hymnal and sang whatever she requested. She became stronger and stronger until she finally took her first step.

* * * * *

At the same time, news was erupting about the deadly attack at the Libyan American Embassy in Benghazi. Four Americans had been killed, including the U.S. Ambassador, Christopher Stevens. Every day we would hear about another anti-American protest at U.S. embassies in the Middle East and Africa by the radical Islamic movement. People were dying and getting injured. The more the anti-American protests happened, the more my concern grew about our embassy date in Ethiopia. I knew Ethiopia was considered a Christian nation. They had a Christian president too, but they also had a large growing number of Muslims, some of whom were radical.

When I returned to Tennessee, I emailed Pochi to find out if there had been any incidents at the Ethiopian U.S. Embassy and to ask if any travel warnings for Americans had been issued there. She quickly responded that Ethiopia was safe. She also informed me that the foster mother would be taking Favor back to the city of Debre Birhan, where the regional government adoption office was to let that office know Favor would be leaving for the U.S. soon. Favor had also said she wanted to see her friends at the Covenant Orphanage location where she had lived for a period of time. My heart stopped and I quickly sent an email back, begging her to not take our daughter back to Debre Birhan.

We heard nothing for three days.

* * * * *

The next time we heard from Pochi, we learned that Favor had already been taken back to Debre Birhan against our wishes. In our hearts, we had known that was going to happen, and there was nothing we could do about it. I wrote Pochi back through tears of pure frustration and anger:

> Mark and I don't understand why Favor was taken back to DB (Debre Birhan). We understood from her that she did not like it there. The men scared her that came to that orphanage. We are praying you remove her as soon as you can, as we don't want anything to happen to her. We were under the understanding that she is considered our child at this point and the foster care is no longer an issue. This is very confusing...

Again, we found ourselves having to trust that God would take care of Favor, halfway around the world. We were confused by what was happening, and it felt like we weren't being told the whole story. In the turmoil, all we could do was look up.

* * * * *

My friend Lori contacted me to see if I wanted to go see Chris Overstreet, a well-known evangelist from Bethel Church in Redding, California, speak at a local church near our home in Franklin. She and I had gone to see the film *Father of Lights (featuring Overstreet)* that powerfully depicted the greatness of God.

Mark decided to join me, and we experienced a wonderful gathering with individuals who loved God and people. Toward the end of the meeting, Chris was pulling various people up and prophetically releasing words of encouragement to them as God directed him. I was hoping that either Mark or I would receive a prophetic word or prayer to let us know that the situation we were going through would turn out okay. Just as I had those thoughts, Chris looked right at me and asked me to stand. Lori turned the recorder in her phone on to catch what he was saying: "...I see like a golden path being laid out in front of you, Missy, right now, and it's just like favor, favor, favor. Favor on your life in the area of influence."

I had to giggle. There was that word: favor! Lori started giggling along with me.

"I just want to give you some scriptures God is giving me for you," Chris continued. "Ephesians 3:20, 'Now unto Him who is able to do exceeding abundantly above all that we ask or think, according to the power that works in us,' and Philippians 1:6, 'Being confident of this very thing, that He which hath begun a good work in you will perform it until the day of Jesus Christ.'"

There it was. God was going to complete what He'd started in our lives concerning Favor and this adoption. I could feel myself calm down about Favor being taken to the city of Debre Birhan. Everything was going to be all right, and He had given me the promises to stand on. We had no idea how important these words would be in the days to come. It's not exaggerating to say that they would be our lifeline.

* * * * *

I received one last email from Pochi before we got word to travel:

> Missy, don't worry about anything. God is in control, and your child will be home with you soon.
> God bless you, Pochi.

Within a few weeks we received the email securing our embassy date. At this point, Mark had decided that it was an easy pick-up-and-come-home trip, and he wasn't excited about returning after he had spent the last trip sick and hovering over a toilet bowl. McKenzie, our 11-year-old daughter, loved Ethiopia, and we wanted her to have extra bonding time with Favor. So, Mark bought tickets for McKenzie and me, and made reservations at the Hilton in Addis Ababa again. The staff at that hotel had treated us well, so Mark felt we would be safe and well-cared-for on our return trip. On the other hand, I had an unrelenting, uneasy feeling about Mark not traveling with us.

* * * * *

Everything was ready to go. However, we hadn't heard a word from Pochi. We contacted EAI America, and we were told that everything was fine and were advised to make the trip.

Still no word came from Pochi.

Five days before we were scheduled to board Ethiopian Airlines, Mark had a growing unrest in his spirit. We both felt something was really wrong. Pochi always returned our emails within a few days; to hear nothing from her for so long was alarming. Mark decided to check into a ticket so that he could come with us. To his surprise, the price had stayed the same, and he knew that there was a reason why God had made a way for him to join us. I was so relieved.

Finally, two days before our flight, we received a message from Pochi. It wasn't good news.

Another adoptive couple from the United States had gone to Ethiopia for their child's embassy date, and the Debre Birhan officials would not release their child to them. The couple had been sent back to the States empty-handed and broken-hearted. They had not even been allowed to see their adopted child.

Mark immediately reached out to Adeferese at EAI Ethiopia and asked him if he was aware of what had happened with this couple and their adopted child. Mark wanted to know if we would face a similar problem, and if so, what was being done about it. He also reached out to several U.S. attorneys who had knowledge of Ethiopia and their laws. All the attorneys knew Adeferese and his reputation. They let us know we were in good hands because Adeferese had the power and influence to get things done.

We then called EAI America again, and they encouraged us to travel because Favor, by Ethiopian law, was our daughter.

Adeferese emailed an hour later, telling us they had a plan in place to get Favor and they wanted to try it before going to court. *A plan? Court?* With each email, we realized our concerns were warranted about not taking her back to Debre Birhan, but that was water under the bridge now. *Where was our daughter?*

A few hours later, we received a call from EAI America. They had spoken to Adeferese, and he was now saying that we should *not* come to Ethiopia. We needed to let them figure things out first. They had no more details to share, but things weren't looking good.

I silently sat on our bed after hanging up the phone. Something wasn't right. Words weren't matching with actions being taken. *What or who was everybody so afraid of? Who could we trust?* I looked up at Mark, who stood at the end of the bed. Helpless, we said nothing. In our minds, we had completely lost control of this situation. We didn't know who had our daughter or if she was scared or safe, and we'd been told *not* to come and pick her up just after we were advised to go and bring her home.

Why was there such a battle for this little girl, and why did we both feel we had no other choice? We had to go get our daughter.

CHAPTER 7
FLYING INTO THE STORM

"I didn't have time to entertain fear when I knew God's promises had given me permission to be brave."

—Missy Maxwell Worton

My mind was racing, replaying the conversation that Pochi and I had about the devil worshiper who wanted to foster Favor, and the plight of the other three children in this foster care situation. I didn't want to believe that somehow the local government was involved in corruption, nor did I want to think that my daughter's future was at stake because of some sinister plan. The reality of what was happening slapped me in the face—no matter how we looked at it, it was a form of child slavery. I couldn't bear to think of Favor being put in a home that didn't love or value her. Mark and I were determined not to allow her to be taken from us—but where would we start?

We knew we were being kept in the dark on the details, so we decided to try to call Pochi in Ethiopia to get more information. As I dialed her number, I prayed that she would pick up. I held my breath until I heard the connection and the rings begin. On the second ring, to our relief, she answered. She was anxious to speak to us.

"Is Favor okay? Is she in a safe place?" were the first questions out of my mouth.

"She is in Debre Birhan," Pochi began. "When the foster mother took her to the official's office, he decided that Favor should stay in Ethiopia in the foster care system. He does not want to release her to be adopted." My heart felt a dagger strike, but I remembered—and held on to—God's promise that she would be mine. We had come too far to not have victory. I remained calm.

"Where is Favor now?" I asked.

"Right now she is safe with the foster mother," she said.

"How long is she with the foster mother, Pochi?" I hoped there would be a window of time to do something before she would be put into the hands of someone else and we would lose her forever.

There was a pause on the other side of the phone.

"Pochi, did you hear me?" I asked.

"Yes," she said slowly, "she is safe. You don't need to worry about her."

But she wasn't in the orphanage, and she was now under the supervision of someone who had the power to keep her from us. Something in me broke. "Pochi, why did you take her to Debre Birhan?" I was frustrated. "We begged you not to take her. Now we could lose her because you didn't listen to us!" I wanted to yell at her in that moment, but I held back, knowing she was the only link I had to Favor.

There was dead silence on the phone for a minute or so. Then Pochi softly responded, "I know, I am so sorry, but I did what I felt I had to do at the time. I didn't think they would keep her and stop her from being adopted. We were promised."

"How could you trust them?" I asked. "I begged you not to take her back there."

"Don't worry...we have a plan with Favor's aunt to get her out of this foster care either Monday or Tuesday," she said. "We will get her back."

"Is this the plan Adeferese was talking about?" I asked.

"Yes," she said, "we are working with Adeferese and Favor's aunt to get her back from this local government. We are hoping this will work. Pray."

Hoping it would work was not what we wanted to hear. We wanted a guarantee. I didn't know what to say. I was so angry that Favor had been put in this situation to begin with.

"They told us not to come to Ethiopia," I said. "What do you think, Pochi?"

"This is up to you," she said. "I cannot promise you that if you come, you will leave with Favor. I don't know what will happen. We are hoping that this plan will work, but I cannot promise you anything."

I sat quietly on the phone. *We had done everything right. Why was this happening?*

"Favor's aunt does not want her to go into the foster care system," Pochi said. "She wants her to go to America with you. She says Favor belongs with you."

"Will they give Favor to her?" I asked.

"She is a close living relative, so they should," she said. "Have you thought about getting an attorney?" *What?* Now she was talking about us getting an attorney when she was the one who should've just listened to us! Why did *we* have to pay for the attorney? We were in this situation because of someone else, and I was having a little pity party over it.

"Everyone seems to believe Adeferese has the influence to take care of this for us," I responded. "Do you really think we are going to need to hire a lawyer too?"

"I don't know," Pochi said. "The couple that just left without their child hired a woman that used to be the judge for adoptions. I think she only cost them a thousand American dollars. She knows what's going on, but you might want to wait and see how it goes Monday with the rescue."

We hung up feeling no better off than before we called. There was no certain outcome, just more questions and more money leaking from our checking account. I had to get out of the house and pray about what to do. The one thing this battle had done well was to drive me to my knees. I was beginning to wonder if that was the purpose of this trial.

* * * * *

Another problem was stirring out in the Atlantic Ocean—a massive storm called Hurricane Sandy was set to hit the East Coast on the same day that our flight was scheduled to fly out from Washington, D.C. Hurricane Sandy had been nicknamed "Frankenstorm." The news channels were calling it "epic," and it seemed to be getting worse as it inched toward its impact zone.

My emotions were having their own "epic Frankenstorm," and I badly needed to calm my mind. Between the call to Pochi, our agency saying not to travel, and now this hurricane approaching, I felt everything converging on us—fighting against us. Everything was screaming not to go, saying we had no possibility to get our daughter, telling us to just give up. *So, why did I not have the peace to stay home?*

"Father, we need answers," I prayed. "What are we supposed to do?"

Silence.

My mind went to the moment that I said goodbye to Favor, standing outside her orphanage. I remembered the promise that I made to her looking in those tear-filled brown eyes. I had promised that I would come back to get her and take her home with me. I had to go, but would I even have the chance to see her? Everything was such a mess—and I felt so out of control.

"If You say go, I'll go," I prayed. "I'm not afraid. I just don't want anything bad to happen to Favor. If You say stay...I paused...I'll do it, and I will choose to trust You to keep her safe."

I kept praying, then I stopped and just sat still, quieting my mind and spirit, dumping all the noise that was filling my head. I took a deep breath and waited, and waited.

Then, as clear as a bell, I heard His answer: "When your foot touches Ethiopian soil, the victory will be yours." I was suddenly overcome with peace and confidence that we needed to go. There was no question—I still believed going to Ethiopia was the only option. I had to win this battle and bring Favor home. Now I had to tell Mark.

I walked into our bedroom. Mark was resting on our bed. His eyes opened and he gave me a knowing look.

"Mark," I started, "I believe that God has told me if we set our feet in Ethiopia, the victory will be ours. Just like He did with my mom."

"Okay," Mark said without a beat. "I agree. We need to go."

* * * * *

Mark's mother, Kathy, arrived two days later to take care of the boys for the week. Mark had decided to honor our word that McKenzie could go with us. Things had drastically changed, and I was a little nervous about taking her, but we both had peace that she would be okay. We quickly pulled everything together and caught our flight to Washington, D.C. The feeling of the unknown was all around us, but the peace that surpasses all understanding was also strong within us.

Shortly after we arrived in D.C., we once again met up with our close friends David and Kathleen. As we sat and talked this time, a few weeks later, we could see their excitement for this adoption, but we could also feel their underlying concern. None of us had ever experienced anything like the run-around, cryptic information we were currently receiving. Our first adoption from Ethiopia had been so smooth. We discussed the fight that we felt we were getting ready to face and the potential issues we would be battling. It seemed very poetic that we were flying out of one storm—Hurricane Sandy—and into another potential storm of a different kind.

I also shared with David and Kathleen the testimony of what had recently happened with my mom, and how much that dream and following God's leading to her healing thus far had built my faith. I had a new level of trust, and I was starting to open the Bible and just say, "Yes!" I was excited for the fullness of what God had for His children. We talked the hours away, until we knew that it was time to get some rest for the long flight in the morning. They took us back to the Embassy Suites near the airport.

At the hotel in a large water exhibit, two swans named George and Martha kept following McKenzie's every move as she walked back and forth in front of them and around the exhibit. The swans' behavior gave her and the other kids watching something to laugh about. The swans reminded me that our God is always near us—no matter where we go. David and Kathleen prayed with us and gave us an awesome care package to take, and we went our separate ways.

After we were settled in our room, I called to say goodbye to my dad. My mom was still at the regional care center where they were continuing her physical therapy. I didn't tell him all the details, but I did mention that we were going to get a new granddaughter for him and granny to love. He could sense beyond my words that something must be wrong. He began to weep and to tell me that he loved me. He was ready to meet this little girl named Favor, but he also wanted his daughter safe.

* * * * *

The next morning, we arrived at the airport under the heavy, foreboding clouds announcing the oncoming storm. Many flights had been cancelled coming into Washington D.C., and of the flights still in operation, only a handful were running on time. Thankfully, ours was still listed as one of the on-time departures. As we waited for our plane to board, I shot off an email to an amazing group of prayer warriors who I knew would be standing in prayer with us.

I had barely sent the message off when the airline announced a one-hour delay because of a mechanical problem on our plane. Soon, one hour turned into two, and we were getting closer to having to cancel because of the impending storm. I continued to pray, knowing that victory was ours once we set foot in Ethiopia.

Mark reached over and grabbed my hand. "Are you doing okay?" he asked.

I nodded my head. He knew me. I used to be a white-knuckle frequent flyer. Any sign of mechanical trouble would make me panic, and turbulence would shake me to my core. I had been known to walk off a plane before it took off because we were going to be flying in cloudy weather. I preferred the clear blue skies with little to no chance of bad weather, and long flights were my biggest nightmare. I had tried every crutch you could think of to overcome my fears. Waiting for our plane, I realized that was the *old* me. Although fear kept trying to whisper in my ear, I knew I had changed when I gave my life fully to God, and had died to self. Fear of dying left—and freedom came. I started to live.

And today, I had a mission. A purpose. I had a little girl waiting for me. Somehow, knowing that mission fueled strength from somewhere deep inside. Every fear that tried to creep in and whisper was completely silenced. I didn't have time to entertain fear when I knew God's promises had given me permission to be brave.

We boarded the plane two hours late. We found our seat in the back, snapped a picture of the three of us in our seats to post on Facebook, and said a prayer. As we started to roll down the runway, I could feel my heart pounding with a new adventure. The airplane lifted into the sky. As the engines roared toward the clouds and oncoming rain, I could feel my spirit soar. We were physically flying into a massive storm, and barreling like a projectile toward our own personal storm waiting in Ethiopia.

After a long delay...we are heading to Ethiopia!!! We know and believe God has already won this battle for us!!!

Facebook post just after boarding to return to Ethiopia for Favor.

This time, McKenzie is with us, and we are flying over Hurricane Sandy..."

CHAPTER 8
PUT YOUR FEET ON THE SOIL

"Like a child who trusted without question, she knew every word from her Father's mouth would happen."

—Missy Maxwell Worton

It had been a long night. We had just flown through the roughest turbulence that we had ever experienced. I was sincerely surprised that the plane could handle all the pounding and jolting drops that it took. The airline hosts looked worn and exhausted, probably rethinking their career choices and insurance plans.

Breaking through the clouds, we could see the sun rising in the distance, as if to say, *Welcome to a new, calmer, less bumpy day.*

I wanted to sit up taller in my chair to see if we were still over the ocean, but I couldn't move. Somehow in her sleep, McKenzie had thrown her body over mine and was half on the floor and half on my chest. About that time, a loud flight attendant came by with breakfast. She pointed to McKenzie and said, "Wake her up! She needs to eat." I managed a smile

Sunrise in Ethiopia

and tried to wave her off, but she insisted. So, I woke up Sleeping Beauty.

It wasn't pretty.

During the next few minutes, I played peace keeper between the sleepy, grouchy tween and the grumpy flight attendant. McKenzie took one bite of the airline food and growled, "Really, you woke me up for this!"

"And...wow, look at that!" I said, looking past her to a golden canvas beneath us. We had flown completely out of any cloud cover and were flying somewhere over Egypt. The land was brown with golds, oranges, and tints of red weaving through it. It had an enchanting beauty, even with no sign of water.

Finally, we could feel the plane start to make its descent. As we came closer, I watched the ground below me. Our view that once was desert had changed into miles and miles of green, lush land. Farms of various crops were growing in rectangles and squares below us. Although we could see the homes showed a level of poverty, the land of Ethiopia was beautiful and bursting with life.

As I watched the buildings get larger, I knew I was closer to the promise that God had given us. If we would just put our foot on the soil of Ethiopia, the victory would be ours. I looked over at Mark and grabbed his hand. "I can see the soil of Ethiopia," I said. "Can you?"

Mark looked past me to the window. "I wonder what God is going to do," he said.

"Something great!" I said with confidence.

Once we landed, we stepped off the plane onto nothing but concrete.

I started looking for soil to put my foot on. I was taking God literally when He said to put my feet on the soil, and I didn't want to waste any time staking claim to my victory! Finally, I found a little patch of soil off to the side of the terminal. Going against the flow of people, I anxiously weaved through them to get my foot on that dirt. I looked up at Mark in triumph the moment my foot touched it, and I stood on it for a moment, letting it sink in.

Victory!

I wondered to myself what had been activated in Heaven. *Were angels celebrating and spiritual breakthroughs launched at that moment?* McKenzie smiled, then rolled her eyes, like she usually does when Mom goes into her "crazy" zone. Mark just looked like he wanted to get to the hotel as soon as possible.

We went through customs, got our luggage, and looked for Josiah from EAI Ethiopia. He was timidly standing off to the side. His countenance was different this time. Instead of the friendly, warm welcome that we had received before, he cautiously approached us, said that he didn't have enough room in his car, and told us that we would have to take the hotel shuttle. He confirmed with Mark that he would pick us up the next day for our embassy date, then he quickly left with a woman who had also flown in from America. We were bewildered. The agency had always picked us up in the past... and why was Josiah acting so weirdly toward us?

Mark smelled his armpit. "I don't think I smell that bad," he said.

"Uh, Dad!" McKenzie said, acting disgusted. "That is just gross!" I started laughing—I knew we could come across as a strange crew. Maybe Josiah just didn't want to be seen with us.

* * * * *

The Hilton had been our go-to place—the staff was friendly, it was secure, and the points Mark had managed to earn while he was traveling made it close to free, which was perfect for our dwindling budget. While Mark checked in, McKenzie and I plopped ourselves down on the nearest couch. Our travel delay had caused us to arrive close to two hours later than planned, and we were exhausted.

I started watching the people around me while McKenzie fell back asleep. Some people were busy, walking off the elevator and quickly out the front doors looking straight ahead. In the corner, some well-dressed men were enjoying the Ethiopian coffee ceremony being served by a beautiful Ethiopian woman in ceremonial dress.

I heard the elevator ding again. This time, a couple walked out, looking around. I immediately recognized Chris Overstreet—the man who had prayed for me a few weeks ago at a church in Franklin—but what were he and his wife doing in Addis Ababa? They walked by, stopped, turned around, and came back to where I was sitting.

"Are you stranded here because of the storm?" Chris asked.

I stood up. "No, we're here for our embassy date," I answered. "We're adopting."

"Whoa, that's awesome!" he said. "Really awesome!"

"Thank you," I said. "So, are you stranded here because of Hurricane Sandy?"

"Yeah," he started. "We just finished up doing some mission work in Uganda and Mozambique. It was awesome there. Anyway, we were just on our way back to the U.S. when our plane suddenly got diverted to Ethiopia. It was crazy. The airline put us up in another hotel, but we felt we were supposed to come over here and stay one night. We got the last available room. We're just on our way out to check on flights."

I listened in amazement. *I knew Chris was sent by God to remind us of the promises that He had spoken to me through this man.* I also realized that if our plane had been on time, we would have never run into Chris and his wife, because we would have already been in our room asleep when they were in the lobby. God was telling me to take notice, remember, and be encouraged in His words. He had orchestrated another miracle on our path to Favor—diverting a plane to Addis Ababa and Chris switching hotels—all for this moment.

"Are you adopting a little boy or girl?" his wife asked.

"A little girl," I answered. "Actually, we really need prayer for our predicament. There's been a real battle over this adoption, and she has been taken out of the orphanage. Today or tomorrow we have a rescue mission planned to bring her out of this corrupt situation and back into our arms."

"Well, let's pray right now!" Chris said without hesitation, and both he and his wife grabbed my hands and began to pray.

> Father, we lift up this situation to You. Nothing is too big for You, and we know how much You love the orphans and how You have put this family with this little girl. I lift up this little girl before You, Lord, and I see favor going before them in this situation. Lord, I pray You will give them favor with this rescue, and Lord that they shall have victory and favor in all that they do! I just ask, that in everything You do for this couple, You will pour out Your favor and bless them for taking care of the orphan. Amen!

I started giggling after Chris had said favor for the fourth time. "Did I tell you her name was Favor?" I asked.

He got a huge smile on his face. "No way!" he said. "God is so awesome. That's a great name!" He raised his hand to give me a high five. "Man, I just kept hearing you would receive "favor." My name is Chris Overstreet by the way, and this is my wife, Stefanie." He extended his hand to me.

"I'm Missy," I answered as I shook his hand. "The girl sleeping on the couch is my daughter, McKenzie, and my husband, Mark, is checking in. We went to see you speak at an event near Nashville, Tennessee, and you gave me a word there. I really think that word was for right now."

"Really?" he said with amazement, "That is so cool! Now, here we run into you in Ethiopia...wow! God is so cool like that!"

I couldn't agree more.

We finished up our talk, and both Chris and his wife gave me a big hug before they left the hotel. I stood in awe at what had just taken place. When I told Mark, we both realized that God was using this moment to build our faith and to show us that we were in the right place. He could bring anyone into our path and meet us where we had a need. At the time, we knew what had happened was amazing, but we didn't know how important these few minutes would be to us in the coming days.

* * * * *

After we took a quick nap, we made our way to the lobby to see Pochi. When we saw each other, we rushed to hug. She held me as if to not let go. I could tell that she was broken and hurting. We were both in a place we had never been before, and all our feelings were revolving around a little girl. After the initial greetings, we found a quiet place to sit and talk. Pochi looked in every direction to make sure no one was within earshot of our conversation.

"We need to be very careful," Pochi said, leaning into us. "You never know who could be listening." Mark and I looked around. We were alone. "I'm sure you want to know what is going on."

"That would be good," Mark said.

"As you know," Pochi started, "when Favor's aunt found out that they were not going to release Favor to you, she took a bus two hours to see the government official in Debre Birhan. She told him she didn't want Favor to go into the foster care program, and she said that she would take her home with her to prevent that. She argued that as Favor's aunt she had the right to do that. She was very careful not to mention you."

Mark and I glanced at each other.

"She is very brave," Pochi said. "She convinced the official of her plans and he told her to come back Monday or Tuesday of this week and fill out some paperwork. Then they would release Favor, only to her."

"Can she get in trouble for bringing Favor to us?" I asked.

"We'll talk about that later," she said, holding her hand up uncomfortably and pausing for a moment. "The plan is for her to take the bus up to Debre Birhan, either this morning or tomorrow. She will sign the paperwork and then be given Favor. She is going alone so that they don't suspect anything. She wants to bring Favor to you here, at your hotel."

"That'd be great," Mark said.

"But, I talked with her this morning," she continued. "She is in the hospital. She got very sick a few days ago."

"Is she the only one the official will give Favor to?" I asked.

"Yes, she is the only one, and she says she will go tomorrow," Pochi said, "even if she doesn't feel well. She is very happy that you came. She was afraid that you wouldn't come when you heard about the other family."

"What do you mean, *the other family*?" Mark asked. "Are you talking about the family who came back without their child?"

"Yes, the family that came for their embassy appointment last week," Pochi cautiously said. "Their little girl is at the same place as Favor. When they came to pick her up, they weren't allowed to even see her. They went back to America after two days, and hired a lawyer to handle it for them. But their case is not going anywhere. It doesn't look good. Nobody cares, and there is just too much corruption."

"Where is the corruption?" Mark asked. "Did this happen to just your orphanage or are there others?

Pochi looked uncomfortable as she glanced around. "The regional government office targeted three orphanages. My orphanage was the only one with older children, so they decided to put four of them in a foster care that UNICEF created to keep children in their birth country. But they are never supposed to take children out of orphanages. These children were in the process of adoption."

Mark felt his stomach tighten.

"By the way," Pochi said, changing the subject, "when I spoke with EAI today, at first they said they had no knowledge of you arriving in Addis."

"But, Josiah talked to us at the airport!" I said. Mark and I were shocked. *Why were they pretending that they didn't know?* Now Mark was concerned about getting to the Embassy tomorrow.

"I don't know why they said that," Pochi said, "so I just acted like I knew nothing about you as well."

"Well," Mark said, "that explains why Josiah acted the way he did."

"But, when I called back, another lady told me that Josiah was told not to bring you to the EAI office," she said. "They are trying to avoid you. The EAI office is still denying that you are in Ethiopia."

Mark and I sat silent. We felt like the ugly step child. EAI, as our agency, was supposed to be on our side, but the people there sure weren't acting like it.

"I am so sorry this has happened to you," Pochi said apologetically. "I would never have taken her back to Debre Birhan had I known this would happen. The foster mother was afraid the regional official would do something to her if she didn't take Favor to them before she left for America. Now they know where Favor is. The official went back on their word. They don't want her to go to America."

"Do you think the plan to rescue Favor will work?" Mark asked.

"Nothing is for sure," Pochi said, shrugging her shoulders.

We didn't know what to say. We were in way over our heads. We prayed with Pochi before she left, then got McKenzie from the couch, and walked outside to the pool area. We stared blankly at the people laughing and splashing around. McKenzie ran over to dip her toes in the warm mineral water.

"I still feel like there is something Pochi isn't telling us." I said, looking straight ahead.

"I agree," Mark answered. "I feel it too."

I looked down. I was standing on a grassy area. I slid my sandals off to put my feet on the soil as a reminder of the promise I had received before we came. The soil was cool to the touch and the wet dew started to cover my toes.

I prayed silently...*Jesus, my feet are on the soil, but I feel like my victory is so far away and untouchable. I'm trying to be positive and trust Your promises, but really, I'm scared. We need Your help, Lord. I don't want to leave without her.*

"Dad," McKenzie's voice startled me, "can we go swimming?"

"Yes," Mark answered. "Let's grab breakfast first, and then come back down."

McKenzie jumped up and down, clapping her hands. Like a child who trusted without question, she knew every word from her father's mouth would happen. She had been looking forward to coming and getting her little sister since the day we told her we had decided to adopt a little girl. She seemed unaffected by what was happening around her. Joy and expectancy filled her every word, and she was embracing every moment. McKenzie was a picture for Mark and me depicting how we could also behave in this difficult situation. We needed to trust without question that our Heavenly Father would be faithful to His word. We had done our part—our feet were on the soil. We were in Ethiopia for a victory—whether it felt like it or not.

CHAPTER 9
RESCUE MISSION

*"God deliberately chooses imperfect vessels—
those who have been wounded, those with physical or
emotional limitations. Then he prepares them to serve and
sends them out with their weakness still in evidence, so that
his strength can be made perfect in that weakness."*

—Christine Caine, *Undaunted: Daring to do
what God calls you to do*

It was 4 o'clock in the morning. Today was the day of the rescue. Mark and I laid in our bed wide awake. Our night had been restless, and we hadn't slept much. My whole body shook with exhaustion and nerves.

The Islamic call to prayer went out about the time that we realized we were both awake. I admired that they started their day with prayer, but I wished they would've found a closet to take it to. I got up and shut the sliding glass door, and as they sang their morning prayers, I turned my prayers to Jesus. I longed for peace, and I could feel my spirit longing to be with the Father.

A few hours passed, then Pochi called with a nervous excitement in her voice. The rescue mission had begun. Emebet, Favor's aunt, had left the hospital that morning and caught the early bus to Debre Birhan. She had just been at the official's office, and had signed the papers to release Favor into her custody. Soon, she would be on her way to pick Favor up at the disclosed location. At this point, the official did not suspect a thing.

* * * * *

After all we had learned from Pochi, we were surprised when Josiah from EAI actually arrived to pick us up for our embassy appointment. We knew Josiah was a good guy, and maybe he was acting on his own and just keeping his word to us. But we also knew someone at EAI was avoiding us like the plague—someone who may have had influence on Josiah's employment. So it didn't surprise us that Josiah was more than 30 minutes late. The van was a sight to see—Josiah had to bang on the side door to get it open. The vehicle had one row to sit in, and it was against the back of the van. We stepped over a wheel to get to our worn leather seat. Jamila, the woman who had gone with us to our court date in August, sat in the passenger seat in the front of the van with a stack of papers on her lap. She never looked at us. Mark and I remained quiet during most of the drive to the Embassy.

Mark looked at his watch. It had been 30 minutes since we had heard from Pochi. "They should have picked up Favor by now and be on their way here," Mark whispered to me.

"They have picked her up?" Jamila's voice startled us. She looked shocked about the news and shot a glance toward Josiah. In that instant, Mark and I knew that we needed to be more careful around anyone from EAI. We hoped that we had not just unraveled the rescue plan and put Favor and her aunt in danger.

When we arrived at the Embassy, Josiah let us out on the curb and said he would be back after dropping off Jamila at another location. He assured us that someone with EAI would be waiting for us. We nervously went through security and into the waiting area. Other than the security officer at the door, no one greeted us. The room was filled with adoptive families and their sweet babies and children in their arms. My heart ached for Favor.

We felt out of place, and we didn't know what to do next. Mark approached one of the windows to ask for directions while I looked around, hoping to see someone from EAI. I recognized a woman who had been working in the EAI office the day of our court date. I walked past her to make sure. She glanced up at me then quickly looked down at the floor.

Mark came up behind me, "Hey," he said, "recognize anyone from EAI?"

"Maybe," I replied, as I pointed her out to Mark. "See that woman in the black, long skirt? I think she was the one that processed our paperwork last time we were here."

"She is. Has she seen us?" he asked.

"She looked right at me and back down," I said, "quickly."

"Maybe she doesn't recognize you," he said.

"Let's go re-introduce ourselves," I said with a mocking grin. We then started walking toward her. You could literally see her trying to disappear into her chair as I approached.

"Hi," I said with a huge Tennessee smile. "Do you remember us?" She looked up with knowing eyes and said nothing. "We're the Wortons. We're here for our embassy appointment today."

"Josiah said someone from EAI would be here, and here you are! Yay!" I said, putting one arm up in a victory wave. She continued to sit in silence, staring at me, expressionless. It was an awkward moment. "Alrighty then...Do you know English?"

"Yes," she shot back, obviously offended, "I know English very well. I know who you are."

"Oh good," I said. "I wasn't trying to offend you. You weren't saying anything. I thought I'd better ask." It was clear that we were the last people in the world that this woman wanted to be near, no matter what I said or did. Everything in me wanted to be rude and forget all about showing any type of love or kindness.

She jumped out of her seat, walked passed us and up to the window, where she began a conversation with an Ethiopian gentleman. We continued to wait until Josiah arrived a few minutes later. His smile was welcoming. If he knew anything, he wasn't letting it interfere with the way he treated us.

"Worton, Mark family," came through the sound system. Mark and I walked up to the window. The vice-consul stood on the other side of the bulletproof glass. He was an all-American-looking, tall, blonde man. He was young, maybe early 30s at the most. He had a friendly face and a way about him that put us at ease.

"Hi," he said as he glanced up at us. "You're Favor Mark Worton's parents, correct?"

"Yes," Mark said. "She isn't with us...is that a problem?"

"No," he responded. "We're aware of the situation in Debre Birhan. This is the second child we've had to deal with concerning this problem."

"Is there anything you can do to help us?" I asked.

"We plan to send someone to the court hearing tomorrow," he said. "We would like to dig a little deeper to see why they went into the orphanage and removed the children. Once we have more information, we'll do what we can."

We finished the remaining paperwork, and we were told to come back at 10 a.m. on Thursday for Favor's passport/visa and the packet that, once she arrived in the U.S., would make her an official American citizen.

"Will we still be able to get her passport and visa if she's not with us?" Mark asked.

"I see no reason why you wouldn't," he responded. "She is your daughter."

* * * * *

On the drive back to our hotel, my heart suddenly started beating faster, and my spirit leapt. I looked around and saw that we were passing a bus station. The way my body was responding in this particular moment, I felt like I would see Favor. My eyes scanned the crowds of people, but there was no sign of her. I looked at my watch. It was 12 p.m. The rest of the drive, I felt like my heart would beat out of my chest if I didn't hold it in.

"What time did they tell you to return to the Embassy to pick up her passport and visa packet?" Josiah asked.

"Thursday morning at 10," Mark answered.

"I will pick it up for you and bring it to your hotel," Josiah said.

"I'd like to go with you," Mark said.

"This is not necessary. We always pick up the packet and bring it to the families."

"No..." Mark responded, "I would like to go."

"Okay." Josiah shrugged his shoulders. "This is a very unusual request, but I will pick you up at your hotel on Thursday when I go to pick up your packet."

* * * * *

The phone rang the moment we walked into our hotel room. It was Pochi. "Hello," she said with a flair. All the nervousness was gone.

"Hey, Pochi!" Mark said. "Do you have some good news for us?"

McKenzie squealed with excitement as she heard her dad's comment. She ran over and hugged me. "Is she here, Mom? Oh, please let her be here."

"I think Dad's trying to find out," I said. We both quickly hushed and got as close as we could to hear the telephone conversation in progress.

"They arrived at the bus station at 12 p.m. and immediately called us," Pochi said excitedly. "Oh, she wants to see you so badly. She is already asking, 'Where is my momma? Where is my dad? Have they come for me?'"

Our eyes filled with tears.

"When can we see her?" Mark asked.

"Favor's aunt wants to meet you at the EAI office to get the papers that prove you are Favor's legal guardians," Pochi said. "This is her insurance that what she is doing is totally legal. She doesn't trust these people to not come after her and put her in jail, once they find out what she did. She is being very smart about this."

"We understand. When can we meet?" Mark asked.

"Right now," Pochi said. "We will be at your hotel in five minutes to pick you up. Pastor, who works with the orphanage, will drive Favor and her aunt to EAI and meet us there!"

Mark hung up the phone, and the screaming of the girls began! McKenzie's joy was almost uncontainable as she jumped up and down, clapping her hands with excitement.

"We gotta go," I said as I grabbed my video camera. We bolted out the door to meet Favor.

"Did I hear Pochi say they arrived at 12 p.m. today?" I asked.

"Yeah," Mark answered.

"We drove past the bus station at 12 p.m.! My heart knew she was there! We were so close, I could feel her."

* * * * *

Pochi picked us up within minutes. A man we didn't recognize was in the front seat. Sensing our apprehension, Pochi told us not to worry because he was from her church.

"McKenzie," Pochi asked, "are you excited to meet your little sister?"

"I can't wait!" McKenzie replied.

"She will look a little different when you see her," Pochi started. "They shaved her head. She looks like a boy."

"What?" I said. "Why would they do that to her?"

"No reason," Pochi said.

"What do you mean, no reason?" I asked. "That had to be devastating to her. She loved her hair."

"Favor wouldn't say why," Pochi said. "She just wanted to keep peace with this woman. Her aunt is very mad about it."

"That is so mean," McKenzie said. "I feel bad for her. I'm going to love on that cutie and not even notice."

I tried not to assume things, but I knew that sometimes to shame a girl, they would shave her head. Then I wondered if they were trying to change her look, or if she had lice. Why on earth would you shave a little girl's hair off? I longed to hold her and make everything better. What else had happened to her since I saw her last? My heart ached and I was angry they had put her through something so traumatic.

"Oh," Pochi yelled back at us, "EAI is still denying that you are in town."

"Well," I said, "it'll be tough to deny we're in town once we show up on their doorstep."

"They did not want you to come here," Pochi said. "But the aunt demanded a copy of the court decree and Favor's birth certificate."

* * * * *

We finally pulled over outside of the EAI offices. I could see the blue gate that we had passed through after coming back from court last time we were in Ethiopia. *How would they respond to us showing up?* Mark and I didn't know what would happen next. All we could concentrate on was being reunited with Favor. I handed my video camera to Pochi's friend from church in the front seat and asked if he would record our reunion with our daughter. I wanted the moment when she would be back in our arms captured.

We waited about three minutes, and then a red truck pulled up behind us. I could see that the Pastor who Pochi had mentioned was with Emebet. He was a tall, husky man with a smile that put you at ease from the first moment you saw him. I'm sure he had a name, but everyone who knew him affectionately called him Pastor. Then I saw a little figure pop up from the back seat between them. It was Favor! When her eyes caught ours, she began to jump up and down.

"There she is!" Pochi announced. "She is so happy to see you. Look at her!"

I couldn't get to her fast enough. Emebet jumped out of the front seat and threw her arms around me first.

"Thank you," I said. "Thank you for what you did for us today."

She held me tightly and whispered in my ear, "Please take her to America, quickly! Please, promise me."

"We will, we will," I said. "I promise you. Thank you, Emebet!"

The back truck door opened, and I saw Favor's little feet hit the ground, running toward me. I scooped her up in my arms. We both screamed with delight as I swung her around, kissing her precious face. McKenzie was right behind me and when their eyes met, Favor reached for McKenzie. They embraced like long lost sisters. Favor showered her big sister with kisses on the cheeks, amidst the squeals of joy. Then Favor saw her daddy and her arms went up.

"There's my Princess!" Mark said, as he picked her up. He held her tightly. She was safe in her father's arms.

CHAPTER 10
BEHIND BLUE GATES

*"Courage is a demonstration of faith.
The Lord never promised that His way would be easy,
But He has assured us that it would be worth it."*
—Rick Joyner, *The Final Quest*

A small blue door swung open within the large EAI gate and Jamila stuck her head out. "Come into the office area," she directed us with her hands.

Our moment had been abruptly stopped, but the joy continued, especially for McKenzie and Favor, who were unaware of the underlying situation.

Once we were inside, Jamila closed the door and then disappeared through a side door. Mark and I looked at each other, not knowing what to do, so I pulled out my camera and asked Pochi to take some pictures in front of the blue gate that separated us from the outside world.

It is often said that a picture is worth a thousand words, and if our picture could've had a voice, it would've said something that would be etched in our minds forever. My arms were wrapped around Favor, saying, "I will never let go of you again. My arms are holding on, no matter what may come." Favor's little hands grabbed my hands, saying, "I've got my mom, and I'm not letting her out of my sight." Her little head leaned toward McKenzie, and McKenzie's head leaned back into Favor, saying, "I want to get close to you. I'm excited to have a sister." Then there was Mark, who wrapped both arms around his wife and girls, saying, "This is my family who I love, and I am their protector."

At one point, I took Emebet aside to talk to her privately. I could see by her eyes that she was very sick. She was a private person, and I knew my questioning would embarrass her, but I was concerned for this newly-discovered heroine standing in front of me.

"You were in the hospital?" I asked.

Mark and I being reunited with Favor, and McKenzie and Favor meeting for the first time behind the blue gate at EAI Ethiopia.

She nodded yes. I could tell she was already a little uncomfortable about the topic, but I had a motive. I saw how God had healed my mother, and I believed He could do the same for her. Favor was back in our arms—and it was all because of the risk that Emebet had taken to bring her to us. I wanted to ask God to give her back something of value: a gift of healing—straight from God to her.

"Do you believe that God loves you and can heal you?" I asked.

She smiled and nodded yes.

"Can I pray for you to be healed?" I asked.

"Yes, please," she responded.

As we both bowed our heads, I prayed a simple prayer that God would touch her and heal her body. I prayed that He would bless her for what she had done for us. When the prayer was done, Emebet wrapped her arms around me.

"Thank you!" she said through tears. Her eyes still showed me sickness, but faith said she was healed.

* * * * *

A young man came out of the building and invited us inside. As we walked in, Jamila walked up to Emebet and whispered something in her ear. Without a word to us, Emebet followed her down a long hallway.

Pochi leaned into me and said under her breath, "Jamila is trouble. Many say she is very much trouble. I don't trust her." My stomach turned. *What if we had been led into a trap?*

I sat down, and put Favor between McKenzie and me. It was clear that Favor wasn't letting go of her new big sister. She had both arms wrapped around McKenzie's neck and had crawled into her lap. Mark nervously paced back and forth, glancing down the hallway from time to time.

A man with glasses appeared at the end of the hallway and asked for Mark and me. Pochi stood up.

"No," he abruptly said, "only them." Pochi shrugged her shoulders and sat back down. I told Pochi not to let the girls out of her sight, and then I walked with Mark down a hallway lined with offices.

We stepped into a crowded office. Adeferese sat behind his desk. Jamila was on his left, sitting quietly with her hands in her lap. Emebet was sitting closest to the desk with some papers in her hand. She looked up and gave me a nervous smile. I grabbed Mark's hand in mine as we took a seat directly across from Adeferese.

Adeferese looked up at us briefly, then back down to a paper on his desk. The room was silent. A woman's high heels clicked down the hallway, coming toward us. The noise was coming from the same woman we had seen at the Embassy, who had been wearing a long black skirt. She placed some newly-copied papers in front of Adeferese. He glanced over them and handed them to Emebet, who examined them closely. Adeferese impatiently watched her for a few minutes, then said something in Amharic. She shot back confident words, as a woman unmoved by anyone else's schedule. When she finally finished reading the papers, she thanked Adeferese, who nodded at her and dismissed her. Adeferese then asked everyone to leave the room except Mark and me. We took a deep breath, unsure of what was happening.

Adeferese took a long pause, playing with the pen in his right hand, then looked up at Mark and me. I could feel the tension in the atmosphere.

"You are lucky to have your daughter," he stated in a matter-of-fact tone.

Mark and I remained silent.

"You are very lucky," he said again, as if we hadn't heard him the first time.

Mark and I said nothing. *Where was Adeferese going with this?*

"You do know that there was another family that left last week without even seeing their daughter, don't you?"

I nodded my head. "It would be very bad if this family ever finds out that you got your child and they did not," he said, raising his eyebrows to put an exclamation point on it. "You need to keep this very quiet. Do not tell anyone... understand?"

Mark and I sat motionless, watching Adeferese stare us down. Mark made a quick nod toward him.

"You tell nobody that you were here! If anyone finds out about this, we could be in trouble over what we did today. I don't want you to have any more contact with us while you are here. Do you understand me? Do not say anything to anyone." He looked over his black-rimmed glasses at me.

Was I missing something? We had done nothing wrong. Why would anyone get in trouble? I looked him in the eyes and for the first time, spoke up. "So, you want us to say we never saw anyone from EAI, although we are sitting right here?"

"Yes!" he said.

"Okay?" I said.

"Good," he said. He put his hand out to shake Mark's hand, then he looked at me and paused before extending his hand.

I noticed.

"Mr. Adeferese," I said, "we did nothing wrong today. A little girl has a family who will love and value her. People prayed. We know God did this, not luck. We should be celebrating."

He rolled his eyes, withdrew his hand, and shook his head. He was done with me.

"Thank you," Mark said, and we walked back toward the girls and Pochi.

Pochi gave us a questioning look. "What was that about?" she asked.

"Not sure," I whispered. "All I know is we're not really here."

About that time, the gentleman who came to take us back to the office was telling Pochi and Pastor that Adeferese needed to talk to them. As they got up, Pochi gave me a look that told me she did not trust what was going on.

* * * * *

We waited for what seemed like an hour. Then I saw Pochi come out of the office with a look of disgust. "Are you ready to go?" she asked, then looked past me, "I will tell you in the car."

We said goodbye to Emebet and thanked her again for her bravery. Then we piled in the car and headed back with joy-filled hearts, despite the confusion of the afternoon.

"What did they say to you back there?" Pochi asked.

"They just wanted us to deny that we ever had contact with them," I said.

"He made it very clear that we are not to have any further contact with the EAI office while we are here," Mark pointed out.

"He said the same thing to me," Pochi said. "He threatened me to not say anything. They are afraid we will tell the other family that you got your child and they did not. This is foolish. Why would I do such a thing? He is so concerned with how this looks."

"He says that he knew nothing about what the regional government office did to these four children, until last week when I told them," Pochi continued, "but I told him back when it happened months ago. He saw the paper the official signed to let her be adopted. He never has come to visit my orphanage to see if the children are okay and being taken care of. Never. He should've fought for those children and for the families that were already adopting them. He does not care."

Mark and I listened as Pochi unleashed.

"He sits in his office, and he has no idea what we do for these children. He doesn't care that we believe every child is carefully placed with the families we choose. We pray for God's direction. God puts families together. Adeferese—he doesn't care." She threw her hands up in frustration. Whatever was said in that back room between her and Adeferese had stirred a fire within Pochi—her passion for the children fueled her.

"He says," Pochi continued between breaths, "why must they have *this* child? We have plenty of orphaned children. They can pick another one. We have people who want them here. Of course, he doesn't say they want the orphans to cook, clean, take care of their kids, or whatever they want to do with them. They don't want these children to love as *their* children."

The picture of who this man really was became increasingly clear the more Pochi vented. He saw no value in placing children within families who would raise them up to fulfill their God-given destiny and purpose. He saw them as commodities, and these four children who interrupted his world were seen as a problem. But he now had a bigger problem on his hands—us—and we weren't going away.

* * * * *

Our second evening back in Ethiopia was filled with firsts. McKenzie showed Favor the drawer that we had filled with new clothes for her. Squeals of excitement came from both of them as they would grab an outfit and run into the bathroom to try it on. We were happy that Favor had taken to her sister. McKenzie was the perfect, loving, big sister—and from that moment on—they would remain side by side.

When we settled in for the night, I made a decision to not post anything on Facebook until we were past the Embassy and held Favor's passport and visa. Although Favor was in our arms, an unsettled feeling was in the air. The events and conversations of the day bothered us. Something wasn't right. We could sense something lurking in the shadows, watching and waiting to pounce. An underlying fear was steadily growing...

Would they try to take her from us? Our thoughts were filled with what-ifs, and so went another sleepless night.

* * * * *

The next day, we grabbed a quick swim at the hotel before Pochi and Pastor came to pick us up for our trip to the Covenant Orphanage in Holeta where Favor lived when we met her on our first trip. This visit would give Favor a chance to say goodbye to her friends before heading to America. We were thrilled for another opportunity to love on the children. Pochi had done a wonderful job with bringing them from a traumatic time of loss to a place of acceptance and healing. With every child, you could see that they felt loved and valuable.

We had driven about 20 minutes when Pochi looked in her rear view mirror at us. "Adeferese called me today," she said.

"Everything okay?" Mark asked.

"He is concerned about you leaving the country with Favor," she said.

Mark and I glanced at each other. Our hearts sank.

"Something has happened, and he is changing his mind concerning letting you leave with her," she said.

"How could he do that?" Mark asked. "She's our child!"

"You may not be able to take her until everything is cleared up with the Debre Birhan officials. He wants me to pressure you to stay. He said, 'We can't let them leave with the kid.'"

I looked at Mark. My heart was in my throat, and all the fears that kept us awake the night before were now a reality. All I could think about was getting out of the country as soon as possible before we lost our daughter. I waited until Pochi was looking straight ahead, then mouthed, "We need to get out of Ethiopia!" Mark nodded in agreement. An urgency was burning in my chest to leave. If it had been humanly possible, I would've started walking home.

We arrived at the orphanage. Favor grabbed McKenzie and showed her around the place while they waited for the children to return from school. Mark and I removed ourselves to the garden where we could talk without being overheard.

"We need to get the earliest flight out of here when we get her passport and visa. I can pack tonight," I whispered.

"I agree," Mark answered. "I'm going to the Embassy when they open to see if I can pick up her documents. I don't trust EAI. They're not going to give us her passport."

"I know," I said. "I feel it too. They're turning against us."

"Something must have happened since we saw Adeferese," Mark said.

"I wonder if he is getting pressured from someone more powerful?" I said.

Mark looked at me for a moment.

"What?" I asked.

"I hope we can get a flight out with Hurricane Sandy stranding so many here," he said. "A lot of people are trying to get back to America."

"I don't care where we go. Let's just get out of here," I said in despair.

Mark nodded his head in agreement.

We grabbed hands and looked at each other. We were on the threshold of making a life-changing decision. We were going against the norm of doing what we were instructed to do for the sake of saving our new daughter. We had to rely on a higher wisdom than our own.

"We should pray," I said, and without hesitation Mark started.

> Father, I pray for protection over our family. I ask You to give us a clear path to get out of Ethiopia safely with Favor. Help me get the passport and visa without delay, and Lord, please give us wisdom, so that above all, we are in Your perfect will and not doing things in our own strength or ways. In Jesus' name. Amen.

We took a deep breath. We could feel the weight and anxiety of stepping out beyond our comfort zone. We had to continue walking one step at a time, placing our trust in the promises that God had given us. He would finish what He had begun in our lives, but it was scary to believe what we had yet to see. Abraham in the Bible dared to believe that God would do the impossible in his life. He went blindly, moving by faith. That unknown place was where we found ourselves in that moment. We were believing that God was able to do above and beyond all that we could ask or think, according to the power that was working in us...faith.

CHAPTER 11
A CHANGE OF PLANS

"Sometimes when you're in a dark place you think you've been buried, but you've actually been planted."

—Christine Caine, author

The children, returning from the nearby school, busted through the orphanage's blue gate door with anticipation and excitement. Isabella, a beautiful 10-year-old girl with long, braided ponytails, immediately spotted Favor. With squeals of joy and outstretched arms, the two friends ran toward each other. Isabella's brother, Fikadu, was not far behind with exuberant hugs. Fikadu patted Favor on the head and asked where all her hair went. Favor shrugged her shoulders, grabbed Isabella's hand, and the two friends ran to McKenzie. You would've thought McKenzie was the Queen of England with the way Favor and Isabella gathered around her.

After greeting all the children with hugs and kisses, Mark and I settled back into the main living room, where Pochi was sitting with one of the babies. She was an incredible orphanage director. She poured out her love on these little ones, playing with them as though she was a child herself.

Mark was in a different world. I could see his mind turning and figuring out what he should do next. I could recognize that "fix it" spirit anywhere, usually kicking in moments after I would express a concern that something wasn't right. Fix-it Mark was coming to the rescue, and this time I was okay with it.

"Pochi, do you know someone who could drive me to the Embassy tomorrow morning around 8 a.m.?" he asked.

Pochi looked up at him. "Are you trying to beat EAI to the Embassy to pick up her passport?" she asked. "I don't blame you. I will call someone and let you know."

"Thank you," Mark said. The fewer people who knew about our plans, the better. He also wanted to protect Pochi from EAI. She could honestly say that she knew nothing. The problem we faced was that EAI knew where we were staying and when we were flying out. They had our entire schedule. If they wanted to stop us, it wouldn't take much.

After a few quiet minutes, as if knowing our thoughts, Pochi suddenly looked at us with a deep concern in her eyes. "You are not planning to leave early, are you?"

We both took a sip of coffee to avoid being the one to answer.

"That wouldn't be good," she said. "There are three other children trapped in this foster care, too...not just Favor."

Mark slowly lowered his cup and took a deep breath as Pochi kept her eyes planted on him. "We need to decide what's best for Favor," Mark said. "Favor is our child and it's up to us to protect her."

Pochi was visibly shaken by the possibility of us leaving early. "That could affect the other three children they are holding in the foster care system!" she said, shaking her head in disbelief.

Mark put his coffee down, got up and walked out of the room. Pochi looked at me. "You have to do this the right way," she said.

"What if the right way for Favor..." I paused, "is to leave?"

"I understand that you don't want to lose her," Pochi pleaded, "but this might affect the others."

"Pochi, we can't take that chance."

Pochi didn't respond. I could tell she was very emotional. We couldn't understand why she wouldn't want the best for Favor. One child getting safely home was better than taking a chance that none would see freedom.

The drive back to our hotel was very quiet. A lot was left unsaid. In the back of my mind, I knew Pochi didn't want us to leave for the sake of the other three children, but all I could see was my child. While the other kids would be going to people to cook and clean, Favor was going into a potentially life-threatening situation. In our resolve, there was no room for negotiation.

* * * * *

That night, after the girls had fallen asleep, I turned on my computer and wrote to our faithful prayer warriors. It had been two very full days. I knew I couldn't give every detail yet, but I wanted them to know we were okay and tell of the marvelous grace we had been given over the past few days.

> I know all of you have been praying and wondering how everything went with the rescue. Let me say this, we are still in a battle! Keep praying! We need prayers to get us safely out of the country without any delays. We need prayers for protection and favor over the orphanage director and the precious people who have helped us. Wish I could say more, just know we appreciate you all so much.
>
> We did have to go to our embassy appointment without Favor, but we now hold her official birth certificate and court decree, which states that we are her legal guardians. We see God moving supernaturally in every step we take. His grace is evident.

> Also, we now know that there are three other children involved who are being held back from their adopted families for this "foster care." Please pray for their release to be reunited and placed with their forever families. I know these families have to be brokenhearted. God so loves these children. I can't imagine why anyone would keep them from being adopted into a loving family. It is clearly not God's plan, but the enemy's.
>
> We serve a greater God and I'm believing all these children will be able to go home with the families who love them. Thank you so much for your prayers! Be sure to read my status...just another way God is going before us and performing miracle after miracle on our behalf.
>
> Love, Mark and Missy

My heart was so thankful for these individuals. I hit the send button, and started to shut the computer down and go to bed, when suddenly responses started filling my page. The prayers and words of encouragement filled my heart and brought tears to my eyes. I knew that they had been faithfully waiting for a word just to know we were okay.

While I was reading the comments, Mark laid in bed quietly. His mind was racing with different scenarios of what he would do if EAI showed up while he was at the Embassy. What if they beat him to the appointment? Would he have to fight for the passport and visa or would they try to take it from him? He faced another night of no sleep and no food in his stomach.

I quickly jotted an extra note to our prayer warriors and answered a few of their questions.

> One more thing—tomorrow is going to be very important for us. We need your prayers for divine favor with who we come in contact with: the Embassy, government, airlines. It will be a miracle to find a flight back to America. There

> are so many people stranded here because of Hurricane Sandy. The next 12–24 hours, we need God to show off! I'll let you know if the first hurdle is cleared by 10 a.m. Ethiopia time. You are 8 hours behind us so I'm sure most of you will be asleep.
>
> I know a lot of you are asking...and, yes, my arms are really happy right now!!! Can't wait to share more. Steve, love on Dad and Mom for me!
>
> Please don't post anything other than we need prayer covering in the next 24 hours. Thank you! Love you!

I sent the message, and within moments, the "hallelujahs" began to pour in. Tears, joy, thankfulness, and praise—they couldn't wait to hear more "happy arms" stories. Many of my friends from all parts of the world were responding and offering up their homes, saying we could fly into their country until we could get back to the States. I was engulfed in love and in their amazing hospitality. I couldn't believe my eyes as I heard from the many who would travel hours to come to our rescue. Seeing this kind of outpouring made the bad that was happening seem so small. An army of saints was assembled, ready to do whatever they could to bring us safely home, and it touched me to the depths of my heart. Tears started to flow.

* * * * *

We had another long and sleepless night. Our hearts raced and our stomachs hurt from not knowing what the day would bring. I had an urgency to leave. I felt claustrophobic and trapped in Ethiopia, and the need to leave on an airplane overwhelmed my every thought. I shared with Mark the strong, pressing feeling that I had to leave. I told him that it was imperative that we got out today. I knew it in my gut. It felt like a volcanic eruption was about to go off under my feet. I had no reason to feel the way I did, but I couldn't shake the anxiety and the feeling of danger. Maybe my mind was starting to imagine things, but the urgency to leave overpowered all my senses.

Mark quietly got up and got ready to leave early. He wanted to be at the Embassy before they opened. When he arrived downstairs, he met Dave, the man Pochi had sent from her church to be his driver. He was early and had already been waiting for Mark for 10 minutes. Dave was a handsome man in his early 30s, and the peace and love of God radiated from him. When he smiled, his eyes would disappear. Mark knew that he was in the presence of a man he could trust.

Mark arrived at the Embassy and requested to speak with the vice-consul who he had talked with a few days before. Dave waited in the car, praying.

* * * * *

Back in the hotel room. I sat quietly as the girls slept in the bed next to mine. They were entangled from head to toe. It looked very uncomfortable, but the smiles of contentment on their faces exuded peace and utter relaxation.

I was in a quiet place of peace, but I still couldn't shake the feeling that we had to leave today. I turned on my praise music and let it calm my spirit, taking my emotions to a place where they could connect with the things that are unseen. I was exhausted, but I couldn't sleep because of the nervous energy. I had to pray. Mark should be at the Embassy by now. I didn't want to think about what could go wrong, so I took a deep breath and stilled myself. Then I felt like someone had placed a warm comforter over my shoulders and placed their arms around me. I could feel God pulling me into the throne room. All I could do was kneel at His feet, and I felt His overwhelming love around me. I felt Jesus' hand touch my face, and as I looked up and saw His beautiful eyes, it was as if He was saying, *Missy, the battle was won when your foot hit the ground. Your obedience will be rewarded.*

I opened my eyes and looked around the room.

Everything was the same as it was a few minutes ago—the girls still in dreamland, the computer screen lit up. I could see we were getting messages from America, although it was the middle of the night for some of them. Prayer warriors were lifting our arms on this battlefield. No wonder I had felt such a strong presence of the Holy Comforter. Prayers of the saints were going up for us. I knew God would get us safely home with Favor. I could trust His word, and His word alone.

* * * * *

After 30 minutes, the vice-consul called Mark to the window. Mark apologized for being early and told the vice-consul he was concerned about Adeferese and EAI. The fact that they didn't want us to leave the country with Favor alarmed us. The vice-consul quietly listened, then asked him to wait while he gathered everything we would need for Favor's packet.

Adeferese's unusual actions had stirred up every kind of concern that an adoptive parent can have. So, when the vice-consul came back to the window and handed him the packet, Mark asked again, "So, are we okay? We did everything, right? We don't need to worry about them taking her away from us? The vice-consul reaffirmed that Favor was legally ours and we were fine to leave.

Mark took the packet from the vice-consul and opened it as he walked away. To his surprise, the packet wasn't Favor's information at all—it belonged to a five-year-old boy. His heart rate quickened as he returned to the window and asked to see the vice-consul again. Fears about the trustworthiness of the Embassy were seeping into his mind. *Why did he receive someone else's information? Did Adeferese have connections within the American Embassy?* Mark, more adamant this time, showed the packet to the vice-consul, voicing his concerns, but talking under his breath to avoid being overheard.

Suddenly an alarm went off in the Embassy. The vice-consul gave Mark the signal to step back as the guard rushed over to see if there was a problem. Apparently, Mark had moved too close to the bulletproof glass so others wouldn't hear his conversation with the vice-consul. Every time he would lean in to tell the vice-consul something, an alarm would be triggered. Seeing the problem, the vice-consul had a better idea. "Meet me in the courtyard," he said.

Mark made his way toward the courtyard. As he opened the door to step outside, he could feel the sun shining down, warming the Earth on this beautiful morning. The U.S. Embassy was newly built, and the landscaping captured a piece of America with the nicely mowed lawn and trees with flowers surrounded with flowers. The Embassy hardly looked like it was in a third world country.

"Okay, so you're asking if it's legal for you to leave early with her?" the vice-consul said as he came out the side door with Favor's packet.

"Yes," Mark answered. "We've heard that our agency said that they don't want us to leave with her."

"There's no reason for that," he said. "There seems to be some confusion concerning what is happening at Debre Birhan. We have someone attending the hearings tomorrow to find out more. As for your case, everything looks good according to Ethiopian law and now American law. You did everything right. She's yours. Leave whenever you want."

"Okay," Mark said, looking for anything in the vice-consul's eyes that would say otherwise.

"Listen," the vice-consul said, sensing he was dealing with a man on the adoption edge, "Here is my private cell number and email if you need to reach me, but I can assure you, you'll be fine. There is nothing they can legally do to you." He added his personal information to his business card and handed it to Mark.

Mark looked at the card. "Thank you," he said.

"Glad to help. Congratulations on your new daughter!" he said, smiling at Mark as they shook hands. Then he turned and walked back toward the Embassy door.

As Mark left the Embassy, he scanned the streets for any sign of someone from EAI. Nothing. Fortunately for him, they never ran on time. He never heard a word from Josiah or EAI, and they didn't come at the scheduled time to pick him up for our embassy appointment either. We will never know if they heard that we had already been to the Embassy, or if they never intended to pick him up in the first place.

* * * * *

"Praise God!" Mark said, entering the hotel room. "We have everything. Favor is ours!"

"Oh, thank God!" I said. "First hurdle cleared!"

"What do you mean?" McKenzie asked. "She has always been our girl." Favor grabbed McKenzie around the waist, giving her a big hug. The girls were ready to have a day at the pool.

"Did you check flights going out today?" I asked.

"We can't get a ticket. It's packed with people trying to get back to America," he said. "They've been stranded here since Hurricane Sandy."

I knew my husband wouldn't lie to me, but sometimes I had to clarify things. "Did you actually check with the airlines, or just assume there would be no tickets? What about going through another country?"

Mark looked exasperated. "No," he said, "let me go down there right now."

"Check on flights going anywhere…just please get us out of here."

"Mom," McKenzie said, "we're hungry."

Mark stopped at the door in hopes I'd postpone checking on tickets for food, but my mind was made up—we had to get out of Ethiopia.

* * * * *

The Ethiopian Airlines service center was packed with people trying to get flights back to America. Mark walked up to the exasperated agent. When he asked about the possibility of getting an earlier flight to America, she shot him a "you've got to be kidding me" look.

"Everything is overbooked as a result of the storm," she said. "You'll need to stick with your original flight out. At least you have a guaranteed seat that way."

Mark stood there, silent.

"Anything else?" she asked.

Mark was working things out in his mind: *Should I ask about another country to fly through? That would probably be very expensive, and the checking account is almost drained. It would definitely be more money than our account could cover. The credit card is at its maximum, so there wouldn't be enough room to charge it. The vice-consul said we shouldn't have any trouble, so why worry about this and spend all this extra money that we don't have to get out of the country a day sooner? It's just not affordable. That's it, we don't have enough money. So, I'm going to believe that God will get us out safely.*

"No, nothing else," Mark said, "thank you."

As Mark walked back to the room, he tried to figure out how he would break the news that we were going to stick with our original plan. When he opened the hotel room door, the first thing he heard was that pressing question.

"Did you get us a flight out?" I asked

"There were no flights back to the states because of the storm." Mark said. "Everything is overbooked. We're lucky to have our original flight."

"Well, can we just go anywhere? Another country?"

"No," Mark responded, shaking his head.

"Nothing?" I asked. "We've got people in the U.K., Australia, South Africa, Germany...all over. They're willing to help us get out. Did you check other countries?"

"No, we can't get a flight." In Mark's mind, that meant, *according to our checking account, we can't.*

I was stunned. I really thought God was going to get us out, even if it meant going through another country. Nothing felt right, and the peace I had that morning had vanished.

Mark saw the shift in my personality. "The vice-consul didn't see any reason they would stop us," he reassured me. "We have everything. She's ours."

I sat quietly dealing with a feeling that I couldn't ignore.

He continued, "And even Pochi said there was nothing they could do to stop us from leaving with her, and didn't she say that they can't take Favor away, now that we have her visa and passport?"

Something wasn't right. I wanted to ask him again. Had he checked all flights out? Instead, I did nothing but sit still, resolved that we were stuck and not going anywhere until our scheduled flight the next evening. God had to have a better plan than me, but this didn't feel right.

"I have peace that everything will be okay," Mark said. "Remember God's promises to us. He even sent Chris Overstreet to remind us. God will take care of us and get us out safely."

I couldn't say anything. I felt tremors beneath my feet that said *RUN!* The tremors were similar to the labor pains I had experienced—I knew it was a physical manifestation of what was happening in the spirit around me. I felt a fight-or-flight reaction, but I sat silent, battling with trusting what I was feeling or submitting to my husband's peace.

* * * * *

Resigned, we decided to make the most out of our last full day at the hotel, starting with a lovely breakfast of eggs and waffles served to the girls. We sat beneath a tiki hut overlooking the pool, as birds of varying beautiful colors stalked our table for falling crumbs. The weather was perfect, and the girls were inhaling their breakfasts so they could go swim.

McKenzie and Favor around the grounds at the Hilton Addis Ababa.

We spent most of the morning watching them enjoy the pool, doing our best to live every moment to its fullest. Maybe I was being too paranoid, thinking we should get out today. Sitting by the pool and watching the girls play felt so peaceful, and the girls were happy and having so much fun. Maybe I had overblown everything. The ache in my stomach could be from a lack of food.

Favor was so full of energy that she wore out McKenzie—a tough thing to do. McKenzie dramatically dragged her body out of the pool and said she had no strength left within her. With that, we decided to make our way back to the room and get ready for lunch.

When we stepped into our room, the phone was ringing. It was Pochi. She had just returned from the court hearing concerning the child who had not been released to the parents the week before. She was speaking very fast and was very upset and nervous.

"Adeferese met me outside of the court and said that there was no way we could allow you to leave with Favor," Pochi said. "He told me that we needed to grab her, or they would be in trouble and so would my orphanage."

Mark looked at me. I saw a grave look come over his face.

I quickly gathered the girls into the bathroom and started the bath running so they couldn't hear the conversation in the next room. "Where's the bubble soap?" I asked, turning to McKenzie. "You both need to take a quick bath before we go eat lunch."

"Who is that on the phone, Mom?" McKenzie asked with a look of concern.

Knowing I have a very smart daughter, I said as I looked her in the eyes, "I need you to keep Favor in the bathroom and happy until I let you know what we're doing next. Okay?"

"Okay. You'll tell me later?"

"Yes," I answered, "I love you. Thank you."

I stepped back into the room in time to hear Mark say, "Wait, slow down Pochi, I can barely understand you!"

"When we got to the court hearing this morning, I saw a man waiting for Adeferese," Pochi said. "We went in and gave our information to the judge. Adeferese still had not shown up. When we were finished, we came out and Adeferese was just getting to court. The man I saw waiting was very friendly with him, and then I remembered that he works at the Embassy."

Mark's stomach turned. "He works at the Embassy? It's not the vice-consul, is it?"

"No," Pochi answered. "He is an Ethiopian, but you should know there is someone in there who might be feeding Adeferese information."

"Did he know that I had picked up Favor's passport and visa?"

"Oh," Pochi laughed, "he was furious about that!" Pochi paused. "Something has happened to Adeferese. He's not thinking right. For him to tell me to grab Favor from you... this is crazy."

"Pochi, why would he try to take her from us? Do you think he has others trying to grab her?"

"He does not want you to leave with her," Pochi said. "I told him he was crazy to ask me to do such a thing. That would be kidnapping. She is yours!"

"Do you know if he has others trying to grab her?" Mark asked again.

"I don't know," Pochi replied. "I would not think he would go that far. He is trying to get ahold of you and he is very desperate! I don't know what he will do! I would not answer your phone."

"He told me not to have any contact with him," Mark said.

"Then I would not," Pochi said. "This is better for you."

"Is my family going to be safe here?"

"I would tell hotel security what is happening if he tries anything," Pochi said. "I will call you back if I hear from him."

Mark hung up the phone and sat on the bed. Immediately, the phone started to ring.

We both stared at the phone until it stopped.

"Do you think it's him?" I asked.

"I don't know," Mark said.

"I'm calling Pochi," I said, as I started to reach for the phone.

Chapter 12
Going Stealth

"Peace was leading me
where my mind could no longer go.
In that moment,
I chose peace instead of understanding."

—Missy Maxwell Worton

The loud ring of the phone startled me, and I jerked my hand back from the receiver. After the last conversation with Pochi, we were apprehensive about who would be calling. It kept ringing. Mark and I stood paralyzed, wondering if it would ever stop.

"Hello!" McKenzie's voice came from the bathroom. "Anybody going to answer that?...It's a tad annoying and it's disturbing our fabulous spa experience!" Long pause. "Hello? Am I just talking to myself here? You hear me, right Favor?" Mark and I started laughing. Leave it to McKenzie to break through the tense moment with her off-the-cuff humor.

The phone stopped ringing, so I quickly picked it up and called Pochi.

"Pochi, did you just try to call us?"

"Yes," Pochi said, "but that was a few minutes ago."

"Did you hear anything?" I asked.

"No," Pochi said, "but I hope I did not scare you, Missy. There is nothing he can do. Favor is yours."

"I don't trust him," I said. "To tell you to grab our child from us...our guard is up."

"He is not thinking right," Pochi said. "It is good you are careful. Are you staying at the hotel tonight?"

"Probably," I answered.

"Good," she said. "Dave can come by in the morning to take you to the market if you still want to buy gifts."

"Let me see how I feel about it in the morning," I said. The last thing on my mind was going shopping, but I had promised to take McKenzie for her upcoming birthday.

"Okay," she said. "Let me know by 8 a.m. Dave can be your bodyguard, and I would not take Favor with you."

I felt sick when I hung up, and had a growing desire to leave. The talk of a bodyguard made me feel weary—not secure. The tremors I felt under my feet grew with intensity. I didn't know how out-of-control this man was, and I definitely didn't want him to lay a hand on my family.

It had been a little too quiet in the bathroom, and when I opened the door to check on my bathing beauties, I found bubbles over everything and everyone! Buried within the mountain of bubbles, I saw two very big smiles and two sets of wide eyes looking up at me.

"You said to keep her happy," McKenzie said. "Well, look at her—she's one happy girl!"

I didn't know whether to laugh or cry. I had a treasure in my beautiful older daughter, always bringing light and laughter into every situation. She was comedy in this dark hour.

Favor and McKenzie having a ball in a bubble bath!

* * * * *

After cleaning the girls and the bathroom up, we were ready for a change of atmosphere. The phone had been ringing nonstop since I had hung up with Pochi an hour earlier. Mark's stomach was in knots, and both of us became very suspicious of anyone around us. We kept the girls within reach every moment.

I watched with a bit of amusement as Mark went into stealth mode. You would've thought he knew covert operations. After learning that Adeferese had told Pochi to grab Favor, he never let us catch the elevator on our floor, but instead he'd lead us up or down a few floors to get on the elevator. It became a game to Favor, who would giggle as her daddy would sneak around, but McKenzie knew something was up. Mark went before us and scoped out the lobby before we came in, and then we dashed into the back of the restaurant. He had discovered a perfect hidden area near the Pizzeria that became our go-to place. Those looking from the outside in couldn't see us sitting there, but Mark could watch the entrance to see if anyone—especially Adeferese—might enter. It reminded me of a scene in an old Western, when the man sat with his back against the wall, facing the door in case he had to protect himself or his family. The only thing missing was the gun and the cowboy hat.

As we got back to just outside our room door, we could hear the phone ringing inside. Mark waited until it stopped, then called the front desk to ask them to stop forwarding calls.

Then I called Pochi. "Pochi, did you just try to call?"

"No," she said, "but he is asking where you are. He is so worried that you will leave the country with her. He sounds very agitated."

"Why?" I asked. "You said there is nothing he can do. She's our legal daughter! He needs to leave us alone."

"He isn't thinking right," she said. "Pray he will see what is the right thing to do."

I hung up the phone and went to my computer. I was exhausted, but I knew I needed to touch base with our prayer warriors to let them know our situation.

> Looks like we can't get out until this Friday night. The flights are overbooked. People trying to get back to America after the big storm. We trust that what God has started, He will be Faithful to complete. We fully trust in His timing as far as leaving the country...no matter how nerve-wracking it can be. We will be arriving in Nashville Saturday at 4:30 p.m. I'll let you know if that changes, but I have a feeling God is taking care of everything. The victory was won the moment we set foot on Ethiopian soil!! Hope to see you soon. She is amazing in every way! Such a bountiful blessing! Just can't believe how good God is to us!

I hit the send button. I was so tired. I didn't wait to see any responses, but instead went and laid down on the bed. I thought about what I had written. *Did I really fully trust*

God's timing? Why was the feeling of an impending volcanic explosion still there? If I trusted Him, wouldn't that be gone? I was resolved to the fact that right in that moment, I had no choice but to believe. I was forcing myself to believe it was going to be okay, and I was too exhausted to fight it.

* * * * *

I was abruptly awakened by a loud knock on our hotel door. Mark jumped up and walked cautiously over to the entry. The girls were still sound asleep.

Someone slid an envelope under the door. Mark reached down to pick it up. The hotel envelope simply had our room number "616" written on the front. Mark looked through the peephole to see who had left it, but the person was out of view. He opened the door and warily looked down the hallway.

Nobody was there.

He walked back in the room and opened the envelope. It contained a type-written note from the front desk—an urgent phone message from Adeferese:

> I have tried calling you many times. You need to return the kid. There is a problem with your paperwork and you are unable to leave the country until it is cleared up. You need to call me immediately!
> Adeferese

In that moment, Mark recognized the severity of the situation. His head flooded with a rush of information, falling like dominoes before him and confirming his buried fears: *We had recognized that something wasn't right with Adeferese since the first time we met him. He didn't want anyone to know we were in Addis Ababa. Then there was that awkward talk in his office after Favor was rescued. Pochi warned us that he had told her to grab Favor. He didn't want us to leave the country with Favor. Adeferese is connected to a person at the U.S. Embassy that is feeding him our information. Had the regional office gotten to him? Or the satanist?* All signs were pointing to a desperate man who could ultimately put our family in danger to protect himself.

"I'll be right back," Mark said.

"Where are you going?" I asked. "What did the note say?"

"It's Adeferese. He says we can't leave. There are problems with our paperwork."

"Mark, you know that's a lie!" I said emphatically. "He's lying. He's trying to scare us."

"I know he is," Mark said, "but I have to make sure we are safe!"

"Wait! What are you going to do?"

"I'm going to the front desk and talk to the manager," Mark said. "I'll alert them that we have a person harassing us. I want to make sure they don't give him any information about us."

"Just be careful, Mark," I said as he walked out the door with the note in hand.

I sat on the edge of the bed. I could feel my neck and shoulders getting heavy and tight. My stomach was numb. I looked at the girls, who were still my sleeping beauties. My breathing had become shallow. I wanted to go after Mark and tell him to check again for available flights, but I didn't want to leave the girls in the room alone. I couldn't just sit there. I jumped up and started to pack our suitcases. I knew we might not be able to fly out for another day, but it eased my tension to do something that made me feel like we were leaving.

A few minutes later Mark walked back in. "Okay," he said, "They've shut our phone off so he can't bother us anymore today. I talked to the concierge and he said they are very careful not to allow anyone from the outside to know our whereabouts."

"Can you please go check on flights again?" I asked with a tinge of desperation.

"I told you we can't," Mark said. "The flights are all overbooked to the U.S."

"Check England, Germany...anywhere," I begged. "Just check, please!"

Mark paused and looked down before answering me. "I said we can't because we have no money and our credit card is full."

"So we can. There are flights out. We'll get the money."

"No!" he shot back. "We have no money! We have to rely on God getting us out of here tomorrow."

"Can't we borrow it?" I pleaded.

"No!" Mark said.

My mind was suddenly hit by a shock wave of fear. The reality was that I would've sold our home and everything we owned to catch a flight out of this place. *How could he not see that or feel the same? How did he think everything was going to be okay?* We had a desperate man pursuing us and telling others to grab our child. Now he was harassing us, using lies. It was almost 24 hours before we could board our plane, and I'd never been so ready to leave. I didn't want to take any chances and find out what this man would do next.

I recognized that I was going into a very dark place in my thoughts. I knew they weren't from God, because they were filling me full of fear, anxiety, and anger. *What was that scripture? Be anxious for nothing, but in everything...with thanks and...*My mind went blank. I kept pushing forward. *I will not fear!* I said to myself. *No weapon formed against me will prosper, and I will not be frightened! God, please just calm my heart and mind. I know you won't forsake us.*

I looked at Mark. He was done talking about this, and I could see his mind was made up. I walked to the bathroom, closing the door behind me as I began to cry. I was hurting and frightened. *Where was that fearless woman who had bravely stepped on a plane and flown across the ocean to rescue her little girl?* Instead, I stood like a scared child alone in a cold bathroom, begging her Father to let her go home with her family.

I took a deep breath. "Father, help me please," I prayed. "I am so afraid. Please help me be the warrior You created. Help me to not fear...whatever might come. I need Your strength. I need Your peace—I need You to make a way for us to leave, now."

I sat there in silence, as if I knew that I just needed to wait and be still. I longed to hear or feel something—anything—from God.

All I felt was alone.

I closed my eyes. I didn't feel like it, but I started thanking God for what He was doing in this hour and in my life. I didn't know what that was yet, but I knew I needed to thank Him. I knew we were past the point of changing things. Although I desperately wanted to go, I submitted to Mark's decision, trusting he had heard from God. I was just being over-cautious.

Then I noticed it. Somewhere in between thanking and praising Him, God freed me from the fear and anxiety—and replaced it with His peace, flooding in like a cool glass of water on a parched soul. Peace was leading me where my mind could no longer go. In that moment, I chose peace instead of understanding. I didn't know what tomorrow would bring, but I knew that whatever would come, I was meant to face it with God by my side, with faith held up before me like a shield.

That night I slept like a baby.

CHAPTER 13
FRIDAY

*"And I am sure of this,
that he who began a good work in you
will bring it to completion..."*

—Philippians 1:6, ESV

Friday. The day we would finally be able to go home.

Although we had only been back in Ethiopia for four days, it felt like months. I woke up with peace. The tremors under my feet were no longer there and the feeling of an impending volcanic explosion had vanished.

I looked at Mark. I could tell it had been another sleepless night for him. His eyes were starting to sink in, and the dark circles beneath them were deepening. He was terribly distracted, and every question or comment I made to him went unanswered.

McKenzie, on the other hand, was awake and ready to go shopping. Dave was waiting for us, so we got ready and said our goodbyes. We left Mark looking dazed, and Favor pouting that she couldn't go.

The cultural market shops were just starting to open as Dave pulled onto the empty street. Owners were placing goods outside to draw the buyers in. I glanced at my list of gifts—mostly scarves and coffee—that I wanted to pick up for those back home. Dave parked, and our car was immediately surrounded by the children and teens who lived on the streets. At first I found anxiety rising in my chest, seeing all the people gather around us, but then my heart rose up with compassion. The reality of their brokenness overwhelmed me.

McKenzie cuddled close to me and put her arms through mine.

"Stay in the car," Dave said. "I will come around to get you out." As he walked around to us the kids stepped away and scattered quickly in all directions.

"Wonder what he is saying to them," McKenzie said.

"I don't know," I said. "My heart breaks for them. I know they're just trying to survive."

"Are they all homeless?" she asked.

"Probably."

We got out of the car and briskly walked into one of the shops that we had been in before. I bought several beautiful scarves and jewelry. McKenzie picked out a few earrings and necklaces for her girlfriends back home.

"Be sure to pick out a few things for yourself," I reminded her. "It's your birthday in a few days. It's not every birthday that you can say you shopped in Ethiopia!"

"We'll be home for my birthday," she reminded me. Just hearing her declare being home put a smile on my face.

Within an hour, we were done shopping. We had spent most of our money at the first shop, and had bags to prove it. Every shop we passed after that thought we were big spenders. Dave was great, always close by our side, watching over us and waiting. He had such a sweet and kind spirit about him, but he was also vigilant in guarding us. Walking back to the car, a group of boys made their way to us. They were enamored with McKenzie. Dave had done a wonderful job at keeping them a fair distance from her most of our time shopping, but this time one of the boys ran up to her and put his hand out.

McKenzie stopped in her tracks and looked at him. His face and hands had been disfigured badly by burns. I noticed that he had been following us since we arrived today, but now McKenzie really saw him with compassion. Looking in his eyes, McKenzie grabbed his deformed hand and gently held it with his palm up. With her other hand she reached into her pocket and pulled out a handful of candies mixed with some Ethiopian money. She put it in his hand and closed his fingers around it.

"You are loved," she said to him.

He smiled, gave her a big hug, then stood back and admired her from a distance. He hastily put the handful of goodies in his pocket as other children made their way to her. Dave stood beside us, smiling and watching McKenzie give out all she had in her—and my—pockets.

When we got back to our hotel room, I realized that all the bags we had brought from the market were gifts. McKenzie had used all her birthday money to buy others something special from Ethiopia. She was so happy and exuberant. I will always look back on this day, knowing my daughter got it right. It is so much better to give than receive.

* * * * *

I finished packing, and we all went to eat lunch by the pool.

Mark was on edge, watching every movement around us. For the fifth day in a row, he ordered food but didn't take a bite. I was resolved that this was the set path for us, or we would've flown out yesterday. But deep inside, I could feel the peace that I felt earlier slipping away and an uneasiness creeping in. I wasn't confident that Favor was safe and in the clear.

Several couples came out with their newly adopted children. Everyone was so jubilant, holding their little ones. I'm sure they'd dreamed about this moment since they started their adoption process, waiting and longing for that precious one to be in their arms. Such a genuine contentment rests on you those first days together. There might be a little dash of fear, or that split second when you ask yourself, *What did I get myself into?* But overall, there is unadulterated joy. I wanted to celebrate with them, but all I could do was stare. We didn't have that joy this time. Was it because we both knew, deep down, that a piece of paper didn't protect Favor from this man? We'd been told everything was okay and there was nothing that could stop us from taking her home. *So why did I feel so vulnerable and uncertain?*

I looked around. I felt unsafe...like someone was watching us. I quickly scanned to where the girls were. They were playing in one of the side pools. I looked around again. Everything seemed normal, but my spirit was feeling danger. Something wasn't right.

At 2 p.m., I said that we needed to get back to the room and take showers before we could leave for the airport. Favor jumped out of the pool with excitement.

"America! We go?" She looked at me with a huge smile. She had been waiting for this time since learning of her forever family and her new home in the States.

"Yes," I said. "We need to go get ready, so we can leave." With shouts of elation, Favor clapped her hands together and threw her arms around McKenzie.

We hadn't been in the room for even a minute when the phone started ringing again. When it stopped, I called Pochi.

"Pochi, did you just call?" I asked.

"No," she responded. "I'm certain it was Adeferese. He is acting crazy. He keeps calling, asking me why I have not grabbed the kid back from you. Missy, he is very upset that you have not answered his calls or contacted him."

"He told us not to have any contact with him!" I said in my defense. "He made that rule—we didn't! Besides, why would we talk to a man telling people to grab our child?"

I looked at Mark. He could hear Pochi from where he stood.

"That's what I told him," she said. "He is very upset and says his agency can get in a lot of trouble over this. He is going to try to stop you from leaving with her, but he can do nothing. She is yours. He is just trying to scare you. You should hear what they are saying to Favor's aunt."

I hated that they would bother her.

"They're telling her that she's going to jail for what she did," Pochi said. "She laughs at them."

"She can't go to jail for what she did for us, can she?" I asked.

Pochi laughed. "Of course not," she said. "They are the ones who are wrong in this. They are scared."

"You are sure there is nothing he can do to take her away from us?" I needed to hear a confident reply.

"No," Pochi said. "You have all the papers saying she is yours."

I glanced at Favor. She was bouncing around, digging through the packed bags to find some dry clothes. "Are you still coming to say goodbye?" I asked.

"Yes, of course," Pochi said. "I will be there in about an hour."

Mark unplugged the phone after I hung up. I'm not sure why it took so long for us to figure that one out. I helped the girls get cleaned up and packed, and then jumped into the shower to get ready before our long journey home.

My hair was still dripping wet when Pochi arrived. Favor jumped into her arms and exclaimed with excitement that she was leaving to America.

Without a word, Pochi shook her head and hugged her tightly. At one point, Pochi looked up at me with a telling gaze. I knew the look—it was fear.

Favor ran to her bed and came back with a gift neatly wrapped and handed it to Pochi.

Pochi with Favor.

"For me?" she asked.

Favor nodded her head. With anticipation, Favor watched as if she didn't know what was behind the pink paper, clearly more excited to see the gift than Pochi was to open it. The paper was pulled back to reveal some beautiful purple earrings that Favor had picked out for Pochi to wear to church. Pochi laughed—they were huge! I took a picture of the two of them together.

I could tell Pochi was nervous, and I couldn't wait to find out why. I gave Favor my phone and set up a game she could play while we sat with Pochi and got caught up on the latest.

"Okay," Mark started, "is there anything Adeferese can legally do to stop us from leaving with our daughter?"

Pochi paused, taking a few deep breaths, thinking for a moment before her reply. "The only place you could be stopped would be at immigration, but that is not very likely since you have all of Favor's paperwork and all of the steps to adopt her were done legally. Everything was done correctly."

"Why are you nervous?" I asked.

Pochi looked up at me like a kid getting caught in the cookie jar. "I am very nervous about Adeferese," she said. "He is supposed to be a very good man, but he is very upset about this. Someone has got him scared."

"Why didn't you tell us that immigration could stop us?" I asked. "Nobody said anything about immigration until now. Now it's too late."

"I didn't think about it until now. It's very unlikely though."

"But, it's possible?" I asked.

Pochi nodded her head.

I glanced up at Mark with a piercing look. *Why did I ever stop pushing to leave early?*

We talked for the next hour, then prayed with Pochi and said our goodbyes. I kept questioning why we weren't told, until today, that immigration stopping us was a possibility. *Were we being set up to fail? What if Pochi was in on it? It didn't take a genius to see that she didn't want us to leave.*

I finished the last of the packing and sat down to send our prayer warriors a final message before we would board the plane:

> There is never a dull moment. We are being harassed and threatened by the agency we went through to adopt Favor. They asked the orphanage director to "grab" her from us and return her to them. They are threatening the person who helped rescue Favor telling them that they are going

> to jail for what they did. We have finally unplugged our phone because of the non-stop calls, and I now have a husband who has gone into "stealth" mode! We are sneaking around everywhere! The girls think it's fun. Giggling in the midst of the storm. That's our God!! We continue to know that we are in the palm of God's hand. On a rescue mission for Him. What an adventure. Feel humbled that He thinks we are worthy of this calling...

Then it happened.

Out of the corner of my eye, I saw something white. A second note was quietly slipped under our door. This time the note was handwritten and unsigned. Whoever delivered it quickly got out of the hallway.

> This is to inform you that your court decree is Suspended. You can't take the kid with you, if you already have a plan to do that. The immigration is already notified. I wish this never happened. I could not reach you by any means. I warned you.

We immediately recognized that it was from Adeferese by the way he referred to our daughter as "the kid." You could see the anger in the messy strokes of penmanship. Mark's heart began to pound, and his head started to throb as he rushed downstairs to the front desk. He looked around the lobby for any familiar faces, but saw none.

"Did you see who wrote this?" Mark asked, putting the note in front of the desk clerk. He looked at it briefly, shook his head, then called over the manager.

"How can I help you, Mr. Worton?"

"I need to know who wrote this note!" Mark said. "Did you see the person who wrote this and had it delivered to my room?"

The manager looked at the envelope and called someone over. He asked the man if he saw the person. The answer was the same. Nobody had seen the person who wrote the note or delivered it. Mark could see they had no clue. That in itself made the matter worse.

"This note is from the person who has been harassing us for the past two days and is the reason we've had to ask you to shut off our phone. He is threatening to grab our daughter from us."

The manager's eyes widened with concern as he looked at the note Mark was holding.

Mark was genuinely scared for his family; a man he hardly knew was threatening to take his daughter. Now, his entire family could be put in harm's way because of this man's obsession with getting Favor back for his own benefit.

Mark tried to calm himself before he continued, but tears were welling up in his eyes as he spoke. "The concern I have right now is that this man knows when we are leaving and knows our flight schedule. I am afraid something will happen to my family on the way to the airport. This man is desperate!"

The manager listened intently, then called the concierge over and spoke briefly to him before turning back to Mark. "Mr. Worton," he calmly replied, "we will make sure that you and your family are safely escorted to the airport. We are calling in our best security to protect your family all the way there. I will guarantee your safety, Sir."

"Thank you," Mark felt a little relief, but was still stirred.

"What time do you need to leave for the airport? We will have everything ready." The manager said.

"We need to leave by 6 p.m." Mark replied and took a deep breath. "Thank you."

"We are happy to help you with this. Please don't worry, we will protect your family to the airport."

* * * * *

My heart was pounding as I sat in front of my computer. Was this really happening? I hoped that we wouldn't be stopped at immigration. I didn't want to think about how I would feel toward Mark if we were stopped and put in a situation that could possibly lead to losing Favor. My heart felt heavy, and I could feel hopelessness trying to slither in. I blamed myself for not going down to the ticket counter and buying tickets myself. *Why did I leave it up to Mark? Why did I always think I had to submit if what I was feeling was right?*

My hands were still on the keyboard. It had been a few minutes since Mark had left with the note to talk to the manager. I pushed back the negative thoughts and decided that God could do whatever He wanted too. He had performed so many miracles for us so far...He could perform a miracle again. He could make us invisible if He needed to. Nothing was impossible for our God.

Mark returned to the room. I could feel the tension in his voice. "Okay," he said. "The hotel is going to have security escort us to the airport."

He was stressed and exhausted.

"I talked with the vice-consul and he confirmed that we could be stopped at immigration, but he seriously doubted that Adeferese had that kind of power. So we just need to get through immigration and we're on our way home."

"Why didn't he tell you yesterday that we could be stopped by immigration?" I asked.

"He said that he seriously doubts that we would get stopped!" Mark snapped. "I think we'll be fine."

All I could do was look at him standing there. I hoped with all my heart we would be fine. At this point I knew our story had taken a turn for a different ending. I wasn't sure if it was going to be a miracle at immigration or an extended battle to keep a daughter who I loved dearly. I was committed to her, no matter what this new ending would look like.

With trembling hands, I finished the message to our prayer warriors:

...One more URGENT PRAYER REQUEST. Pray we are invisible to the enemy as we leave and go through the airport, especially through immigration. We've had the Embassy and the orphanage director tell us the only way they can stop us is at immigration. It seems that our case is exposing something the enemy has been doing for some time and it involves some corruption. Our agency knows when our flight is, so we are at a disadvantage. I'm sure they feel that if we get out and expose this, all hell will break loose. The orphanage director came and prayed with us and said many are praying for us. We are so thankful for all the prayer warriors standing in this battle. We know we couldn't have done it without each one of you. We have been stretched and have had to go to a whole new level of faith in this hour. We're soaking in songs like, "Our God," and other songs that declare the awesomeness of our God. We're holding on to all the promises spoken over us. We have been made more than conquerors through the blood of Jesus Christ!

We leave for the airport within the hour and as I'm writing this, we are still being harassed. Our phone is now unplugged. We just received a letter saying our adoption is suspended. It's not on official paper...we know they're desperate. Our flight takes off in five hours. For a person who used to be terrified to fly, I can't wait for the wheels of our plane to be off the ground. Hopefully, the next message I send you will be from America!
Love You! Thank you!
Missy and Mark

CHAPTER 14
IMMIGRATION

"Sometimes destiny takes a path we would never chose on our own."

—Missy Maxwell Worton

The Hilton lobby was bustling with activity when the elevator door opened. My heart was beating outside my chest, and I could tell Mark was in a rush to get to the airport. I grabbed the girls' hands and drew them close. I could sense a bad presence, and I knew it was near—like the feeling you get when walking into a cold, dark room. A chill went up my spine.

"Let's stay really close together, okay?" I said with a forced smile, acting as normal as I could. I glanced nervously at the faces around us as we walked through the lobby. I took the girls and had them stand behind a pillar near the concierge within a few feet of Mark, who was now checking out of the hotel.

I couldn't shake the feeling that someone was watching us. I scanned the lobby again.

Then I saw him.

The girls holding on to one another in the lobby just before we left for the airport.

My heart started racing. I turned to Mark.

"Is that Adeferese?" Mark asked.

I nodded yes. The security guard must have seen what was happening and was immediately by my side asking where he was. I pointed over to the couch he was sitting on. He was gone.

"He was just there! He's gone!" My eyes searched the faces in the lobby in desperation, trying to find him again.

"Do you remember what he was wearing?" the security guard asked.

My mind was racing. *What was he wearing? Think, think! Was he going to try to take my daughter? Was he here to make sure someone else took her from me?* I looked in every direction. *What was he wearing? Think!* Every person who looked at us was suspect. *How much did I remember from my self-defense classes back in Franklin?*

"Miss! What was he wearing?" the security guard asked again. "Did he have glasses on? A hat perhaps?" I could see that I now had three security men surrounding me, asking questions and trying to get information from a mom who was doing her best to not hit the freak-out button.

Suddenly I remembered. "Glasses!" I blurted out. "Yes, he had glasses on...and a striped shirt. Blue, vertical stripes."

"Can you come with us to identify him?" the security guard asked.

"I can't leave my girls."

"I understand," one of the guards said, looking down at my girls who were now tightly fastened to my waist. "Stay here and we'll look for you."

"Thank you," I said. I watched as they searched the lobby and every adjacent room, looking for the man who had been harassing and threatening us for the past 48 hours.

Meanwhile, as Mark was trying to check out, the hotel was having internet problems and our card was not going through. Finally, Mark agreed to sign off on our bill and told them that they could run our card later.

"We'll keep you safe, Mrs. Worton," a voice said. "I have the head of security here to escort you to the airport." As I looked up, I saw the man from the concierge desk talking to me. He had been so helpful and genuine the entire time that we had been at the Hilton. I smiled and thanked him. It was one of the many characteristics that made me love the Ethiopian people so much. They had always been there for us—and now more than ever.

Mark walked up behind me. "Okay, we're ready." The concierge looked at Mark and signaled a tall man who we were introduced to as the head of security. He reassured us that he would take care of us through the airport security so no one would be able to harm us. Two of the security men surrounded us as we rushed out of the hotel to the waiting van. I expected Adeferese to jump out at any moment to stop us, but he never did. Nobody said a word.

As we piled into the van, an unknowing passenger had seated himself in the front seat. I could tell by his posture that he was frustrated that he had to wait for us, and possibly a bit obsessive compulsive. "What's going on here?" he asked, concerned by the amount of commotion around us.

"We're going to the airport," the head of security nonchalantly answered as he jumped in the driver's seat.

The man turned around and looked at me for a moment, then at Mark and the girls, then back to me, narrowing his eyes and trying to figure out what all the fuss was about. Perplexed, he turned back around as the doors were shut and the van sped out of the parking lot. We turned right instead of left to the airport, sending the passenger we didn't know in the front seat into a panic mode. "Why are you going this way? We never go this way! I could swear the airport is that way," pointing in the opposite direction.

"We are taking a shortcut," the driver answered. "Don't you worry about it, sir."

The man didn't miss a breath, "But I know the airport is that way," he said as he desperately pointed the opposite direction. "Now, where are we...?"

Suddenly, the driver took a right off of the main road onto a dirt road that had mounds of dirt piled everywhere. It looked suspect to say the least. The skeptical passenger in the front seat searched in desperation for something to hold onto. We were bouncing around like Mexican jumping beans, and by the stares we were getting, I don't think this neighborhood was used to seeing a Hilton van drive through these parts. Favor and McKenzie giggled with delight as they bounced off their seats and crashed back down. I caught myself laughing. We must've looked ridiculous. God had an amazing sense of humor, and we were living out a comedy scene.

"This isn't even a finished street!" the man exclaimed. He was clearly confused and getting quite agitated. About that time, a herd of white goats marked with hot pink hair on their heads crossed in front of our van and we came to a complete stop.

The extra passenger was annoyed. "Oh great—goats! Are you serious?"

"That is so cool!" McKenzie said with excitement. "Look Favor, goats with pink hair! They're stylin' goats!"

I glanced over at Mark, who was deep in thought. He was playing out in his mind what would happen if Adeferese showed up at the airport. His only concern was the safety of our family.

The passenger in the front seat was about to have an anxiety attack. The driver calmly reassured him: "I promise. I will get you to the airport — no problem. Don't worry."

* * * * *

As we approached the airport, the driver abruptly stopped, pointed to the man in the front seat, and said, "You, get out here! This is your exit!"

"Here?" the man asked, confused. But aware that this had not been the normal ride to the airport, his resolve to get out overwhelmed his desire to argue.

"Thank you, sir!" the driver said hastily as he gave him his bag. "You have a nice flight home." We quickly drove away. I looked back to see the man shaking his head, wondering what had just happened.

The head of security drove us to the far left of the airport where he jumped out and started pulling out our bags and placing them onto a cart. "Just follow me," he directed, "I will get you there safely and nobody will bother you. I promise." I grabbed the girls, covered their heads with scarves, and made sure we had removed all of our things from the van. We followed him up the ramp, running past a line of people waiting to go into the airport.

"Why are they all staring at us, Mom?" McKenzie asked.

"I'm sure we're quite a sight right now," I answered.

One of the guards put his hands up to stop us. Our driver told him we were Americans and the guard quickly waved us by. Americans still have so much grace and favor as we travel abroad.

Everything went smoothly as we all made our way through security and to the check-in gate. It looked like God was clearing a path for us, just like we had prayed.

"Are you going with us all the way to immigration?" Mark asked.

"You'll be fine," he said. "He won't be able to stop you. No one is allowed past this point."

"You're positive?" Mark needed confirmation.

"Yes!" He said reassuring Mark with a pat on his shoulder. "He does not have that kind of power. I wish you and your family well and a safe journey back to America!"

We thanked him for his kindness and said goodbye. Mark tipped him and made a beeline to the ticket counter. Quickening my pace, the girls and I caught up just in time to be handed immigration paperwork. I quickly filled them out and handed the papers to Mark as we stepped up to the counter. Then we waited for what seemed like eons.

To pass the time, I looked at the people checking in at other counters. I couldn't believe my eyes—I recognized someone from America! Julie Hedberg was standing there with her mother, Sue! Julie had lived with my next door neighbor Cindy this past summer. It was surreal to see her standing there at the airport in Addis Ababa. I tried to get Julie's attention, but she was focused on helping her mother check in.

"Mark, it's Julie! I can't believe she's right here!"

I didn't even get a grunt out of Mark. He was in another world. His expression was as clear as if he had said, *I've got the world on my shoulders right now—so don't talk to me!*

"Okay, well I thought that was totally awesome," I said, talking to myself.

Mark turned to me with the tickets in his hand, "So far, so good! Now let's just pray we get through immigration." I followed Mark with the girls jumping up and down behind me, rolling their carry-ons.

"Mom," Favor said in her thick Ethiopian accent, "America, airplane, America...We go now?" I smiled and nodded my head, praying that going to America would be the outcome. Favor's smile was bright, and her sparkling eyes were filled with the excitement and anticipation of going to her new home. She could hardly contain herself as she walked with a little bounce in her step, giggling with McKenzie.

I could tell Mark was nervous by his pace. I prayed silently, *God, please get us through. I know You love the orphan. I know You love us. You promised me if I just set foot on Ethiopian soil, the victory would be ours. I trust You and I thank You for letting us walk through these gates with Favor. I know the battle is won. I know You will get us home safely.* Suddenly, I heard a song come from my spirit. I began to sing it to myself as we approached the immigration booths. *I have given you this battle, put your trust in Me alone. Hold on to My promise, I'll complete what I've begun.* I kept hearing the song rise up in me. I could feel the victory was within my reach.

"Next," called the guard sending us to the immigration booth. I took a deep breath. I was trying to contain a nervous energy as I kept praying silently.

Mark handed immigration his passport. He stamped it and handed it back. Favor's passport was next. Mark's heart was beating hard. Favor was giggling with McKenzie about riding the airplane. As the immigration officer opened Favor's passport to the visa inside, he studied the screen before him. Suddenly he looked down at a piece of pink paper next to his keyboard. Mark glanced at me with a look of concern. We both watched in disbelief as he quickly got up, left his booth, and rushed toward another immigration officer, obviously his superior. My heart sank. Noise filled my head and I felt everything start to go in slow motion.

"They're stopping us," Mark said, almost in tears.

I took a deep breath. *This can't be happening...we did nothing wrong!*

"Mom, what's happening?" McKenzie nervously asked. "Why did the man leave with Favor's passport?"

"I'm sure they're just checking out something," I responded, "just keep Favor near you." We followed the immigration officer over to the doorway that held their offices. A crowd of officers started gathering around us.

"What is the problem?" Mark asked. "Why are you stopping us?"

No one answered him. They kept talking among themselves and looking at Favor's passport. I brought the girls into my arms. Mark dug into his briefcase and pulled out a file filled with all our important documents proving Favor was legally ours. The head officer briefly looked at the documents, her birth certificate, and the court decree, as Mark desperately tried to influence her to allow us to go. She looked up at Mark and firmly stated, "I'm sorry, but she will not be able to travel. I have been told to collect her passport."

Mark shoved the documents at them, "I have everything that says she is our daughter." Mark pleaded, "What right do you have to stop us?"

The lead officer handed Favor's passport and visa to a man, who then walked through a doorway that was labeled "*No Entrance to Public.*"

"Wait!" I yelled. The officer ignored me and kept walking. I felt a tinge of hopelessness as I realized that we weren't leaving Ethiopia any time soon.

"You don't understand!" I pleaded, almost in tears. "We have to get her out of here." I knew that a dangerous man wanted her as his own. I wondered: *What kind of power did this man have enabling him to reach immigration and stop Favor from leaving the country?*

"We have been told to take her passport and visa," another officer said in broken English. "We don't know why." He then turned to answer the head officer in Amharic. As they talked between each other, Favor's face changed from excitement and joy to despair and uncontrollable sobs.

"Mom, what just happened?" McKenzie asked. "Favor is crying...bad." I looked down and saw that Favor was inconsolable. Something came over me. I'm not sure if it was the mother bear in me or the lioness—it might have been both—but in that moment all fear left and I turned to the officers talking.

"What did you say?" I interrupted. He looked at me for a second, shocked that I was so brazen. "You said something that upset my daughter. She understood you! What did you say?"

He looked at Favor and for a moment I saw a hint of sympathy, "I said you can go, but she is not allowed to go with you to America."

Favor started crying harder. I got on my knees to embrace her and look in her eyes. "Favor," I said, searching for eye contact, "I'm not leaving you."

"We're not going to leave her," Mark said to the officer. "Who do we talk to so we can get this fixed? Our plane leaves in two hours."

"We cannot help you," the officer said, "a court order was written to stop you. We were not told why."

"When did you receive the court order?" I asked.

"At five o'clock," the officer in charge responded.

"Today?" I asked.

"Yes," she said, "just a few hours ago. We do not know anything, but only to stop her from leaving Ethiopia. Two of you can leave, and one of you can stay, if you don't want to leave her."

I looked at Mark. My pain was so deep in that moment that words wouldn't come out of my mouth, but I felt screams of agony from my soul. Tears welled up as I mouthed, "I am not leaving her."

Mark looked at me and at our two daughters. McKenzie had her arm around Favor, who continued to sob. All he could think about in that moment was the fact that he had not tried harder to leave the country as I had urged him.

"I'm sorry," was all he could say. "I'm sorry." I knew he meant it by the emotion he carried and how he looked at me—but all I could feel was pain.

Fighting back tears, I put my hand up to stop him. *No, don't do this now. Don't say anything.* No words were spoken, but he understood. I felt myself pushing him away, and by the look in his eyes, he knew what was happening. I was angry, afraid, and hurt. I knew there was a price we would all pay because of his choice. I couldn't look at him. In that moment, a barrier came between us...a severing of my trust.

Mark watched, helpless to change the path we were on. He knew the financial decision he had made might cost him his daughter, and he could see that a wedge was quickly separating him from his wife.

CHAPTER 15
HELP COMES

"Our story had taken a turn for a different ending..."

—Missy Maxwell Worton

I heard a voice coming from the line behind me. "Do you need help?" It was my friend Sue, Julie's mom. She was an adoption agent, and if ever there was a voice for orphans, Sue was a strong one. She would take the hardest orphan cases—special needs, sibling groups, AIDS—and find them loving, forever families in America. We couldn't have run into a more qualified person to help us. She had dealt with any and every adoption problem you could come across.

"Yes!" I answered. She turned from the immigration window and began walking toward Mark and me, still surrounded by immigration officers. She had two Ethiopian little ones—one in a stroller and one holding tightly to her hand. She was taking them to their family in America.

"You cannot go over there!" The officer yelled, trying to stop her.

"I can and I will! They are with me," Sue replied, putting the officer in her place. "What is going on?" I could barely speak before I was overcome with emotion. She hugged me and said, "Do you need me to call the Embassy?"

"Yes, they took her passport and visa from us," I choked out.

Sue looked up at the crowd of officers and then back at me. "I've never heard of this happening. Do you know why?" she asked.

I shook my head no.

"We have everything. We passed the court, the Embassy..." Mark said as he showed her all our papers.

"Why did you take the child's passport away?" Sue asked the head officer.

"We have orders to stop the child from leaving the country," the officer answered.

"But, *who* stopped us?" Mark pleaded, although inside we knew this had to be connected to Adeferese.

Sue pulled her cell phone out of a jacket pocket and gave it to Mark. "Here, dial up the vice-consul. He's in my speed dial. He can help you." Mark took the phone and walked away from the officers to make the call.

"We do not know. We just cannot let her go. Sorry, we cannot help you!" the immigration officer responded to Sue and me. I could tell that some of the officers were kind and wanted to help us, but there were others that were sharp and unyielding to our pleas.

"Is there a decree stopping them? A piece of paper?" Sue asked politely.

"There is a court order," the officer turned to me. "We were just told to stop you. We cannot help you. You come back after you go to immigration offices on Monday." She handed me a pink slip. "You take this and they will give you the passport back."

"I don't understand what's going on," Sue said. "Maybe the U.S. Embassy will be able to help you out."

My head was spinning. I looked up at Mark, who was finishing up his talk with the vice-consul at the U.S. Embassy. The defeat on his face told me the news wasn't what he wanted to hear.

"The vice-consul said there's nothing they can do tonight. We'll have to stay here over the weekend and find out Monday why we were stopped. He doesn't know why. They can't help with Favor because she's not an American yet. We might need to go through the courts to get this cleared. He said it's in the hands of the Ethiopian government now." Mark took a deep breath. "He also said we'd need an attorney. He can recommend one."

"You go to the court Monday and ask why they stop you," a young, female officer spoke up. "It will all be okay, you'll see. You'll go to America soon." She smiled and looked at me with such compassion. I knew she wanted to help.

One by one, the officers returned to their various posts, except one—the head of immigration, who had a hard look and had been deaf to our pleas. She watched us in silence and satisfaction, looking so smug and arrogant. I checked my "love" meter. As much as I wanted to attack her with words, I knew she was only doing the job she had been hired to do. I knew there was nothing we could do at this point—neither words nor tears would move them to let us pass through. I looked at her leaning against the wall, watching us walk away. Did she have any idea that not letting Favor go to America could put her in danger or seal her into a life of slavery? I turned away, but secretly I was praying God would keep her up all night.

* * * * *

"I don't understand why this is happening to you. In all my years, I've never seen this," Sue said. "Do you have a phone? An Ethiopian phone?"

"No," Mark replied.

"My daughter Julie is staying here. She just dropped me off—she can pick you up and at least find a place for you to stay for the night, until you can figure out what you're doing." Sue handed us the phone, "Here, take my phone as long as you need it. It will be no problem for Julie to come back and pick you up. She'll be thrilled to see your new little one."

"Are you sure?" Mark asked. We didn't want to be a burden, but we knew we couldn't return to the Hilton. That's what Adeferese would expect us to do.

Sue reached out and gave me a long hug. "It's going to be okay. I'll be praying for you. I'll do all I can from my side." At that, she turned and walked through the immigration gate pushing a stroller with one of the little ones and the other child clutching her hand. What I would've given to be able to walk through that gate with them and head home to America.

Mark rushed over to the ticket counter to stop our luggage before we would be stranded with only the clothes on our backs. I walked out of immigration and into the crowded check-in area with the girls. I looked over and saw the sweetest couple standing in line with two older Ethiopian children, whose faces were bright with anticipation of their journey. *That should be us,* I thought as I walked past. My heart ached at the very sight of them.

"God, I don't understand this, but I trust You. I trust You," I whispered. "Please give me strength to walk through this."

* * * * *

I looked up to see a large crowd of women covered in black burkas waiting—for what, I don't know. The stares were piercing as we moved against the flow of traffic to get to the baggage claim. The girls and I sat on a bench and waited for our luggage.

"Mom, what's going to happen to us?" McKenzie asked as she put her head on my shoulder. I moved my hand on her head to comfort her. "We aren't going to lose Favor, are we?"

"I'm not sure, Sweetie," I answered. "I know God is with us. I know He wasn't surprised by this, so, we have to trust that He knows what He's doing. We just can't see it right now." Favor laid her head in my lap. She was exhausted, and I could see a weight on her that I had not seen until now. "Favor, we're not leaving you," I said. She looked in my eyes, finding the truth she heard. I wiped her tear-stained face and smiled at her. Her sparkling eyes were now red and disappointment replaced the joy that was there just minutes ago.

"Mom, I don't want to lose her," McKenzie said, as I felt a tear drop onto my shoulder.

"I don't either." There was nothing more to say. She was family now.

Mark was nervously making phone calls. One of those calls was to Pochi. He told her we had been stopped at immigration and that we had a place to stay for the night. She said she and Pastor from the church she attended—Covenant Church—would be there in the morning to pick us up. She was in shock, but she encouraged Mark that God had a plan. She also said she and the church would help us every step of the way.

Fighting back tears, we walked out of the airport. The head of security ran over to us and offered to help in any way possible. When he realized that we could not return to the Hilton, he brought us all cold waters, which in that moment, was the kindest thing he could've done.

Julie spotted us immediately as we came out of the terminal, and she ran over to give us a hug. Even though it was a bittersweet reunion because we were in emotional shock, it was so good to see a friend from America.

"So this is Favor," she said, bending down to give her a hug, "the one you've been waiting and fighting for—for so long." The words hit me like a sledgehammer to the stomach. We had waited and fought so hard and long for her. It couldn't end this way. *Where was our happy ending? Where was our victory once we set foot on Ethiopian soil? Had God forgotten His promise to me? Did I not hear God?* My mind struggled to grab any words Julie and the driver were saying to us. I did my best to make conversation on our ride to the guesthouse.

Mark was in a different world. He had stopped talking and tears were gathering in his eyes. He was in a daze—a fog that wouldn't let up—and the accusing words, *What have I done?* kept repeating in his head.

* * * * *

The gate to the guesthouse swung open, and we were greeted by the owners. They had prepared a dinner for us.

Mark and I fed the girls and did our best to eat something, but we had no appetites. After the meal, I took the girls upstairs to our room and opened the suitcases. I had packed them just hours before, but it seemed like years. I was happy to have what few clothes we brought. I found the girl's pajamas and had them brush their teeth and get ready for bed. They went into the bathroom without a word, with their shoulders and heads hung in exhaustion.

A platter of Ethiopian food served on Injera bread.

Downstairs, Mark had opened our email to find an urgent message from Adeferese. He made it clear that he was the one who had stopped us by convincing the judge that we were doing something illegal in our adoption. He said he was protecting the reputation of EAI, and any attempt to take Favor would make things complicated. He stated that he had recently seen a video of a ceremony where the four children had been handed over to the zonal officials for placement with foster care. He was convinced that the orphanage had misled all of the adoptive parents and he now believed that Favor had never actually been in their custody. All of Adeferese's claims in this email were lies. We had first-hand proof that Favor had been in the custody of Pochi's orphanage. The email made Adeferese and EAI sound like they were completely justified in trying to stop our adoption, because they made it appear as if they were only doing what was in the best interest of the child. Yet we knew the real story: Favor and the three other children were in the middle of the adoption process with their forever families when they were removed from Pochi's orphanage and placed with a foster mother who worked at the orphanage. I thought about the dream Daniel had about the python. It was becoming clear who the snake was—and that snake was holding back four children from their forever families.

* * * * *

I walked in to see Mark clicking away on the computer. His eyes and nose were red and swollen. I could see that my husband was carrying a huge weight on his shoulders. I paused, not sure if I wanted to interrupt. He stopped and looked up at me with eyes that still said he was sorry.

"Who are you contacting?" I asked.

"Just some prayer warriors, friends, travel agent," he said. I nodded my head, still unable to hold eye contact with him. I turned and started to walk down the hallway to return to our room. I stopped. I had to know. I had to ask. The reality that his decision could cost me a daughter was sinking in. I had to understand why he didn't trust my instinct to leave. I slowly turned around and walked back to where Mark was. I stood in front of him, choosing my words. He stood motionless, bracing for what would come.

"I have to know why you didn't listen to me!" I said. "Aren't we supposed to work together? I begged you to leave on Thursday! We would be home now and Favor would be safe!" I lowered my voice, trying to control my anger. All I could think about was what I thought should've been. "Was it the money? With you it's always about the money. What was it, a few hundred to change our flights?" I wanted answers and I wasn't hearing anything.

"It's all on me. I know that." Mark said, and looked down.

"How do I trust you? I was your partner, telling you what my spirit was saying, 'We have to get out of here, now!' Do you not trust that I hear from God, too?" Mark had no response. He just stood facing me. "We could lose her! Why didn't you listen to me?" I said, overwhelmed with the thought.

Silence.

"Don't you think I have realized the cost of my decision?" he said after a minute or two, totally broken. "If we lose her...I'm the one who'll live with that the rest of my life."

"No, you're not the only one who will live with it," I said under my breath and walked away.

I felt drained. The hallway was dark and all I could see was the light under our door. I walked in and saw Favor with her face toward the wall, resting. McKenzie was lying in bed, her eyes heavy with sleep.

"Mom, where are we going to go?" McKenzie asked.

"I don't know," I said, running my fingers over her arm.

"Oh, that feels good." Her eyes closed. "What's that noise?" she said as she yawned and drifted into sleep. I could hear the sound of a large airplane starting to take off.

"An airplane," I said, glancing at my watch. It was 10:30 p.m., and I realized it was our flight. I looked at McKenzie who was now fast asleep, pulled the covers over her shoulders, and walked over to the open window next to their bed. I pulled back the curtain. In the distance, I saw our plane—the Dreamliner we were scheduled to be on—power into the open sky above us. My heart sank further as I read "Ethiopian Airlines" on its side, knowing our four seats would be empty. My heart felt sick, like someone was squeezing the life out of it. I was so homesick that I could barely breathe. I wanted to hug my boys, see my dog, and sleep in my bed. I felt like I was in a movie with the wrong ending to my story. Suddenly, amidst the tears, a peace came over me. I knew God was in control. I knew He was a God who worked out good things for those who loved Him, and He was working for us in this hour.

* * * * *

Later that sleepless night, I got on Facebook and wrote to our faithful prayer warriors:

> We know God is in control. We know all things work together for good for those who love Him. God is working on our behalf. We did get stopped at immigration and they took Favor's passport and visa. If you've ever seen a beautiful young girl go from excitement to pure fear and tears...it's devastating. I held her tight and she is still with us. This momma and daddy are not leaving without her. We have to stay in Ethiopia until we can go to immigration and prove our case. The Embassy is with us, but can't go over the government's head concerning Favor because she is not American until she sets foot in the U.S. We don't know how long this will take.
>
> We are exhausted and need prayer to just keep our heads above water. Pray for wisdom, divine connection, and that this will be resolved quickly. We need protection

desperately. We are safe in a wonderful Christian guest house tonight. God never said it would be easy. Sometimes we have to kill a few more giants than we have strength for. In this case, God is fighting for us so we don't have to have the strength because it's His battle. It never was ours. We just have to trust Him.

Truth be told, we're in shock, but we also know God's promises are true. We know we can expose some things in this country that are hurting adoption and these precious orphans. Maybe that's why God has us going through this, so we can bring light into a dark place and situation. We then are happy to be used for the Lord. He loves these children, and we are fighting not just for our child, but all those who might be put in harm because of this corruption. We have nothing to hide and bringing this to light might help some other families not go through this. We're warriors for those who have no voice and they messed with the wrong children of God. All this did was get our fighting spirit going to see that justice is done.

Trusting God to do great things!!

Love you!

Mark and Missy

Chapter 16
ANGEL ARMIES

"Therefore I take pleasure in infirmities,
in reproaches, in necessities, in persecutions,
in distresses for Christ's sake:
for when I am weak, then am I strong."

—2 Corinthians 12:10, KJV

Within minutes of posting a status on Facebook, our friends were responding with prayers and questions. We couldn't tell them much, but we found ourselves encouraged and filled with hope. Our hearts were still heavy, but we knew that God most certainly had a plan for us in Ethiopia.

One of our relatives sent a private message about a connection he had who was very familiar with the corruption we might be facing. He had called a special agent, who gave us instructions to not allow Favor out of our sight, or we might never see her again. He told us we had done the right thing by staying, but now it would be best to go into hiding and to retain an Ethiopian attorney through the Embassy. My mind went into overdrive thinking of the danger we could be putting McKenzie into by having her there. One of us should take her home, but neither one of us wanted to leave Favor, or each other. All I could do was pray for God's protection.

I finally shut my computer off at 2 a.m. I was tired, and knew that I needed to sleep if I was going to think straight the next day. I could tell Mark was still awake, but we didn't say a word to each other. Although mere inches were all that separated us, we were a world apart.

A pack of dogs barked in the alley outside our window all night. At one point, by the sound of it, I could tell a neighborhood cat was having a really bad night. I don't know if I was feeling the cat's pain or just my own, but ironically I found myself totally relating to an unknown feline.

I was glad to see the dawn break. It gave me an excuse to get up and stop trying to act like I was sleeping. Looking outside, I was amazed at how peaceful it looked—so quiet and still. I could feel the presence of the Lord, and I felt safe, although everything happening to us was telling me we were in danger. I ran the bath water and got myself ready before the girls woke up. I wasn't sure what we would be facing. We were now in uncharted territory. My usually strategic mind couldn't think of what I needed to do next. All I could do was to trust God in what He was doing now. He doesn't make mistakes, and He is never random.

I started thinking about where we would go. We didn't know anyone in Addis Ababa except for those at the orphanage and Julie, who lived in a small apartment with several other girls. We had to leave the guest house early because a large group of medical missionaries was coming in. Our money was almost gone, and the credit cards were maxed out. Where would a family of four go that wouldn't cost much and be a safe place to hide? *Lord, I know You are my provider. I know I don't need to worry about You taking care of us. Please help us find a safe place that we can afford. You know exactly what we need,* I prayed silently.

Mark was up checking emails when I returned to the room. I started catching up on Facebook posts from the night before. There, in the comments, waited the answer to my prayer. Jody had friended me three years ago after meeting our son Shewit—at the same orphanage where they adopted their daughter. She had sent me pictures of Shewit taken while they were picking up their new daughter, and we had remained friends. Her family had moved to Addis Ababa two months ago to do missions. Later, I would find out that they arrived months ahead of schedule because they were able to raise money so quickly for their mission work. Jody had commented several times on our Facebook posts to contact her because she wanted to help us. This time, she offered her home as a place we could stay in Addis Ababa until we could take Favor home. I hesitated. I didn't want to be a burden. But here, right in front of me, was the answer to my prayers. God's provision arrived just in time, and my pride was threatening to step in and take it from me.

We packed up our belongings and dragged our bags downstairs to wait for Pochi. The medical missionaries were starting to arrive. I noticed Mark was pacing out in the courtyard. He still couldn't bring himself to eat, and I could see his eyes were red and swollen from crying. As he paced, he cried out to God to fix the wrong decisions that he had made. He was begging God to protect his family from the danger he had put them in. He prayed that God would forgive him for his unbelief.

Inside, I sat down with the girls and made sure they had a good breakfast before we left. One of the missionaries sat across from me and wanted to know what brought us to Ethiopia. I started to tell her about our story and the battle we were facing with the foster care system that was trying to stop our adoption. Mark walked in as she began to share that these foster care systems were being created by UNICEF.

I told Mark about Jody inviting us to stay at their home, "Does she know that there are four of us and that we have no idea how long we are going to be here?" Mark asked.

"I'm sure she knows, but I'll make sure," I said. "What else can we do? We are running out of money, and we used up all our points at the Hilton."

"Adeferese is probably looking for us at the Hilton," Mark said. "We need to find a place to hide."

"I'll give Jody a call, but I believe God sent her to help us. It's no coincidence," I said.

"You're right." Mark said, "It seems like God has it all planned out."

* * * * *

About that time, we heard honks from the car with Pochi, Dave, and the Pastor coming to pick us up at the front gate.

Pastor stepped out of the car, and when he saw Mark, he opened his arms to embrace him. I could see Mark's shoulders shake as Pastor held him like a father. Mark was in so much pain, but even tears didn't seem to bring much relief from his agony.

Pochi ran up and gave me a hug. "Oh, you look so tired! Be happy, Missy! God is going to do something big! He is in control!"

I stared at her, unable to respond.

"Missy," she said, "this is about so much more than you can understand right now. You could've left, but you stayed in the battle. You are fighting for those with no voice. You can help uncover something that needs to be stopped—a corruption hurting these children."

Something she said reminded me of a Nashville pastor's fairly recent prophecy, which stated that Mark and I would both help expose corruption and be used as God's secret agents to advocate for orphans and human traffic victims. It sounded so exciting and cool when we first heard it... but not so much now as we were beginning to live it out. Yet, God's prophecy was defining us for the work in this moment. We could see ourselves differently—through His eyes, instead of what we were feeling in our stage of weakness, pain, and exhaustion. *He* was defining us—not our circumstances.

"We have a meeting with our attorney this afternoon," Pochi said. "He will know what steps you need to take next. We can take you to a guest house and get you settled for now."

Mark looked at me to see if I would say anything.

"Pochi," I interrupted, "let me call a friend who lives in town before we go to the guest house. She lives in a compound where we could possibly stay."

* * * * *

Jody answered on the first ring.

"Jody, this is Missy."

"I'm so glad you called! I was hoping you would take me up on my offer."

"Jody, there are four of us, and we don't know how long we will be here. It could be a long time. We just don't want to be a burden."

"You will not be a burden," Jody said. "We would love to have you. We're on an eight-acre compound. There are many kids around for the girls to play with, and we have several armed guards protecting us 24 hours a day, every day. So when can you be here?"

"Well," I asked, "how long does it take to get to you from near the airport?"

"About half an hour. We're at The Academy, if your driver knows where that is."

I turned to Pochi, "Do you know where The Academy is?"

A big smile came over Pochi's face as she replied, "Of course I do, my nephew goes there! Tell her we'll bring you right now, if that works."

* * * * *

We loaded our bags into the cars and headed toward the compound. As we pulled onto the highway, Pochi was encouraging us in the Lord, but I could see Mark was getting frustrated by each word she said. Finally, Mark turned to Pochi and unloaded his pain and frustration. "Why did you take her back to Debre Birhan when we asked you several times not to? Missy begged you not to take her back!"

"I know you are very tired and upset, but this will all work out, Mark." Pochi calmly responded, then took a deep breath. "I made a mistake. I should've never taken her back, but the woman who was acting as her foster care mother said she would be in trouble if she did not let them know Favor was leaving for America. The officials wanted to see Favor before she left."

"But that was a lie!" Mark shot back. "They didn't need to see her. She was released from that foster care days after she was dragged out of the orphanage. The judge wouldn't have approved us at court and given us irrevocable rights as her parents. They had no right to know anything about our daughter after they signed that release!"

"Mark, I know you are upset," Pochi was trying to put out a fire that wasn't going away until he had answers. "I am sorry. I should not have taken her back. I didn't think they would keep her, or try to stop your adoption. They gave me their word."

"Do you know how much danger you have put my family in?" Mark asked. "How much hurt you have caused us by not just doing what we asked? You have no idea how much pain we are feeling."

Our car was quiet. Mark turned his head to look away from Pochi. I could see his face in the side mirror and it told a story of a man past his threshold of pain. Pochi quietly answered him, "I never meant to bring Favor harm or put your family in a position that would endanger them. I give my life for these children. I love them with all that I am. We have four children that need to get to their forever families. If you would've left, we might not have had any chance of freeing them to go to their families. You see one child. I see four."

Mark started to respond, but no words would form, so he sat silently in his suffering.

* * * * *

About 20 minutes into our drive, I noticed a shift in the atmosphere—more than just a physical shift—it was something I was feeling in my spirit. I had that undeniable, uneasy feeling come into my stomach that wasn't my exhaustion or the conversation that had just taken place—it was something deeper—some kind of spiritual warfare going on around us.

We finally arrived at the tall black gate at the end of a long dirt street. Barbed wire was circled around the top and as promised, we were greeted by some very serious and strict security guards. Jody had to vouch for us before they would let us pass. Once we were inside, I felt safe. We parked near the gym, which was lined with flags from the countries representing the students who attended The Academy. Just seeing the American flag made me proud. The buildings were in good shape, and a peaceful feeling surrounded us from the first moment that we came in. We could see that some of buildings were used for classrooms. Everywhere we looked, we knew this was a place for kids. The playground would have been illegal in the United States. No plastic, unappealing labyrinths to explore here. Everything was metal and looked like an adventure—or a hospital visit waiting to happen. Either way, it was going to be a bright, fun spot for the girls. There were huts we could sit in and birds singing in some nearby trees. They even had a little coffee and snack shop.

Walking up the path was a woman I only knew from pictures, but by the smile on her face, I knew it had to be Jody. I couldn't wait to reach out and hug her.

"Thank you so much for allowing us to stay here," I said. Then I introduced her to Mark and Pochi.

"I'm so glad you took me up on my offer. What a crazy time you're having!" Jody said in an apologetic tone.

"Yeah, a little crazy," I said. "Hopefully, God will somehow use it. We're meeting with someone at lunch to see what the next step is."

"Well, I can't wait to see what God does. It does sound like a great book or movie though." Jody smiled at me, "Don't you write? You never know!" I laughed at the thought of writing my own adventure story. Things like this don't usually happen to middle class families who decide to adopt. I know hundreds of adoptive families that never had any problems adopting—including us.

"I was going to have you stay in my house, but there is also another option: My husband, Pat, found out we have a small apartment available, which is really unusual, especially right now," Jody said in disbelief. "We never have apartments available."

I knew God was taking care of every detail.

"You are welcome to use it anytime while you're here. I know there's a small fee, but I don't think it's much," Jody continued. "You might just want to be together with your new family after all that's happened. I know you're transitioning with Favor, and I remember how tough that can be."

Mark didn't hesitate, "That would be awesome. Would you mind if we just start in the apartment?"

"It would be no problem at all." Jody turned and walked toward the office behind us. "Let me grab the keys."

The small apartment was located over the kindergarten classroom in a building near the entrance of The Academy. We went through the teacher and administration lounge area, up some beautiful mahogany steps, and then up a few more steps to our door. The computer classes were right next to us. Mark was excited that we'd be getting a good internet connection. We walked in and saw a small apartment perfect for a single adult. It had the feel of an older cabin with a slanted ceiling. The first sight from the doorway was the "U" shaped kitchen, stocked with all the utensils and cooking necessities we'd need. I noticed a few extra buckets, but I didn't question why they were there. In the living room was a couch and a small table. The bathroom, the same size as our half-bath at home, had a sink snuggled up to one side of the toilet with a small shower on the other side. The bedroom, in the back of the apartment, had a bed under a slanted ceiling and a small armoire for our clothes. The ceiling had a sliding door that revealed a skylight, which doubled as our light during the day. The apartment was perfect, and it would serve as our home for however long we would be here.

Our apartment located above the Kindergarten at The Academy.

Our girls were excited to check out the rest of the compound, but that would have to wait until after our meeting with the orphanage's lawyer.

"I'll bring some mattresses for the girls and some towels for you," Jody said as she glanced around the apartment looking for things we'd need. "We don't have air conditioning, so windows stay open all the time. You'll need to boil your water, and the big containers are for your purified water. I'll show you where that is."

"This will be perfect, Jody. Is there a place where I can buy food?" I asked.

"Actually, we'd love to have you for dinner at our house tonight—if that works for you," Jody said. "I can take you shopping tomorrow at a little store we go to. It's the only place that I'll buy meat from, and there's a fruit stand that we'll visit. Oh, and if you hear something above your heads tonight, it's probably the resident mongoose."

"Is it a pet?" I asked, trying to remember what I could about the species.

"Oh, no, no, it's completely wild—so don't try to pick it up or anything like that," Jody told the girls.

"What does a mongoose look like?" McKenzie asked.

"Well," Jody explained, "it looks like a giant cat with a flat face and a really bushy tail. Just go the other way if you see it."

"It sounds so cute!" McKenzie said.

"Really," Jody warned, "they're not cute. They'll attack if they feel threatened." At that, the girls' eyes got as big as saucers.

* * * * *

Later that day, Pastor and Pochi drove us to the guest house, where they had suggested we stay earlier that day. There, we would be able to print some needed documentation for the court and for our next meeting later that day. When we walked in to the guest house, I recognized the other adoptive mother who was adopting through EAI. She had been on our flight to Addis Ababa, and she was the lady who Josiah gave a ride to when he relegated us to the hotel shuttle. We now realized that God's protection had steered us to stay with Jody and Pat instead of the guest house because EAI might have found us if we had stayed there. Mark hurried to print all the correspondence between us, Adeferese, and EAI. We wanted to leave as soon as possible for our safety.

I joined Pastor and Dave, who had been our driver and bodyguard, at the dining room table. They were talking about timing. A man in their church had brought Psalm 57:1–6 to Pastor three weeks ago. God had shown this man that this passage was the promise God had for those of us going through the fire of the enemy right now. In this Psalm, even though David was fleeing from Saul into the caves, David was praising God for His protection and refuge. His soul trusted the Lord, he had confidence that the truth would prevail, and he was seeing God's great mercy in the midst of his enemies. The trap Saul was trying to set for David ended up being the one that would entrap Saul. As I read this passage, I marveled at how many times I had read that psalm, but now I related to every line of it—in every fiber of my being.

Our next meeting with the orphanage's lawyer was across town at a luxury hotel. We sat in the huge marble lobby as they served us coffee and soft drinks. Pochi told the lawyer everything that had happened leading up to us being stopped at immigration. Mark showed him the note that was slid under our door at the Hilton. The lawyer began laying out a plan for us.

The girls were getting fidgety, so I took them exploring up and down the eight flights of marble steps to the floors above. I felt like I couldn't take my eyes off Favor for a moment. It was exhausting on a normal day to follow a high-spirited and active seven-year-old, but today was even worse because I was running on no sleep. At one point, the girls got far ahead of me, and I could no longer hear them. My heart started beating faster as I charged up the steps and into a room that overlooked a dark ballroom. The girls were nowhere to be seen or heard. Then the elevator opened...it was empty. I went up a few more steps and saw a couple eating outside their room. They had not seen anyone. I rushed back down the steps, praying that nothing bad had happened to them. I looked back over the balcony in the ballroom. Then I heard giggles behind a table, and I knew the joke was on me. I had only feelings of relief that they were safe.

After that trick, the exploring came to an abrupt halt, and the girls were entertained with a soft drink while I shot down a strong cup of coffee. I was hoping it would jolt my body awake, but I must've been too exhausted for the coffee to make a difference. As we waited, I listened to the lawyer's different strategies. The first was to go directly to the president of courts, but after he made a call and had an appointment set, he felt it was in our best interest to go through the lower courts first to prove our innocence. He kept asking Mark what else had happened between us and Adeferese, because this looked like a personal attack on us. Adeferese was telling the court lies about us being involved with illegal activity. He was even suggesting that we were human traffickers. Why would he do that unless he wanted to get us back for something we'd done to him? Mark and I sat there at a loss, knowing we had not done anything wrong, nor had we done anything personally against Adeferese.

"Can you represent us in court?" Mark asked the lawyer.

"I can't," he said. "I represent the orphanage. It would be a conflict of interest."

"Then let me ask you," Mark asked, "who would you not want to go head-to-head with in court? I want that guy!"

The lawyer thought for a moment then said, "I think I might know someone. He is smart and is a very good man. I will get back with you on this. I believe the president of the courts will be willing to help you, but first let's see if the judge will clear whatever charges are against you. In our culture, I think this is the right way to do it. The judge is the one who can get Favor's passport and visa back into your hands."

* * * * *

Mark and I felt a little better after speaking to the lawyer. We trusted him, and he seemed to know how to work the system correctly. He also had the connections we needed in the event that our case went terribly wrong. Both Mark and I believed the lawyer, and felt like we wouldn't be in Ethiopia that much longer.

Driving back to The Academy from our meeting with the lawyer, I noticed that the area we were in was predominantly Islamic. In every direction, I saw signs of Islam—from the mosques, which seemed to be around every corner, to the women, who were covered in their burqas and khi-mar head-scarves. As I watched the people around me, I couldn't help but notice that not one person was smiling and no laughter filled the air.

"I never knew how large the Muslim population was in Ethiopia," I said.

"It has grown in the past 10 years, but this area has the largest population in Ethiopia," Pochi answered.

"This area?" I asked. "The place where we are staying?"

"Yes," she said.

I didn't have a problem with Muslims, but I did know that some Muslims, who are radical, have a problem with Christians. I also knew that in the last few months, American Embassies in nations surrounding us were being taken over by radicals who burned American flags and put up black Islamic flags in their place. Then there was the horrific attack in Benghazi that left four Americans dead, including the ambassador. My exhausted mind went negative, my heart started beating faster, and I found myself fearing the worst. I questioned God for placing us in the middle of an Islamic area. I felt like I was already living a nightmare, and now I was about to go head-to-head with another one.

* * * * *

When we got back to our apartment, we found our counter and refrigerator filled with yummy comfort items, snacks, and bread. I knew these items had to be from Jody. The girls taste tested everything, like they hadn't eaten in a week. I started unpacking and tried to make our little apartment feel like a home while we were there. I took the wooden cross that we had bought for our home and hung it where we could see it...a reminder of where our salvation came from.

Mark quickly checked our emails. One was from the U.S. Embassy in Ethiopia. He became suspicious when one message stated, "Adeferese was working in our best interest, and we needed to work together with him and keep the lines of communication open." Mark couldn't believe what he was reading. He knew someone in the Embassy was working on behalf of Adeferese. Most likely that person was completely unaware of our side of the story. Our trust level dropped knowing that we had been falsely accused by the man who they were now asking us to work with. Another resource that we had hoped would stand with us had just fallen through.

The next email Mark opened was from U.S. Senator Bob Corker of Tennessee, wanting to see how he could assist us. The email after that was from Tennessee Congresswoman Marsha Blackburn, seeking more information to help us with our dilemma in Ethiopia. I knew that Marsha was a strong advocate for orphans and adoption. It seemed that our friends back in Tennessee had been busy calling our senators and state representatives—giving us a possible lifeline.

Favor kept asking when we were leaving for America. I could only say, "Soon." Her question broke my heart, and I knew she was wondering why we were still in Ethiopia. I checked Facebook and cried as I read the prayers that filled my wall. There were words of encouragement that helped me see things from a different view—a heavenly perspective. These words and prayers brought such peace and life into my battle-weary soul.

* * * * *

We joined Jody's family for dinner that night. They were warm and encouraging. We knew that they were very conscious of our emotional state. As Jody prepared the meal, I tried to help as we got to know each other. Her heart for Ethiopia amazed me, and her ability to take things in stride was delightful. She told me all about the things that she had learned since moving to Addis Ababa a few months ago, including the trouble her four girls had adjusting, and the things she missed most about America. Skittles, pretzels, and a bag of chips were like gold to them. On the bright side, it seemed like everyone who moved to Ethiopia from America dropped 10–20 pounds in the first few months they were there. I'm sure that had something to do with the lack of processed foods.

Jody's husband, Pat, confirmed that we were in the heart of an Islamic area, and also near Mercato, a place that people in the States had warned us about.

Walking back to our apartment after dinner, we met a giant tortoise coming down the hill. McKenzie couldn't believe her eyes.

"That is the biggest turtle I have ever seen!" She blurted out as she ran toward it. "Can I ride it?"

"That's probably not a good idea," Mark warned as McKenzie stopped in mid-stride with one foot held in the air. We were so thankful she was with us. Favor loved having

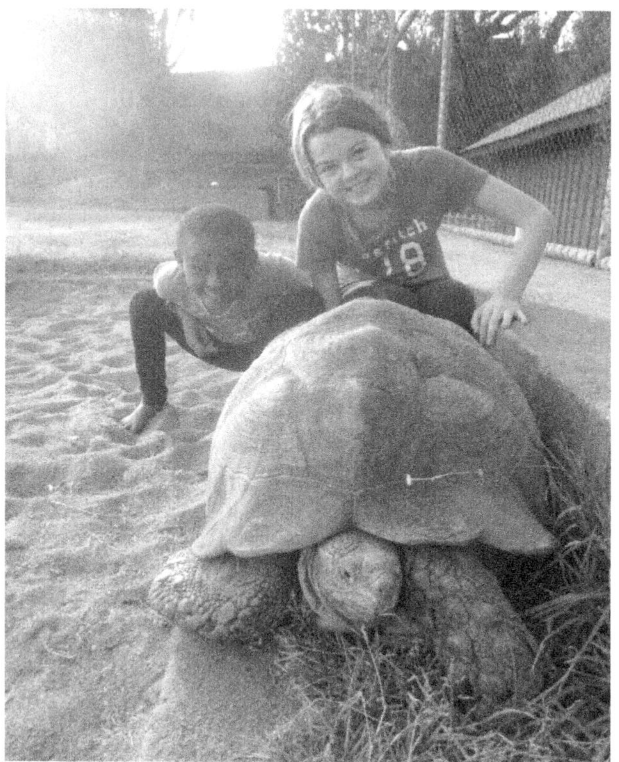

McKenzie and Favor meeting one of the turtles on The Academy's grounds.

a big sister, and McKenzie's cheerful disposition was a light in a very dark place. As we all continued to walk toward our apartment, I looked up and noticed how beautiful the night sky was. Mark reached out for my hand, and without a thought, I grabbed it. As mad as I was at him, it felt good to have him by my side.

* * * * *

That night, we couldn't wait to crawl into bed. We were completely spent. The girls were asleep the moment their heads hit the pillows, while Mark stared at the ceiling, 36 inches from his face. I quickly drifted off to sleep, but I was awakened a few minutes later by the Islamic call to prayer blaring through the loudspeaker next to the compound.

The streets were alive and noisy, and I knew there was no way I was going to fall back asleep. The four mosques surrounding us seemed to take turns seeing who could be the loudest. Although I had heard the call to prayer many times on our overseas trips, something was different about it here. I couldn't understand much of what they were saying, but I knew a spirit of war was behind it. The crowds outside became louder and more aggressive in their chants. Mark and I became more and more painfully aware that we were in the heart of Islamic territory. I tried to pray, but the people were so loud I couldn't think. I checked the girls and they were still sleeping. I thanked God that they were both heavy sleepers.

We heard what sounded like a riot all around us. I made a mental note to find a bugle and blow it as loud as I could in every direction first thing in the morning. Then I decided that the right thing to do was pray for their salvation and that they would come to know Jesus's love. After an hour, all grace left and I found myself praying for a sudden onset of laryngitis and narcolepsy to come upon them all. I thought about blasting some loud music out of our window, but I realized that I would be as annoyed as they were. I tried desperately not to think about Benghazi and what the radicals did to the Americans there. My spirit was so stirred, my body was so tired, and my heart was pounding within my chest.

I reached over and found my iPhone in the dark. Even at 2 a.m., it sounded like the crowds in the streets were just getting warmed up. I could feel my anxiety level rising. I searched for a worship song that would set my mind and spirit on the things of God and drive away the fear that was trying to take over and torment me. I found some music by Alberto and Kimberly Rivera. Within a few minutes, I could feel my spirit settling and tension leaving my body. I kept worshiping and thanking God that He was with us and taking care of us.

* * * * *

I'm not sure if what happened next was a vision in my spirit or an actual out-of-body experience, but as I lay there, I found myself being "caught up." I could hear everything around me as my body kept rising toward the heavens, looking down from where I was, high above the city. I could see the perimeter of the compound where we were staying, including a creek which ran on the back side of the area. I could see the homes, mosques, and people in the streets all around us. Then I looked at the top of the brick walls, and I could see large 9- to 12-foot angels facing out, standing guard around the entire compound. They were beautiful and mindful of their surroundings. Each had long swords to their left side, and they stood in silence. Suddenly, I felt my body being pulled toward the front gate. As I turned, I saw the most amazing and majestic being rising up in the midst of these angels. I watched in awe as this mighty host angel stood up and took a commanding stand before me. He was the most magnificent being I had ever seen, towering into the sky. His knees came to the top of the three-story gym to his left. He had a radiance illuminating from within him, his forearms were covered with gleaming gold armor vambraces, and he carried a massive sword in his right hand. His breastplate and body armor were like iridescent gold, which seemed to shine with a light of its own. The colors looked alive. His lower legs were protected with golden greaves. I watched as he looked toward the darkness that was surrounding us, and I saw the enemies instantly take flight in every direction when they saw him. All of them were completely terrified at his presence. They looked like ants next to him. The glory that he carried took my breath away.

I knew God had sent him for us, and I knew God wanted me to see His immeasurable power in this moment. As I watched in awe, I was aware that the mighty God I served, Who created me, was this mighty angel's Creator. Jehovah God was so much bigger and greater than I had made Him. In that instance, all fear left me, and in its place, came love. I was filled with wonder and reverence that the God of the universe was mindful of our need, and I knew we were there for a Godly purpose.

As suddenly as I was "caught up," I returned to my bed. Peace and love had replaced the fear and anxiety. I looked over at Mark to tell him what God had just shown me, but he was asleep, and I knew he needed rest. Within a few moments, I had drifted off into a restful sleep, safe under the protective watch of an army of angels.

CHAPTER 17
FEARLESS

"Sometimes, feeling unqualified
to take on the task God has put before you
is the very thing that qualifies you."

—Missy Maxwell Worton

I woke up the next morning to the sounds of birds singing outside our bedroom window. It was quite an amazing contrast to the sounds that filled our room the night before. A new day had begun, and my spirit felt alive and awakened like never before.

I looked toward Mark lying next to me, his eyes searching mine for any forgiveness or encouragement. "God showed me an amazing vision last night," I started. I shared everything I had seen from the night before—the angels encamped around us, the skyscraper-sized war angel that came out from the midst of them, how the darkness fled at the sight of him, and how my fears were instantly gone.

"Why didn't you tell me last night? I didn't sleep at all," Mark said, disappointed.

"I thought you were asleep," I apologized.

"No, I was awake, but I'm encouraged," he said. "God obviously knows we're going to need it."

"He obviously knew I needed to see that vision last night," I said. "I was battling overwhelming fear until I remembered to put praise music on. The enemy never likes to be reminded that he got his butt kicked on the cross." My little aggressive comments about the enemy usually make Mark laugh, but I could see he was worn out and operating on no sleep.

The girls ran into our room to pounce on us when they heard us talking. We all cuddled up together, and I told them my vision about the angels. They wanted to go outside and see the angels right then! I love children and how their minds aren't cluttered with the message of the world. They still believe because they don't have to work through all the ideologies we do. Their God is already outside of the box of conventionalism. They were excited that God was looking out for us with so many beautiful and mighty angels.

We ate breakfast bars and had some mango juice before we got ready to meet Jody and her husband Pat, who were so generously providing a place for us to stay. On the way to their church fellowship community, they were going to drop us off at Covenant Church, where Pochi and Pastor attended. But first, we would have to drive again through Mercato—the place we had been warned about because of its reputation for muggings, murders, rapes, and beatings—not exactly your family-friendly destination. This time, however, all the things I knew about the area couldn't stir up any fear. I knew my God was greater than any evil that thought it could harm us. People were glaring at us as we drove by, and they would approach the van when we would slow down in traffic. I watched in disbelief and sadness at some of the cruelty that I saw, and I cringed at the level of poverty that was everywhere. This time I was different though—I found myself praying for them instead of fearing them. I realized that my heart was so full of fear before, that it had no room for love. When I released all that fear, God filled me with His perfect love. Love had replaced fear.

* * * * *

Pat dropped us off on a dirt road that Pochi said would lead to her church. When we opened the car door, we could hear the praise coming from a building right down the road. My spirit leapt. I turned back to thank Pat and grab my purse, but my body could not wait to be near the worship. As we walked up to Covenant Church, Favor ran into Pochi's arms. Pochi then greeted us and introduced us to a young man, who would translate the message for us.

We walked into a metal-framed building with dusty, cement floors, vibrating from the music. The pews were metal frames that held two pieces of wood, one to sit on and one to lean back on. The worship leader was singing his heart out at the front of the room, where there was a large white cross with the church's name and some gold drapes covering the wall behind it. Some blue-and-white wilting balloons were placed around the front from a wedding the day before. The band played off to the side of the small platform, and people of all ages were dancing and singing to the music. They had so much freedom as they praised God! Seeing the wave of energy as they worshipped with their whole bodies was electric! When they were exhausted, they would take off their outer shirts and circle them above their heads. We weren't sure what the words they were singing meant, but the joy that filled the sanctuary immediately lifted our spirits and made us feel like family.

For much of the next three hours, God's spirit ministered to us in a language we didn't understand. At one point we got a shout out from the preacher—it would be the only English we would hear: "Mark and Missy Worton from Texas!" We laughed. Everyone thinks you're from either Texas or New York if you're from America. What we did understand, though, was that this little church and the people who filled it were full of the presence of God. His Spirit was prevalent in the worship. The message was sweet like honey. We read line-by-line just after the translator wrote it in English for us. We needed to feel God, and we yearned for Him more than water in a desert—more than life itself—and He was there.

After church, we went to the front to see Pastor, who welcomed us with open arms. He told us that he knew we were sad, but this was God's fight. The people at his church had been praying, knowing that we were in a mighty battle, but they believed God had sent us to help the orphans. We were humbled to think that God could use us in our current state to help anyone, but we thanked them and asked for their continued prayers.

* * * * *

That afternoon, I went with Jody and some other ladies to buy food for the coming week, while Mark got beat in a one-on-one soccer game with Favor. We had run out of Ethiopian Birr, so I had to ask Jody for a loan until we could have money wired to us.

The first stop was a two-story grocery store. I followed Jody around like a lost puppy dog. I started laughing when she spotted a recent delivery of Mountain Dew. "I've never seen Mountain Dew here," she declared, as she excitedly began filling her basket with cans. "I am so excited! I can use these for Christmas gifts or a special treat!" She kept grabbing cans until she had successfully cleared the shelf on which they were displayed.

The prices and packaging for items was different than America. The cream cheese cost more than $9.00 for what I would usually pay $1.00 at my grocery store back in Tennessee. The milk was packaged in a bag instead of a box, and meat was sold by a butcher. You could tell if your meat was prepared by a Muslim or Christian based on the symbol of a cross or the crescent moon and star displayed above the meat.

McKenzie wanted to get her dad some peanut M&M's, his favorite, to hopefully bring a smile to his face. In her 11 years, she had never seen her father cry, and now she was seeing him in pain daily. As we were shopping, I noticed two teenage boys following us around the store. They were mesmerized by McKenzie and trying to get her attention. McKenzie was oblivious. Finally, one of them yelled out in broken English, "You are beautiful! Please marry me!" McKenzie froze, gave me a confused look, glanced at them, and then quickly walked behind me, shaking her head no.

"Did that boy really just ask me to marry him?" she said. The boy grabbed his chest, acting like it was broken. All I could think about was that my daughter's first marriage proposal was in the candy section of an Ethiopian grocery store. Although broken-hearted, they were kind enough to carry our groceries out to the van for us. I think it was just so that they could be near my daughter.

My favorite stop was the fruit stand, run by a group of local men. These men loved to see the women from The Academy arrive to shop and to give them extra attention. We bought eggs, fruits, and vegetables, and when we were all done, I walked away with a box of various produce items for under six American dollars! The bargain shopper in me was thrilled.

Jody had prepared me by telling me beforehand that we would be surrounded by beggars as we left and that we needed to use wisdom in our interactions with them. One woman came up with a two-year-old child and asked for money. I gave the little boy a banana and the woman a few birr that I had left from the day of shopping. She looked at what I had given her and gave me a look of disapproval, then abruptly turned and walked away without a word. I understood why the others had ignored her and gotten in the van—they had obviously experienced her less-than-grateful attitude. I had to laugh—I had just handed her the last money I had, still knowing her life was a lot worse than mine.

* * * * *

That night I made spaghetti on the one burner that worked in our kitchen. It felt like a little bit of home. We found a candle and burned it as we ate our meal and talked about the day. After the meal, McKenzie had Mark close his eyes then ran to the freezer and came back with the M&M's she had bought. When he opened his eyes he was humbled at what McKenzie had done. She had shown kindness at a time when he didn't feel strong but like a failure. I was glad McKenzie was taking care of her daddy. Even though I could see he was hurting, I had no comfort to give him. I wasn't mad or angry anymore, I just felt numb when I looked at him.

* * * * *

Monday morning started off with a call from Pochi saying Mark needed to meet DJ at a government office to sign over our Power of Attorney before 12:30 p.m. that day, so our attorney could stand on our behalf. DJ helped the orphanage with paperwork and some of the legal aspects. There was no transportation, so Mark had to get a cab. I didn't have to go because I had already signed my Power of Attorney over to Mark. I stayed with the girls at the compound and worked on our timeline for our new attorney, Mesfin. The room was quiet and peaceful. I grabbed my iPhone and listened to some soaking music. Within moments of worshiping God, I found myself in the Throne Room, crawling up in Father's lap. I could feel the movement of His chest against my head and His breath upon the top of my head. There were no words, just rest that I needed in that hour. I could feel His spirit washing over my hurting heart, and somehow I knew I would be okay—no matter what the day might hold. I knew Who was holding me.

As I was worshiping, the cabbie was taking Mark a different way to the office. Sitting there, Mark realized he had no idea if he could even trust this driver. Was he a friend of Adeferese working on his behalf to take Mark to another destination? The road was unfamiliar, and Mark didn't communicate with the cabbie who didn't seem to speak much English. Mark's imagination started stirring up crazy scenarios. He shook off the feeling and tried not to entertain those thoughts, but he found himself unable to easily trust anyone.

Finally, Mark arrived at the government office and saw DJ standing on the curb with a friend. Mark was relieved and felt compelled to give the cabbie his $20 sunglasses along with the tip. The driver was very grateful and told Mark, "Whatever you need, I will be there for you." Mark then realized the cabbie probably could speak English well.

Once they went inside the government facility, Mark followed DJ through the process of signing documents. Everything was flowing smoothly until they arrived in the particular office where they would need four verifying stamps to move forward. The first stamp was easy, but at the second counter, the lady wouldn't approve the Power of Attorney because I was not there to sign for it.

* * * * *

The phone in the apartment rang, shaking me out of my tranquil setting. I jumped over the girl's mattress and ran to grab it before the girls woke up. It was Mark letting me know that he was sending a cab to pick me up in the next 15 minutes. He needed me down there immediately before they closed the office in the next few hours. I stood there in my nightgown with my hair going in every direction, wondering how making that journey was even a possibility for me.

I woke up the girls, told them what was happening, and let them know that I would be leaving for just a little while. I called Jody and asked if she could help me by staying with the girls, and she was quick to come to my rescue. We didn't feel safe taking the girls out unless we had someone to watch them constantly.

Somehow I made it to the cab, and off the driver and I went. Traffic was intense. It seemed like we were parked more than we were moving. At one point, the driver told me to roll up my windows and lock the doors. We slowed to a stop, and the car was surrounded with people looking in at me in the back seat. I felt like a fish in an aquarium. People were banging on the windows and were calling out "Faranji" (fah ran ge), which meant "foreigner." This word was like a signal to others, and more people gathered around the car, asking for money. I asked the driver where we were, and he said we were in Mercato Fruit District. He told me to ignore all the people surrounding the car or it would become dangerous. I looked up ahead, noticing that we had a truck carrying bananas blocking the road in front of us. Behind us, a huge truck was pinning us in. I yearned for my serenity moment, doing my best to grab hold of the peace that I had experienced that morning. I took a long, deep breath. Then I remembered the angel that God had sent the night before. *God, please make a way for us.* Almost immediately, the banana truck drove out of the way, and we sped up the street—away from the Fruit District and all the onlookers.

* * * * *

I had been in the back seat of the cab for almost an hour now. I had received a few marriage proposals, and seen a few things my eyes would've been better off missing. Then the driver's phone started ringing. It was Mark, wondering what was wrong and why it was taking us so long. It had only taken Mark 30 minutes to get there, and time was running out to get our three remaining stamps and signatures for our Power of Attorney.

I heard the driver say, "We are right around the corner. She is safe." He hung up the phone and smiled. "Your husband—he think I kidnap you. He is very worried where you are." I nervously smiled it off, but knew this had been the longest 30-minute ride I had ever taken. I couldn't imagine how Mark felt on the other side, waiting.

The driver asked me who I thought would win the American presidential election, which was the next day. I knew who I hoped would win, but didn't see any clear winner. I had to start laughing when he told me how proud people in Africa were that America elected a man born from there. "So you really think Obama was born in Africa?" I asked.

"Oh, yes! Everyone knows this here," he proudly proclaimed. "We do not understand why people from America do not want to admit this."

"Well, it could be that if he was proven to be born in Africa, then he couldn't be our president," I told him.

"Why would that matter?" he asked.

"We have a law that a person can only be president if he or she is born in America," I shared. "I've adopted two amazing kids who would probably make wonderful presidents someday, but they were born here, so they are not allowed to run for president of the United States—ever."

He kept asking questions about politics, but the subject started to stress me out. I looked at my watch. It had now been more than 20 minutes since he had told Mark we were just around the corner. "Are we almost there?" I asked.

"Almost," he said. The phone rang again, and the driver answered.

I could hear Mark say, "I thought you said you were around the corner? How close *exactly* are you?"

"We are driving up the road to you," the driver said. At that point, he slowed down and stopped on the six-lane highway.

Across those lanes, I could see my husband desperately waving him over from the far side. The driver made a U-turn in the middle of the traffic and drove across all the lanes to Mark. My door opened and I was whisked away by DJ and Mark as they threw some money at the driver and thanked him.

"Come on, we have to run to make it," Mark said. "What happened? We were afraid you weren't going to get here in time." We were running down a long set of stairs and down a dirt road, about a block away.

"The traffic was just really bad," I tried to answer as we ran faster and jumped over rocks and holes in the road. Then we turned and ran up to a white building. We went through security and it was then that I saw Mark's hands shaking. The elevator was full. "We don't have time to wait...let's take the stairs," Mark said. *I should've worn my tennis shoes*, I thought.

Finally, we arrived on the fourth floor to a packed room of people. The room was sweltering hot. I looked at all the people sitting on the chairs and standing around every inch of wall. Every attendant had a line waiting for their attention. How would we be able to pull this off before they closed in ten minutes?

"Mark Worton," the man from behind the desk called out as if he saw us walk in. We all glanced momentarily at one another, not believing what we heard. The man waved his hand to come to the farthest desk. Within a few minutes, we received the third stamp, and then the fourth and final stamp. We paid the attendant just as they were starting to close up for the day. We took a deep breath as we turned to walk out of the room. Mark looked up at the clock, "12:30 p.m., not a moment too soon," he said. But at least now we had the documents we needed for an attorney to be able to speak for us.

"Wasn't it you that said that God is never late, but He may make you wait to the last minute to answer your prayer?" I teased. "He's just trying to build your faith."

Chapter 18
Meeting Mesfin

"The journey was not about us.
It was about what God could do through us."

—Missy Maxwell Worton

Later on that day, Dave picked Mark and me up at The Academy so that we could go meet an attorney by the name of Mesfin. We didn't know much more about him, other than he came highly recommended by Pochi's attorney. Dave turned up a street that was under construction, and we were immediately greeted with a dust cloud that had us rolling our windows up at record speeds. We made our way to the top of the hill, and we parked next to a four-story building. No one seemed to be on the streets, but who could blame them? We looked like a mud bath gone wrong.

We continued to wait. And wait.

"So," Mark asked, "have you ever met this guy?"

Dave looked at Mark with a smile and shook his head, no.

"Does he know who you are?" Mark asked.

"No," Dave said.

"How are we supposed to know this guy when we see him?" Mark asked.

"He will know you," Dave answered. *Oh, that's reassuring,* I thought. *Here we sit on a dusty side road, waiting to meet a stranger, and none of us know what he looks like.*

After a few passes of the roller equipment that sent dust into our lungs, there was a tap on the driver's window from a person outside. Dave quickly rolled his window down. The two spoke a few seconds and then he turned to us. "He wants me to move the car, and you two get out and follow him," he said.

"Is that Mesfin?" Mark asked.

"I don't know," Dave said. "I believe so."

Mark and I made our way to the sidewalk where this man was standing. He was tall at six foot one, with broad shoulders that made him look larger than life. His face was framed with a well-groomed haircut, mustache, and goatee. He was soft-spoken as he offered his hand to Mark. "My name is Mesfin," he said.

Mark shook his hand and introduced him to me. He briefly shook my hand then looked around as if to see if anyone was watching or following us. Without a word, he motioned for us to follow him into a four-story building. We could see that he was a very quiet individual, one that said very little, if anything at all.

We walked in and went through a security system while the guards sat in their chairs. We obviously didn't pose much of a threat. The building looked like it was pulled out of the pages of the past. No lights were on. We followed Mesfin up to the third floor, and we stood in the dark hallway as he fumbled with his lock. Mark was watching his every move. We had already been turned down by several lawyers before we came. We knew Adeferese had powerful influence over the city, and anyone who would stand up against him might easily be intimidated. Would this man stand up for us? He had a lot to lose, but if he didn't stand for us, we had everything to lose.

He finally opened the door to his office. It was cold, like the rest of the building. It reminded us of a scene out of a 1960s movie. The lights seemed to struggle to come on and warm the room. In the center of the room was a metal desk with a beautiful mahogany bookshelf standing behind it, sparsely decorated with a few legal books. The walls were stark white, waiting for something to dress them. His desk was clean—not even a phone or picture sat on it. He laid the pile of files that he was holding on the center of the desk and seemed to place them in order. Finally, he sat down, pulled his chair in, drew his hands together, and looked at us for a moment. Mark wondered if this was the man who would be able to help us leave Ethiopia with our daughter.

The meeting began with an awkward silence.

A couple minutes later, Mesfin said, "I've talked to a few people about your case. They think I should run the other way."

Mark and I sat, not sure if we should say anything.

"I have never dealt with the adoption courts. I work with companies. What am I doing taking such a case?" Mesfin mused.

We didn't know what to say. Was this his way of bailing out too? Our hearts sank.

"I want to hear what happened from you," he said. "Tell me your story. Why is this man after you?" He unfolded his fingers and leaned back in his comfy chair, ready to hear every detail.

Mark took a breath and looked at me before starting. I nodded for him to be the storyteller. For the next 30 minutes, Mark told Mesfin how we happened to be sitting in front of him on this day. From time to time, I would interject something I felt should be shared about the journey. I watched as Mesfin would nod his head in disbelief, then jot a few notes down on his writing pad.

After Mark finished, Mesfin looked over the notes he'd taken. Then clasped his hands behind his head as he leaned back in his chair. "This is unbelievable!" he said. "I want to know—what does he have against you?"

Mark and I sat silent, shaking our heads. We honestly didn't know why he had come so strongly against us. Deep inside, we had a strong sense that he was not acting on his own.

Mesfin spoke again, "He has to have *something* against you to act like this."

"Nothing," Mark said.

"Nothing?" Mesfin asked. "There has to be something. This is a personal attack on you."

"We came when he said not to come," I said. "All I can think is that we went against his wishes. But we would've lost our daughter had we not come."

"You've done nothing wrong," he said. "There's something more here. Something else."

"There's nothing we've done to him or anyone that we know of," Mark said.

"You know that he has accused you of some horrible things..." Mesfin said outright.

"We've heard," Mark replied.

Mesfin looked at us without a word, as if he was trying to see into our souls. He had yet to smile even once since we had sat down in front of him. "I am aware of Adeferese's power," he said, "but truth will always win. You need to reach out to the EAI Agency in America. Outline your case by email, everything Adeferese has done to you, and see if they will drop this. The agency should've come forward long before now to state a case against you." I jotted down his list of to-dos. "Meet me at the courthouse tomorrow morning, and we will go before the judge and see why she signed the petition to stop you." With that, he put his pen into his coat pocket and stood up.

"Do you think we have a strong case?" Mark asked.

"Yes," he said confidently, "a very strong case. There is no precedent for an adoption to be revoked, especially after it has passed the courts. Also, you have done nothing wrong."

Mark and I shook his hand and thanked him for his time.

"The truth will always win." Mesfin said again.

Mark and I knew we had truth on our side as we walked out the door and down the dark hallway. We were hopeful that we had been placed in good hands, and were starting to breathe a little easier.

* * * * *

When we got back to the compound at The Academy, Mark and I talked seriously about one of us taking McKenzie back to the States. She was missing school, and we didn't want her to fall behind. I refused to be the one to leave, and Mark refused to leave his wife and new daughter in a place where he felt responsible for putting them. When all was said and done, we decided the best choice was to stay together. We had Grandma Worton taking care of the boys, and McKenzie was irreplaceable when it came to being a big sister.

FaceTime with the boys that night was hard. I was on the verge of tears, and my arms ached to hold them. When we told them that we wouldn't be coming home, they begged us to find a way. They didn't understand why we couldn't just hop on a plane. Somewhere in all their questions and pleading, I broke down. I had to leave the conversation. I could no longer form words as the tears started to flow. Mark stayed and talked, but as his mom watched and listened, she saw right through his tough exterior and knew that her son was hurting on a level she had never witnessed before.

* * * * *

November 6, 2012. We had now been in Ethiopia 11 days. November 6th was also the day of the U.S. election, our first court date, and McKenzie's 12th birthday. It started with a knock on the door that startled the girls. Mark opened it to find Pochi's nephew asking for McKenzie to follow him. We all knew it had to be something special that he had planned at

The Academy. As we followed him into the sixth grade class, the room erupted in a "Happy Birthday" chorus. McKenzie, still wearing her pajama bottoms, stood with a smile on her face in front of an entire classroom of kids who she didn't know. As they continued in four different languages, she did her best to blend into the wall. I watched with pride at how thankful she was for their kindness, but deep inside, I wondered how this experience in Ethiopia would affect her—even define her.

We had to go to court again. Although we had a lawyer now, we still had to be there in case the judge had questions for us. Julie showed up to babysit with gifts, movies, and fun activities for the girls. Even though I knew that they would have a blast while we were gone, pain and anger swirled around me. I wasn't sure if I was upset to be leaving my daughter on her birthday, or angry that the sacrifices for not leaving Ethiopia early were adding up on my list.

Dave picked Mark and me up, and we once again headed through Mercato. We had almost cleared the worst area when, without warning, a man stepped in front of our car. Dave slammed on the brakes, which threw me between Mark and him in the front seats. The man turned and looked at us. His eyes were wild and red. His teeth, broken and yellow. He looked like he hadn't taken a bath in weeks. Then his eyes caught Mark sitting in the front seat. The man abruptly turned toward the car and slammed both hands on the hood. We all jumped back, looking at him, not knowing what would happen next. He never took his eyes off of Mark. I slowly shrank into the back seat and got as low as I could, making sure I was covered. The man's head tilted to one side. He started doing a crazy happy dance in front of us, smiling with a bit of bizarre insanity mixed in. He was as high as a kite on hash, and he had just hit the crazy train. Suddenly, he threw his entire body down on the hood of our car, refusing to move.

We can't go anywhere. If you hit someone with a car, it's 15 years in prison, even if you're a foreigner. Dave honked and told the man to get off his car. Without warning, the man's countenance shifted from crazy to uncontrollably angry. He demanded money from Mark, who sat quietly in the front passenger seat. With an angry face, the man started spitting out "Faranji," which means foreigner, pointing at Mark. The man then started moving toward Mark's car door, getting louder and louder the closer he got. People started looking toward the commotion he was causing. As the man approached Mark's window, Dave hit the gas and left him standing in the middle of the street.

We were all relieved as we drove down the road for the next few miles. But within moments, Dave was making a right on to a rough road in the Fruit District of Mercato, a very large open-air market area. I recognized it from the day before, and my stomach turned. The area was packed with vendors, animals for sale, people, and stand-still traffic. We came to a stop and Dave told us to roll up our windows and lock the doors. I knew the drill and covered as much of my face and body as I could.

Mark sat quiet, but I could see the stress in his white knuckles holding onto the door handle. For the next 15 minutes, people started surrounding our car and banging on the windows, asking for money or any type of handouts. I wanted to help them—give them anything—but Dave told us to ignore them to avoid having more people than we could handle around us. Finally, the truck blocking traffic moved, and Dave found a clear path out.

I was unnerved by the experience and sat quietly in the back. We had driven this route three times. The reality that this would be a daily experience for us started sinking in. This route was the shortest option between the apartment and the court, where we would be spending most of our time fighting to keep our daughter. I hated it. I didn't like to be looked at like a fish in a bowl. I also didn't like ignoring their pleas for help, because of the realistic fears of causing a riot.

"Can we please not go that way again?" I asked Dave. Mark started laughing and Dave gave me a smile as he looked into the rearview mirror. He didn't say a word. I could tell my request was not being taken seriously, but I was dead serious.

"I'm not joking!" I said, almost in tears. Then all the tension we had been feeling unexpectedly exploded and was released in bouts of laughter. By the time we drove up to the adoption court, we had tears in our eyes from laughing so hard.

* * * * *

Mesfin met us outside at the door of the adoption court. Before we went in, he gave us some final insight. "This is a new judge," he said. "Let me do the talking. If she wants to hear from you, she will ask you to talk. The good news is that she is the same judge who did your court date for Favor, so she is very unlikely to revoke what she initially passed."

I started remembering how upset she was when EAI had brought us to our court date almost an hour and a half late—talk about making a bad first impression.

"I also have been told that Adeferese tends to intimidate others to get his way," Mesfin said. "He is a very powerful man, so he has many people he can call on for favors."

Our stomachs turned. *Was there any way we could win?* Everything seemed to be stacking up against us before we even started.

"I know this judge," Mesfin said. "I don't believe Adeferese can intimidate her. She is about doing what is right and just. From what I understand, she can't be controlled, but we'll see. He did get her to stop you with a court order."

"With lies," Mark said.

"I am confident she'll figure that out," Mesfin said.

We followed Mesfin up the steps to the third floor and started making our way to the familiar waiting room down the hall. Mesfin stopped and spoke briefly to the judge's secretary. Mark grabbed my hand and whispered in my ear, "We need to pray that this judge will not rule in fear of man, but of what is right and just." We stood in the hallway, hand in hand, asking God to intervene for us with this judge.

Mesfin stepped out of the judge's office and paused as he saw we were having an intimate moment of prayer. When we were finished, he said, "The judge will not see us until after 1:30 p.m. I will see you back here at 1:30."

Mark looked at his watch. That was three hours away. Shouldn't Mesfin had called ahead of time? Shouldn't he have known this already? Mark was starting to question if this was the guy for the job. Had Pochi's lawyer recommended the best person to us?

* * * * *

As we climbed back into the car, Dave could see how frustrated we were. It was too far to drive back to the compound to spend time with our birthday girl, and I didn't want to go back through the Fruit District again. We were stuck.

"I know where I can take you," Dave said, with a smile.

He did know.

Dave drove us to a restaurant on top of a mountain, overlooking Addis Ababa. He said he had to do some personal errands, but I think he knew we were in desperate need of some alone time.

Mark and I walked up the steps to a restaurant separated into two dining areas, with an open courtyard connecting them. We picked a lovely table outside, under the shade of a peaceful, beautiful, tall tree. For the first few minutes we sat in silence, until the waitress took our order.

I looked at Mark. He was on the verge of tears. He had lost a lot of weight and looked worse than I've ever seen him in 21 years of marriage. His nerves were completely shot, and he couldn't speak without a quivering lip. I should've felt compassion...that's what good little Christian girls do...but I just wanted to beat him up for not leaving last Thursday. But the phrase, "If you can't say anything good, say nothing at all," kept going through my head. So, I held my tongue, with a bad attitude written all over me. I knew God had a plan, but what if that plan was to get us out on Thursday like I had felt so strongly, and we had missed it? The more I thought about losing Favor, being away from my boys, putting McKenzie in danger, being stuck in a place I didn't want to be in, and driving through the dangerous Fruit District nearly every day, the more angry I got and the looser my tongue became. I loved that man sitting on the other side of the table, but right now I felt like pushing him down the mountain we had just driven up.

"Mark," I said, "I have to know!"

Mark looked at me with eyes that begged me not to ask.

I didn't care.

"I have to know—why you didn't listen to me?" There, I said it. But that wasn't enough—I had more. "When I told you specifically that my spirit was screaming to get out, you did nothing." The dam broke, and all the words I was trying to hold back started spilling out. The questions kept coming, and I was unleashing on my husband like an automatic weapon. I started bringing up things that happened years ago. I watched him flinch in pain, hit after hit. Hurt people hurt others, and I had thrown all caution to the wind.

Mark could see I needed resolution, and he knew I was not stopping until I had some understanding into his thought process of not leaving. The problem was, he didn't have any better answers. Tears started to flow down his face. He knew he had jeopardized our adoption and put his family in harm's way, but he also knew he had lost my trust, which delivered the deepest blow of all.

Mark searched for words to answer my unyielding questions. I could see he was in a fragile state of mind. As he bared his soul, I realized that he didn't know why he had chosen the path he had taken, but he was clearly suffering for it. I began to let up on him, not because I had my answers, but because I didn't like seeing him agonize over something that couldn't be changed. I didn't like hurting him, no matter how badly I wanted to understand why he didn't leave when I'd asked. I'd just verbally beat up my husband, and although I want to say it made me feel better about our situation, I felt miserable.

CHAPTER 19
FALSELY ACCUSED

"No weapon formed against you will succeed,
and you will refute any accusation raised against you in court.
This is the heritage of the LORD's servants,
and their righteousness is from Me."

—Isaiah 54:17, HCSB

A shadow came across the table where we were having lunch. We looked up to see Pochi and Pastor standing over us.

"Mind if we join you?" Pochi asked.

It had to be the worst timing in human history, but Pastor was such a likable guy that I caught myself smiling when I looked at him. When he looked at you, you knew he genuinely loved you. He came over and gave me a hug, which felt like a warm blanket to my freezing soul. They could see that we were both in pain and exhausted. During the next few minutes, they both tried to build our spirits with encouraging words.

They had just returned from a meeting with the director and the lawyer at the Ministry of Women's Affairs (MOWA).

Pastor and Pochi join us at Topview restaurant in Addis Ababa.

It had been a good meeting, and they had been able to present what was happening with some of the children in Debre Birhan being pulled out of the orphanage and put into foster care. MOWA was not happy about what they heard, especially since all the children Pochi was speaking about had families actively working to adopt them. MOWA's top concern was the welfare of children. Pulling a child from an orphanage was illegal unless you were a family member. The regional government office at Debre Birhan had no right to pull any of those children out of the orphanage.

As Mark and I listened to them recount their meeting, my emotions swirled around me. Five million orphans on the streets of Ethiopia, and they march into where our little girl and three other children are, and pull them out. *Why?* It made no sense to anyone. MOWA was going to send a note demanding that the regional offices at Debre Birhan release the children back to the orphanage.

Pochi and Pastor then told the director and the lawyer of MOWA about our case and how Adeferese and the head official at the Debre Birhan regional government office was harassing Favor's aunt, Emebet, for helping us rescue Favor. They were even threatening to send her to prison. MOWA's director and the lawyer could see that Emebet had every right to go get Favor, and that we had every right to leave with her. Those were hard words to hear when you're stuck in a court wormhole to retrieve a visa and passport.

At one point in the conversation, Pochi looked at us sitting across the table. I knew we had to be a sight...no sleep, little food, same wrinkled clothes.

"You were sent for this battle!" Pochi declared. "You were chosen because you are strong. Don't you see? You stayed and did not run away like the others. You stayed to fight for the children!" Just because we didn't leave, we somehow looked like we had strength to Pochi and Pastor. In that moment, though, we had no thoughts of judging the other family for their emotional state or their decision to leave. The reality was that we were all in the same position to lose our children. We were just the ones to have a front row seat to the event.

Mark sat forward in his chair. His lip started to quiver as he pointed his finger at Pochi. "It's easy for you to sit there and say those things to us," Mark said, trying to hold his emotions back, "but the reality is, you're not in the same place we're in. We're on the front lines taking the beating. We're the ones being challenged, threatened, and facing the possible loss of a daughter. We have everything to lose. You're not going through any of this!"

Pochi looked at Mark with a nervous smile. "Yeah," she laughed, "I know."

Her words delivered a gut-wrenching blow to both of us, and I could see it didn't sit well with Mark.

"Why did they come after us and not you?" Mark asked. "We did everything according to the law. What aren't you telling us? I think we have a right to know."

"Mark," Pochi said, "we did nothing wrong. This is a war. The enemy hates adoption and while you're only thinking of your daughter, we are thinking of four children that can hopefully be released to their forever families, because you've stayed to fight."

Pochi and Pastor looked at us from across the table. Their faces had hope and courage beaming from within. Then it hit Mark and me: While all we could see was our losses, they saw four children who could be freed and adopted if we would just fight for them. They were hoping we would hear the call to be their champions. They were believing that we would be the ones who would dare to go into the ring, armed only with faith.

Did God set up this moment? Were there two human collaborators sitting across the table from us, all part of the plan to make a path to freedom for these kids? Could this all be about affecting a change in the system? Was God really calling us up to do something that courageous? How desperate was He? What if we failed? Could we not only lose our daughter, but three others? The last thing in the world Mark and I felt like were prizefighters.

"Adeferese is afraid of you." Pochi said. "He thought you left. The fact that you stayed..." Pochi started laughing.

"It terrifies him," Pastor finished. "He called me up, screaming, accusing me of child trafficking."

"People are asking what is wrong with him," Pochi said. "He's acting crazy, like he's losing his mind over this. It's not like him. He's always been very respected, but now he's lying and harassing anyone involved in this case—mostly us and the people at the orphanage."

"But why has he come after us so strongly?" I asked.

Pochi shrugged her shoulders. "I believe it is because he can't control you, and that scares him."

While we were talking, Emebet called Pochi to see how we were doing. She was no longer answering her phone because of the harassing calls from both the regional office and Adeferese. We had not heard from her since we were stopped at immigration. She was so thankful we didn't leave and stayed to fight for Favor. *There was that word again: fight.* She shared how sorry she was that we had to be away from our other children, but she felt God had sent us for this time. We, on the other hand, were amazed at her bravery. She had no way out of her situation, but she fearlessly fought for Favor. Even in the face of threats to her freedom—here she was—encouraging us.

The case was building. We knew, once again, that this was not about us. It never had been. A shift had taken place in my spirit at some point during our conversation. My eyes were redirected from myself and my needs, and refocused on a greater need. A fire started burning in my heart. It wasn't only about Favor, and it wasn't about these four kids. It was about all the kids who had lost freedom in this nation because of age or corruption. My mind was made up. I would go into the ring and fight for the sake of those trapped in this abusive maze. I wasn't sure if Mark was ready for it, but he was going in too. My strength was starting to mount up. Maybe, just maybe, something good could come out of all of this.

* * * * *

At 1:30 in the afternoon, Mark and I were back from lunch standing in front of the locked doors of the adoption courts. Couples were being dropped off with their agencies for their court dates. The looks of joy and anticipation on their faces were priceless. They all looked so fresh in their Sunday best. I glanced at Mark and myself. We looked like we hadn't got the memo.

I heard a familiar accent behind me, so I turned to see a jet-lagged family trying to manage three children. "Are you from America?" I asked.

"Yes!" she answered.

"Where are you from?"

"Houston," she answered. "And you?"

"A little city south of Nashville," I said.

She looked at me, then tilted her head. "Are you the Wortons?" The question took me by surprise and she obviously could see it by the expression on my face. "My friend told me about what you're going through to bring your daughter home. She said you would be here."

"Wow!" I said. "Small world!"

"You've got so many people praying for you. I just want you to know that you're not alone."

"Thank you," I said as the tears began to well up in my eyes. I was humbled to know that others we didn't even know had our backs in prayer. I gave her a hug. "That means a lot."

The doors opened, and most of us walked up the three stories of steps to the adoption court, while a few braved the rickety elevator. I kept talking with my new-found friend from Houston, while Mark caught up with Mesfin. We watched as, one by one, couples were summoned into the judge's chamber to attend their court date. They all went in so somber, but a few minutes later, they came out with tears of joy in their eyes and celebratory smiles on their faces. What a perfect reflection of how your heart feels after the judge tells you that the beautiful child you've dreamt about and loved for months—the one you've worked towards bringing into your family and giving your name—is yours. From my seat, it was bittersweet.

Mark and Mesfin had their heads together, talking about our case. It looked intense. A part of me was glad to be sitting in a different area of the room.

"Based on what you know," Mark asked, "what are our chances of leaving this week with Favor?"

Mesfin was guarded but positive as he answered Mark's questions. "Nowhere in Ethiopian law has an adoption been revoked after a verdict has been rendered," Mesfin said confidently. "If EAI wanted to challenge your adoption, they should've done it before your court appointment in August. They didn't. Today, I want to find out why you were stopped at immigration. What right did they have to stop you?" Mesfin shook his head. "This is personal."

* * * * *

I tried to write down what I was feeling in my notebook, but the words wouldn't come. Explaining the spectrum of emotions that I was feeling was nothing short of impossible. I was full of hope and purpose, but then I was scared and fearless at the same time. I was on an emotional rollercoaster. I really just wanted to go home and hug my kids, but there was an unshakable stubbornness that would not leave without fighting—for both my daughter and the injustice that had been done.

When I looked up from staring at a blank page, I realized the last couple had just left the judge's chamber. My heart jumped, and I raced to load everything back into my purse before our name was called. The young lady came out and looked around. Mesfin quickly addressed her and asked that we be able to have a moment with the judge. She nodded and ducked back into the judge's chamber.

The door opened, and the young lady came out again. "The judge says she is done for the day," she said. "She will review your paperwork and you can go for today. Make an appointment to see her next week."

What? Mark and I stood there, helpless.

Mesfin approached the clerk and said something in Amharic in a soft, calm voice. The clerk looked up at him, took a deep breath, and went back into the room. A few minutes later, she opened the door and ushered us into the judge's courtroom.

Mark and I were filled with emotion as we entered the room. It looked exactly the same as it did three months earlier, when we were here for Favor's court date. We sat in the exact same seats. We looked into the eyes of the same woman who had declared with a smile that Favor was ours. Now, she looked annoyed as she glanced up at us. We knew that she had signed the papers to stop us from leaving the country, but we didn't know why. We also understood that she was the only one who had the legal power to either take away our daughter for good, or declare her ours for life. It all sat on her shoulders.

"Take a seat please," the judge said. She jotted down some notes, then looked up at Mesfin and spoke in Amharic.

Mesfin stood tall and began to speak. His voice was calm, and his inflections and tone were exact as he spoke to the judge in their native language. Mark and I sat quietly. We saw the judge's emotions rise and fall after each statement from Mesfin. We didn't understand a word that was being said, but we could somewhat decipher the conversation by the judge's voice inflections and responses. Mesfin's demeanor never changed; he remained calm. It didn't look like it was going well from our point of view, and the judge seemed to be on edge more and more as they talked. At one point, Mesfin handed her a few documents, including one of the letters that was slid under our door at the hotel. She began to read it. That's when the fireworks started.

"Who wrote this?" she demanded, looking at us.

"Adeferese," Mark said.

"I did not suspend your adoption!" she said with alarm, as she underlined the word *suspended* on the sheet. "This is not true! I did no such thing." We could tell she was very upset by what Adeferese had done. She started speaking Amharic in a raised and stressed tone to Mesfin, who stood composed, agreeing.

She took a deep breath as she looked down at the paper and shook her head.

"I want to make this very clear," she looked right at us. "I did not suspend your adoption as this letter states. No matter what the agency says, she is your daughter and that has not changed!"

I squeezed Mark's hand. Our spirits leapt at the news. Maybe we could leave tonight if we could get her passport and a flight out.

"The reason I signed the paperwork which stopped you from taking Favor out of the country was because there was another case just like yours. I am concerned with what is happening to these children, and I need to get to the bottom of this. I'm sure you can understand this."

I shook my head in agreement, but my mind was trying to figure out what that meant for us. Could we leave with Favor now, or was she telling us this was going to be a long, drawn out court case as she got to the bottom of this? The bottom could be a long way down.

"I want to hear your story," she said.

Mark and I looked at Mesfin, who had told us earlier not to say a word.

She interjected again, "I want to hear what *you* have to say."

For the next 20 minutes, she listened intently as Mark and I shared our story. We told her everything, from the emails to the conversations we had with Pochi and Adeferese before we arrived in Ethiopia. We told her how Favor's aunt traveled to Debre Birhan to rescue Favor, and the awkward meeting with Adeferese in his office after Favor was in our arms. We left nothing out, even the last few days that were filled with harassment and intimidation from Adeferese, which eventually brought us to her. When we were done, she shook her head with a noted irritation and started talking to Mesfin. Mesfin simply listened and agreed with what she said. Mark and I sat quietly and clueless.

"What did you do to make him so mad at you?" the judge asked.

"We came to get our daughter," I said.

"You know that this has become a very personal attack on you?" she said. "Adeferese has attacked you both, personally."

We had no words. We knew he had accused us of being involved with child trafficking. With all the personal information we had to divulge to be considered for adoption, let alone pass court, you'd think someone would've caught that if it was remotely true. We knew this man would stop at nothing to make himself look good, and that included making us look bad with unfounded accusations.

"I do not like that he used my court to intimidate you and threaten you," she said, but then took a deep breath before she continued. "Because he did, this is now a court problem, and it will have to be resolved in the courts before we can release you to immigration for her visa and passport." The judge pulled out her calendar.

"EAI is due in court to present evidence on November 16th," she said. "You return then."

My heart sank. That was almost two weeks away. I couldn't stand the thought of being gone from my boys, Matt and Shewit, that long. Mark and I stared at Mesfin as if to say, *Help us! We want to leave now!*

"Is there any way we can make it sooner?" Mesfin asked. "They have children back in America that they must get back to."

The judge quickly fingered through her datebook, paused, then pointed at a date. "I can bring you in Thursday the 8th. I will have my office contact Adeferese to be here."

"Thank you," Mesfin said and glanced our way. Our hearts soared and we were excited at the possibility that this nightmare could be behind us within a few days.

"My concern is what has happened to these four children," the judge said. "You understand—I have to get to the bottom of this."

"We understand," I said. We all stood to leave. "Thank you, for hearing us today."

She nodded her head, "I can see you love your daughter very much. I won't change my mind, but I must complete the court process."

My eyes started to water. I said thank you in Amharic and turned to leave before the water works really started.

* * * * *

Mark immediately started questioning Mesfin about what was said in the courtroom.

"I relayed to her the facts," he started. "EAI can't come, after she had issued the adoption decree, with "so-called" evidence to stop your adoption. What is upsetting to her is that Adeferese claims he knew nothing of what was happening to these four orphans. That means he never checked up on an orphanage he was representing."

"How do you feel about our case?" Mark asked.

Mesfin paused, "I feel good," he said. "We should be in a good position. She is a very good judge, and she will hear all the evidence before making a decision. I believe she will do what is best for the child, but we must not let our guard down. He has lied and accused you of very bad things to get you stopped. He is a desperate man."

When we got downstairs to the street, Mark brought up Mesfin's fee. We had heard nothing and were getting a little nervous that it might be more than we could afford. But we were invested, no matter how much it would cost. At this point, everyone who wasn't too scared to take our case had doubled or tripled their fee, with no hope of winning.

"So how much are you going to cost me?" Mark nervously asked.

Mesfin was thinking. He took a deep breath, narrowed his eyes and said, "It will be a minimum of $5,000."

I could see Mark trying to hold his composure as his eyes got big and he swallowed hard before responding. "U.S. dollars?" he asked.

"No," Mesfin quickly responded. "No, no, birr."

"Birr?" Mark asked with relief. One hundred birr was worth about six American dollars. "Is that a fair price for the work you will be doing for us?"

"I believe so," Mesfin said.

Mark paused. Even with his bank account running out back home, he knew Mesfin's service was worth far more. So, for the next five minutes, Mesfin and Mark went back and forth to find a fee that they both agreed would be fair. When all was said and done, both walked away very pleased with their agreement.

CHAPTER 20
STILL ON THE THRONE

"God is orchestrating our story at every turn. He's not missed a single step or need that we've had."

—Mark Worton

Mark and I rushed to get back to The Academy to celebrate what was left of McKenzie's 12th birthday. It was now almost five in the evening. My heart sank—we had been gone most of the day. The moment we stepped into our little apartment, we could see the disappointment in McKenzie's eyes when she looked up from the movie she was watching on our computer.

"What took you so long?" McKenzie asked. "You've been gone all day." I knew she was hurting. In our battle for Favor, we had forgotten how hard this had been on McKenzie. This day was supposed to be a big celebration for her back home, surrounded by friends. We never anticipated that she wouldn't be home for her birthday.

"We brought you a cake and even found a few chocolate chip cookies!" I said, trying to show her that although we weren't with her, she was on our mind all day. "Do you know how hard it is to find cookies in Ethiopia? And nobody carries Blue Bell ice cream." McKenzie shot me a "really, Mom?" look. I knew it so well. "How was your day with Julie?"

"She's awesome!" McKenzie said, giving Julie a big hug.

"Thank you so much," I said to Julie. "I don't know what we would've done without you being here today. The girls would've been bored to death with us."

"Oh," Julie said, "I loved it! I was so excited to spend a day with them."

I walked over to hug Julie and then reached to give McKenzie a hug, but she pulled away. I tried not to take it personally. It had been a hard day for all of us. "Tell me what you three did today." I said. Favor immediately ran up to me with a beautiful new red and orange scarf. She wrapped it around herself and posed from side to side, showing me how ravishing she looked. Then she ran to a bag Julie had brought and started pulling things out one at a time so I could admire all her new trinkets. We loved watching her joy, and I could tell she was a natural-born shopper.

My attention was quickly drawn away by how withdrawn McKenzie was in the show-and-tell. I knew what she was feeling. She was, after all, just 12 years old, and this was her birthday.

"What's in *your* bag?" I asked McKenzie.

"Pretty much the same," she said. "I love everything," she was trying to mask the pain.

"Well," I said, "we want to see."

McKenzie gave us an annoyed look and begrudgingly went into our little room, then emerged with a beautiful blue scarf and bracelet. After showing us all the gifts Julie had brought, she suddenly started ranting about how embarrassed she was when the classroom sang happy birthday to her.

"I'm standing in front of a classroom in my pajamas, with all these kids looking at me like, *Who on Earth is this and why are we singing happy birthday to her?* Awkward! I was so

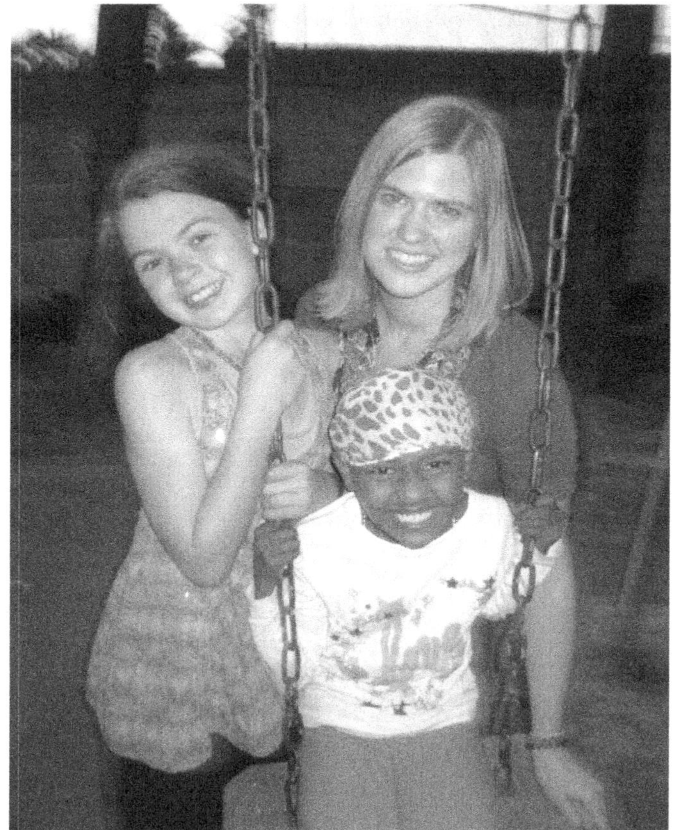

McKenzie celebrating her birthday with Favor and Julie at The Academy.

embarrassed! Never mind the fact that I had just woken up and probably looked like a zombie. I'm sure I made a *great* first impression."

"Kenzie," Mark said, "they were just trying to make your day a little special."

"Did Mom put them up to it?" McKenzie looked at me and narrowed her eyes.

"I didn't do a thing," I said, "Pochi's nephew wanted to do something special for you."

"Well that's pretty special!" McKenzie said, "All day kids were pointing at me saying, 'Isn't that the girl we sang happy birthday to? Hi, Happy Birthday Girl!'"

"At least everyone knows you now," Mark said.

"Great." McKenzie said, "Hi, my name is Happy Birthday Girl." We all continued to laugh as McKenzie went on like it was the end of the world—or at least it was the end of her social life on this campus. A twinkle in her eye, though, told us she was going to be okay.

The night went by fast. We sang happy birthday to Happy Birthday Girl and let her blow out a match that served as a makeshift candle. I could see the day had been a challenge for my 12-year-old, but I was proud of how she was handling it. Things don't always turn out how you think. I'm sure that during those three years she was asking for a little sister, she didn't expect this birthday to be part of the journey.

* * * * *

Back in America, it was Election Day, and Facebook was erupting with various stands and comments on both sides. It was getting ugly. Elections tend to stir the pot and bring out the worst in people.

I sat in bed, looking at all the posts, as one by one, my phone would flash election results by state. Back home, I had been so invested in the election that I'm sure I would have been right in front of my television, watching every talking head give their opinion about who would win based on the exit polls. My emotions would have resembled an out-of-control roller coaster ride, but now I looked on with detachment. Something inside of me had changed. I served a bigger God now. He was a God who had all things in control, and nothing would happen without His knowing. The enemy wasn't going to slip one over on Him. He was almighty, He was all-knowing, He was loving, and He was in charge. I trusted Him with every fiber of my being. No matter who was going to win on this night in America, I had chosen peace. I wrote my status and posted it.

> Regardless of who wins tonight...MY hope is built on a Mighty God, not one man! So continue to stand that in these days we will see Freedom, Justice, and Righteousness! If you have eyes to see, start looking beyond the natural realm. Look to God. Put your trust in God. Do not allow fear to come in and take the peace Jesus has come to give you. God is STILL on the throne!

I wrote a private message to our prayer warriors, then shut down my computer and tried to fall asleep.

* * * * *

The next morning, Dave, our trusted chaperone and prayer warrior, called and wanted to pick all of us up for a little surprise that included a meal.

After a long drive across town, we arrived at a beautiful high rise. We walked through the security and into a lobby that was stunning. The floors and walls were covered with marble all the way to the top floor. It felt like a little piece of America as we rode up the glass elevator overlooking the mammoth lobby. When we arrived at one of the top floors, we were greeted by the entire leadership of Covenant Church. We had just attended this church, which oversaw Pochi's orphanage, the previous Sunday. We couldn't believe their gracious love and support for us. These were men who had been standing in the gap for us, praying unceasingly for our situation since the battle had begun. They were there to encourage us with the knowledge that God was doing something greater than what we could see in this moment.

As we sat around the large table, Mark opened up about how his heart had broken when we were stopped at immigration. He had been walking around in a daze, simply going through the motions as people directed him from one place to the next—not realizing how much God was orchestrating our story at every turn. God had not missed a single step or need that we had.

"Here I am," Mark said, "and all I can ask is, 'Why, God, aren't you getting us out of here?' What I wasn't seeing was how He sent Sue to walk right up when we were in our most desperate moment at immigration, when we didn't have a clue about what to do next. Sue guided us to our next steps. She gave us her phone and contacted her daughter Julie to come get us. Then some Facebook friends provided a place for us to stay. They had just happened to move to Ethiopia a few weeks earlier. It's all been miraculously taken care of. We couldn't have planned it out as perfectly as it has happened. And some of these miracles and provisions we are seeing right now, were set in motion over three years ago."

I watched the men hang on every word as Mark continued to glorify God with our story. They all knew these miracles Mark spoke of weren't coincidences or random chance, but rather God's hand working out His plan for our lives. God had already chosen the cast of people who would be part of our journey—the ones who would step up and pray, the ones who would come against us, and the ones who would fight on the ground with us and for us. *How could we be offended by a God who had not gotten us out of the country, but had ensured our safety and protection for the duration of the journey?*

"Our God is so *big*!" Pastor enthusiastically said. "We have no reason to ask, just trust."

Throughout the next hour, we talked about the move of God that was happening in Ethiopia and other parts of Africa. Reinhardt Bonnke, an international evangelist, was coming to Addis Ababa in a few days, and the excitement for what God was going to do was like an uncontainable wildfire. Although the Covenant Church leaders asked us to join them, we were positive that we would be on our way to America before the

Bonnke event started. We politely declined the invitation, thanked the pastors for everything they had done for us, and said goodbye. We believed that the next time we would see them would be in Heaven. No matter how our journey turned out, we were thankful for the new family we had in Ethiopia.

* * * * *

That afternoon Mark and I took the girls for a walk around the compound. Many of the people who lived at the compound stopped and talked to us. They knew our story and wanted to encourage us.

As we continued to explore, I suddenly remembered the small creek that ran behind the compound, past the large track and field area.

"Let's go look at the creek in the back!" I said excitedly.

"Creek? How do you know there's a creek back there?" Mark asked me. "We've never been back there."

We hadn't been back there, and no one had told me about a creek. *How did I know there was a small creek and why was I walking so confidently toward it?* Then I remembered the vision that I had Saturday night when I couldn't sleep, about the angels who camped around us, and the huge angel who rose from the center. During that vision was the only time I could've seen the creek. That vision was the only way I would've known what the entire compound looked like as if I had seen it before. It wasn't like a dream, but it was more like a real-life experience. I started to walk faster. I had to see if the creek was there. I got to the other side of the field and looked over to where I remembered seeing it in my vision.

There it was.

I looked at Mark in amazement. "I know because I've seen it before," I said. Mark looked at me with a huge question mark on his face. "The night God allowed me to see the angels that were camped around us, and the huge host angel I saw rise up in the middle of them."

Mark and Favor enjoying The Academy's playground.

"I remember...you saw all the way back here?"

"Yes," I answered, "I saw the entire compound and into the streets around us."

I could see Mark take a deep breath and relief come over his face. My vision was a sign of God's great love for us, and He wanted us to know that what I saw that night was very real. He was a big God, and He was with us in this battle.

We stood at the steps going down to a path that overlooked the creek. The girls ran in front of us to explore, but Mark and I just stood gazing at the sight before us, a sign of God's faithfulness for the days ahead. We were being prepared for a big day tomorrow in court, and we knew that we would be coming face-to-face with the man who had falsely accused us—who had us stopped at immigration. We needed to know God was here in a very real way, but we had no idea how much.

CHAPTER 21
BIG BATTLES

"A couple of thoughts...
First, God is never surprised by the
enemies plans and actions.
Second, Big Victories never come
without Big Battles!"

—Ben Wilson, cousin and prayer warrior

We had now been back in Ethiopia almost two weeks. Mark and I woke up with high hopes that today we might be given the okay to leave with Favor. Mark, with faithful anticipation, worked with our travel agent to get credit for our unused airline tickets and rescheduled four new tickets home after our court hearing today. I quickly showered and got myself ready before the girls woke up. I sent off a quick email to our prayer warriors:

> Within the next few hours, we will be facing corruption that has infiltrated the adoption community in Ethiopia face-to-face. We will stand before a judge and hear the argument of the ones who are behind holding Favor

back from being adopted. They are using "foster care" as the reason to keep these children in Ethiopia, but "foster care" is not always a family that wants to take in a child because of the love and goodness in their heart. It is a single man who wants a child to cook, clean, and keep him company. It is a single mother that wants a nanny and maid. It is a form of slavery. We're going in, knowing the battle is the Lord's, we simply stand in the shadow of the Almighty God! The spirit we are facing is a python spirit. Three years ago, one of the orphans had a dream. He saw orphans cornered by a huge python snake who was not allowing the children to get to their forever families on the other side. The children were held captive.

THAT DREAM IS HAPPENING NOW!

Please join us in this spiritual fight...pray, activate every prayer warrior you know. The battle is the Lord's, and just like David, who knew the Spirit of the Living God was with him...we too, are running toward the giant in Victory. Pray the python spirit will be destroyed and all these children will be freed to go to their Forever Families.

Thank you, and may God bless you bountifully for battling with us!

* * * * *

We drove through the Mercato Fruit District with lightning speed, which was a shock to all of us. We decided to look at it as another miracle that God was indeed making a path for us.

On our way to the courthouse, Dave shared a conversation that he had with Favor yesterday while we were at the restaurant. He knew how traumatic it had been for her to be stopped at immigration, and so, he simply asked how she was doing.

Favor had told him, "My God is so good, He is so great. He has given me a mom and dad that love me more than I have ever been loved. I know they are fighting hard to take me home with them. I am ready to go to America with the family God has blessed me with. I think God must really love me to give me a family like this."

Mark and I couldn't help but tear up. We hadn't realized that she was aware that we were fighting for her. Our resolve became even stronger.

We arrived to a courtroom packed with families waiting for their court appearance with the judge. We knew that we would be waiting for all of them to go through before we would be seen. As we scanned the crowd, we noticed Adeferese wasn't there yet. Instead sat the lady who had been in the front of the van when we went to our embassy date, and EAI's lawyer. This man, more than anyone, knew how they had treated us and the truth in our case, but I knew he wouldn't stand up for us. They both looked up and gave us a pensive smile. I smiled back then searched for a seat and sat down with Mark and Mesfin.

It didn't take me long before I was talking with a family who was adopting their first child from Ethiopia. She was a breath of fresh air, and the man that represented their agency was so full of Jesus's love that it almost knocked me out of my seat. I was a tad envious that they had such an amazing representative. When they asked about our adoption, I hesitated to share with so many ears listening in. Instead, I shared the miracles that had happened in our journey, and how God had provided at every step we took. She looked at me with a smile and said, "I know who you are. We've been praying for your family at our church. Favor, right?"

"Yes," I said.

"I've heard all about your story," she said excitedly. "I can't believe I'm sitting here talking with you."

I was speechless.

"God must really want you to know that He has mounted up the prayer warriors for you and *you are not alone!*" she said.

Tears welled up and I gave her a big hug.

"Do you have any idea how many people are praying for you guys?" she asked. "I can't even begin to count how many—it's a lot!"

I was overcome with thankfulness for these individuals. "Tell them thank you for us. We feel those prayers," I said.

I was filled with thankfulness. I remembered how many times I had said that I would pray for someone or commented on Facebook that I would be praying. It really mattered to that person, even if I only had time to offer up a quick prayer. I sat there, unable to express my gratitude in a sufficient way, before she and her husband were called in for their court appearance.

"Pray for us!" she said nervously.

"Absolutely!" I said as we hugged. She walked through to the courtroom, turning around one last time to give me a little wave. "Jesus, bless them with favor today and let their court hearing go perfectly," I prayed quietly.

I looked over at Mark and Mesfin. Their heads were glued together in deep conversation. This man, whom we were initially concerned about, was showing his quiet strength and knowledge of the situation. Mesfin continually reassured Mark that EAI didn't have a case, and he was positive that the judge would rule in our favor. He told Mark, "I have not found any history of a child who has been revoked after the court approved the adoption."

After Mark had finished hitting Mesfin with a barrage of questions about our case, they began discussing the love they had for their families. It doesn't matter where you are from...the way a good man cherishes and loves his family is the same on all continents. They talked about the love they had for their countries and the relationship between America and Ethiopia—how the Americans had always been one of the first countries to help in time of need. They discussed Jesus, and Mark told him about our faith, and about how God had shown up for us time and time again during the past ten days. Mesfin, an Orthodox Christian, was amazed at Mark's faith that God wouldn't let us down—no matter how difficult life was at this moment. Mark encouraged Mesfin to get to know God on a more personal level. He shared scriptures with him that were full of God's promises that He was a personal and loving God.

The waiting room was soon empty except for us and the two people that EAI had sent to represent them. Adeferese didn't show up.

The door opened and the sweet clerk welcomed us into the judge's chambers again. Mark and I took the same seat that we had taken before. The judge gave us a glance and quick smile, then immediately started talking to Mesfin and the EAI representatives in Amharic. We sat there, not knowing what was being said for or against us, unable to defend ourselves or correct any inaccurate testimony.

"Why is Adeferese not present?" the judge asked.

"He had business elsewhere," the EAI lawyer responded.

The judge took a deep breath. We could see that she was not happy. To not show up for a court hearing was a sign of disrespect. Everyone knew Adeferese had crossed the line and was displaying a false sense of authority and power. "He does understand that he is the one who must prove why he had this family stopped at immigration." She began to raise her voice. "He should've made a way to be here. He was the one who started this court case with his accusations against them."

"The burden is on him to prove these things he said. Do you have any proof of what this couple did and why Adeferese says they cannot leave with their little girl?" She looked directly at both of the EAI representatives. We could see they were nervous.

The EAI lawyer cleared his throat and began to speak, "We have evidence that their child was to be remanded to foster care before the adoption had been approved by the court."

"Where is this evidence?" the judge asked.

"We are trying to find it," the lady with EAI said.

"If this is true," Mesfin said, "why did EAI continue to approve the child's paperwork for adoption? Bringing the family to Ethiopia for a court date and approving an embassy date?"

"We weren't aware of it," the EAI lawyer said.

"Do you not know what is going on in the orphanages you represent?" the judge asked.

They stood like sheep going to slaughter. They had no response.

"Honorable Judge," Mesfin said, "is it not in the best interest of the child that she be permitted to go home with her family? The law says that the decision rests on the best interests of the child."

The Judge looked at Mesfin for a moment. We could see that she agreed with what he was saying, but she was deliberating over what her next move would be.

"If they have evidence that she was to be in foster care before the court hearing, this would make the adoption invalid," she said.

The room was silent.

Mark and I noticed the silence and looked at Mesfin, but he didn't return our glance. I looked at the EAI representatives, and the woman had a smirk on her face. My heart sank. We had been sitting in the middle of a heated conversation we couldn't understand, and now suddenly, there was silence. We didn't know what was happening, but we knew what we felt, and fear had crept in. I immediately started praying for God's help. I needed a sign that we had not been abandoned. I wanted to feel God's peace, or see an angel flying outside the court window.

Please God, I prayed through the sounds of my nervously pounding chest, *let me know you are here. Please.* I kept pleading and looking around for a sign—any glimmer of hope.

Then it happened.

I glanced down at the area rug that covered most of the courtroom. It had a large lump in it where it had been pulled up, and air was under it. Slowly, in the middle of the lump,

I could see a large footprint form and compress the rug all the way to the floor. The rug literally started forming around a huge invisible foot!

Is that you, God? I held my breath and quickly looked around for any human interaction that would've caused the phenomena I was watching, or if anyone else had seen it happen. Nothing. No one had moved an inch. I continued to look at the large footprint where something large was standing that I could not see. After about 20 seconds, I watched as the footprint slowly lifted and was gone. The rug returned to normal and never changed again while we were in the room.

I squeezed Mark's hand and whispered in his ear, "God is with us."

In the ocean of silence surrounding us, Mark managed a smile, and I continued to watch the rug.

The Judge looked up from her time of deliberation and said, "I will hear testimony on the 16th of November and then I will decide."

Mark's heart sank. "May I speak to you privately?" he asked the judge. The judge denied him.

"If you have anything to say, it can be said openly, in front of everyone here," she said to Mark.

Mark began, fighting a losing battle to hold in his emotions and frustration as he argued his point. "EAI has been irresponsible in handling our case from the very beginning. They have not checked on Favor *one* time throughout this year-and-a-half process, and now they are trying to prevent us from leaving the country only to protect their reputation."

Thc judge listened closely.

"We have been harassed and threatened by an agency who is supposed to protect and look after us and our daughter," Mark said. "You said the last time we were in your court, that Favor was our daughter. Nothing that EAI said would change that."

"Yes," the judge said, "but I have to hear his side and see the evidence he has to present."

"If they have evidence, why didn't they bring it today instead of dragging this out? Adeferese didn't even show up to defend his case. I am asking you to release us and let us take our daughter home," Mark pleaded.

The judge looked at Mark with zero sympathy. "You need to come back on November 16th, and then I will decide after hearing both sides," she said, shutting her calendar with a slam.

That was it. We were dismissed without another word. Our hopes of leaving early were dashed, and we were now more concerned than ever that we would lose Favor. Adeferese had so much power.

Walking out of the building, Mesfin did his best to calm Mark down, who was now near tears. "Do you feel I disrespected the judge in any way?" Mark asked.

Mesfin paused, then grabbed Mark's shoulder, "It was good that you showed emotion. It will translate to the judge how much you deeply care for this child."

I looked at Mark. He looked sick as he stood there.

"Nothing has changed in your case," Mesfin encouraged us. "We are still in a good place, and the judge will rule in your favor." Mesfin paused before his next statement, "I want to recommend that you reach out to EAI America and request their help."

"What?" Mark asked, confused. "Why?"

"They might be able to get Adeferese to drop the case and allow you to leave," Mesfin said. "Just ask for their assistance in this matter. They might be able to help."

Mark agreed to reach out to EAI America but now, he was concerned about why it was brought up. W*as there a possibility that we could lose?*

* * * * *

The ride back to the compound was quiet. All the wind had gone out of our sails, and we were thinking about numerous decisions. *Do we go home? Do we need to send McKenzie home with Mark? What about McKenzie's school?* She was missing so much. *What if we stayed and lost Favor?* Even if we won, and everything went our way, we were still looking at potentially up to another 14 days before we would see our boys. *What if we stayed and false charges put Mark and me in a third world prison...then what?* We had three other children we needed to think about. *Was it time to just give up?*

One day more in Ethiopia seemed like forever. The thought of 14 more days away from our boys was unbearable. I sat in the back seat, longing to be home and have this nightmare over, but I knew that the moment we left Favor, we would lose her.

"You have to take McKenzie home and go be with the boys," I said. "I'll stay with Favor until it's done. It's the only logical thing to do."

"I'm not leaving you in Ethiopia! We'll figure something out," Mark said.

"She needs to get back to school, Mark, and the boys need their dad," I said, barely able to talk without emotions shutting down my vocal cords.

"They need their mom, too!" he said.

I couldn't think anymore. The hurt I had felt the night we had been stopped at immigration returned in force. There were no words. I was angry. I was questioning every decision I had ever made that led to this moment.

Dave dropped us off, and we made our way to the gym, where a volleyball game was going on—most likely the place we would find our girls. We walked in to find Jody and Pat waiting anxiously for us just inside the door. They looked at us in anticipation of good news. We didn't have to say a word—our disappointment was written all over our faces. Jody's arms immediately went to embrace me, and I put my head on her shoulder and began to weep. I couldn't hold it back any longer—I was tired of being strong. Then I heard McKenzie's and Favor's voices through the crowd. I looked up and both of them were running toward me with expectant smiles. Somehow hearing my girl's voices gave me an ounce of strength. I quickly wiped away the tears and straightened myself out.

"Mom," Favor yelled, "we go home now?"

"Yay! Can we leave tomorrow?" McKenzie asked. Then looked in my eyes and knew something wasn't right.

"Mom? Is everything okay?"

I fought to put a smile on my face. I knew this was the wrong place to break the news that we weren't going home anytime soon.

Mark told Pat everything that had happened. "Adeferese didn't show up," Mark said. "He knew that the judge would have to hear both sides. I'm sure they'd like us to just give up and go home. Pat, I don't know how long this is going to take. Missy and I have to talk about what we need to do."

"Listen." Pat said, "You're welcome to stay as long as it takes. The apartment is yours, and we're all behind you on this. You do what's necessary."

What a blessing this family and community was to us. God had overwhelmed us with amazing people who were making our journey a little more bearable.

As we walked up to our apartment, I could feel the sun beating down on this beautiful day. I knew that despite how I was feeling, God was with us. Mark and I were both contemplating how we would tell the girls, and when we walked into our sitting area, McKenzie wasted no time.

"Mom," McKenzie said matter-of-fact, "I know something's wrong. You aren't excited. What is going on?"

I opened my mouth but nothing would come out. The pain in my heart had made its way to my throat.

"We weren't released to leave yet," Mark said.

"I don't understand! Why?" she cried. Mark tried to explain it to her, but her mind couldn't wrap around it in the emotion of the moment.

Favor ran up and threw her arms around my waist, burying her head into my chest. I knew she couldn't understand the conversation, but she recognized the pain. I held her as tight as I could. I loved her so much, and the thought of losing her again was more than I could handle. I wanted to scream, the pain pushing through was too much for my body to contain.

Mark dealt with the pain by trying to explain what the next step would be, but I couldn't hear a word. I had to get alone. I excused myself and closed the door between Mark and the girls. It felt as if I was going to explode if I didn't release the river of pain flooding my body. I laid across our bed and buried my head into a pillow to stifle my cries. For the first time on this trip, I allowed myself to open up the dam and let it all out—releasing the pain and anguish I felt through my tears and silent groans.

After a while, Mark came into the room to check on me. It hurt too much to look at him. I had nothing to say. He quietly came over and put his arms around me, and for a moment, I accepted his embrace. It settled and reassured me, but then I remembered that I had begged to leave and he had ignored my pleas.

I stiffened and pushed him away.

"I should've made you leave that Thursday," I cried out. "I should've! It's my fault that I didn't push you harder."

"No." Mark shook his head, "It's mine. I take the blame."

"If I had just pushed you," I said, "I should've made you do it. I should've just walked down there with you and made you book the flight no matter how much it was, but I didn't want to be that pushy wife...but, I was right. How stupid can I be?"

The poisonous what-ifs started to rise in me. "We could be home right now. Favor would be safe. I could be holding my boys. Why didn't I push...now look at us! We could lose her, Mark."

I stopped. I looked at Mark's face, and pain stared back. I had said too much. Mark reached out and pulled me to him. "I am sorry," he cried. "I am sorry. I am sorry."

We both stood in that little room, weeping in each other's arms. It didn't matter who was at fault...we were going to go through this battle together.

CHAPTER 22
GOD I LOOK TO YOU

"A Champion is someone who gets up when he can't."

—Jack Dempsey, professional boxer

The next morning, I woke up before the sun, singing the song, "God I look to You." I had sung it several times, but this morning it came from a deep and desperate place—it was my heartfelt prayer. I was at the bottom of what seemed like an impossible situation looking up, and I needed vision beyond what my physical eyes could see or my mind could understand.

Just being in God's presence put me at peace. As I kept worshiping God, I could feel myself being drawn into the Throne Room where Jesus took my hand and let me rest in His arms. As I was resting, He showed me a vision with two paths. I couldn't fully grasp its meaning at the time, nor did I want to see all of it in my pain. Still, the vision was a loving encouragement that I was where I needed to be. This journey was not only about us—it was about what God would do through us. When I came out of the vision, I knew that if I gave in to the thoughts of defeat and depression, I would only be strengthening the enemy and, in the end, lose what I was fighting for. I was determined that every time a negative thought would come in, I would pray that I would have strength to take it captive. Then I would set my mind on the promises of God, focus on what He has done for us, and remember what he has called us to do. I prayed that every beat of my heart would beat for Him, that every word spoken from my mouth would glorify Him, and that my tongue would be used only for worship and gratitude to Him. Thankfulness would be the oil that fueled my survival.

* * * * *

Mark woke up, and we laid in bed, watching the sun rise on the wall. Birds were singing outside our bedroom window—a new day dawned, and with the new day came hope.

I glanced at my computer. I had written to our prayer warriors the night before, asking for wisdom and sharing the hurt and frustration we were feeling. We knew we were being refined, and it was painful, but we also knew that somehow we were in the middle of God's perfect will. Our prayer warriors' responses, prayers, and encouragement lifted our spirits. I could feel the shift in my soul after reading their replies.

"We need to make the most of this," I said to Mark. "We're here for at least two more weeks, and we need to use the time well. We should plan things to do with the girls and use this opportunity to bond with Favor."

"I agree," Mark said. "I need to get some money wired to us too. We're almost out." At this point, money wasn't an obstacle. Mark and I knew God had it taken care of, and what usually would stop us, wasn't even a pebble in our shoe.

"I want to go see Bonnke!" I said, changing the subject, remembering that Pochi and Pastor invited us to go with them to see this evangelist and world changer. "I heard that he's raised people from the dead! Wherever he seems to go, miracles happen. I need to be in that atmosphere!"

"Okay, I'll reach out to Dave, but I don't think we should take the girls," Mark said. "There's too big of a crowd. I don't know who's watching us right now. I'd feel better if we left them with Jody and Pat."

He was right. We would be distracted by watching the girls and not get a thing out of the service. At this point, we also didn't know how desperate Adeferese was to get Favor back into his hands and out of ours. We decided that we were better safe than sorry.

Mark checked the computer. "Hey," he said in relief, "McKenzie's school got back with us. They said, 'There is no better life lesson they could teach her than what she is learning at this very moment.' They just want a full, written report of her experience in Ethiopia when she returns."

"She could probably write a novel," I said. I was so relieved. The thought of Mark leaving me to do court on my own, and saying goodbye to McKenzie, was too difficult to add to my emotional weakness. All we wanted to do was be a family—all six of us. The night before, I had not done well telling the boys that it would be possibly up to another two weeks. I was so proud of how brave they were and the strength they showed. It made me miss them all the more.

* * * * *

The next few days were filled with activities that were being held at The Academy. An Ethiopian track meet is something to behold, and The Academy was hosting one. Ethiopians are beautiful, fast runners!

While I was chasing down Favor and stopping her from joining the races, Mark and McKenzie got us some chocolate-covered ice cream to eat. You would've thought we had won the lottery, but by the second bite, we knew these desserts weren't anything like the ice cream at home. I'm not sure that there was either cream or chocolate in the ingredients, but we were desperate, so we consumed the ice cream in record time and got more for later.

I went with Jody and some of the women who lived at The Academy to get groceries. This outing always included several stops around town to get things on our list. I still couldn't believe that I could walk away with bags of vegetables and fruits for under six U.S. dollars. I bought avocados, mangos, oranges, potatoes, carrots, bananas, and eggs—all of which were organic and fresh. After we got back to the apartment, I gave them a chlorine bath, dried them off, and placed them in my makeshift fruit baskets.

After dinner, we walked down to the gym. Favor was running around with her arms thrown back and her new red scarf flowing behind her. I pulled out my camera and took a quick shot of this beautiful picture of freedom. McKenzie taught us all a few tips in volleyball, but we seemed only to frustrate her when we tried them. We were pathetic. We took a stroll around the compound and headed back to our apartment.

I'm not sure what happened next, but I believe it was the moment that McKenzie and Favor became true sisters. They had a screaming match, and before we could find out what had happened, McKenzie walked out the door, slamming it behind her. Favor curled up on the couch and started crying, while Mark and I stood across the room, staring at each other.

"Do girls always act this way?" Mark asked. I shot him a quick "really?" look.

"I guess I need to go find McKenzie. You stay here and comfort the little one," I said.

"Okay," Mark said. He looked like a deer caught in headlights.

I ran downstairs and looked around the teacher's lobby and everywhere I could think of. No luck. I started walking back to our apartment, looking in every corner to find her. *God, please show me where she is.* When I got to the steps that led up to our room, I remembered the attic where we hung our clothes to dry.

When I looked up the narrow staircase to the attic, my first thought was that she wouldn't have gone up there alone—it was too dark and scary.

"McKenzie?" I called. No answer. But there was a strong pull that kept me moving forward. The only light was behind me as I walked toward the darkness. I got to the top of the steps and fumbled to find anything that resembled a light switch. I walked with unsure steps, my hands reaching out in front of me. I could imagine stepping off of the floored area and dropping in on the apartment underneath me. Finally, I found a string to pull. My eyes struggled to adjust as I looked around.

There, huddled in the corner, sitting on the floor, I found McKenzie, crying. Without a word I walked over and sat next to her, taking her in my arms, as I had done so often. I had no words, so I let her cry. Maybe she had come to her breaking point and just needed to let it out and be a little girl. She had been so strong and grown up through all of this.

"I hate this!" she said through tears. "I hate this, I want to go. I miss my brothers and my friends back home."

"I know you do. I'm sorry," I said.

"I miss my kitten," she sniffled. "He's probably all grown up now. You and dad expect me to be so strong, but I'm not. Why can't we just go home? I hate it here!"

In my fear to not be left alone to fight in court, I hadn't fully considered what this trip had done to McKenzie. I realized how selfish I had been. I knew that no matter how much I didn't want to send her home, it was probably the best choice for her.

"McKenzie," I said, "Dad can take you back home. Only one of us needs to stay."

"Why do you have to stay?" she asked.

"Because we can't leave Favor," I said. "The last time we left her we almost lost her for good. We can't risk that again, but Dad can take you home. You have been so strong and have helped us out so much with her. I don't know what I would've done without you."

"No," she said, "I don't want to leave you—or Favor. But, she's a brat."

I had to laugh. "No way! You're telling me she's just a normal little sister? She's not perfect?"

"Ugh," McKenzie said, as she wiped away her tears with her shirt sleeve. "She cries the moment she doesn't get her way. Don't get me wrong, I love her, but she is so annoying."

"She's a little girl," I reassured her, "and that's a little sister's job."

"Well, she's good at it," she said.

"Hi Mommy!" I looked up to see Favor. She had snuck up while McKenzie and I had been talking, and was standing in between the slats, with no floor boards protecting her from breaking through to the floor below.

"Favor!" I yelled as I reached to grab her, "you can't walk on that. You could've been hurt!" I was talking loud, and I could see in her eyes that she was frightened. I took a breath and pulled her in for a hug. "I'm sorry—you scared me, Baby." I got down where I could look her directly in the eyes, "Favor, that is dangerous. I pointed to the open space where she could have fallen through. "You have to stay on this." I then pointed to the floor beneath us. She nodded her head like she understood, and then hugged me.

Suddenly, we heard a sound coming from the corner. I turned and looked, but couldn't see anything. "Ah, Mom, did you hear that?" McKenzie asked.

"I did," I answered.

McKenzie looked at me with big eyes. "What is it?"

We both looked in the direction of the sound. We could hear something moving toward us, I started recalling everything Jody had said about the mongoose that lived up in the attic. The last thing we needed was to get attacked by a territorial mongoose with rabies.

We scrambled down the steps as quickly as our feet would take us, screaming and giggling the whole way back to the apartment. We were having so much fun laughing together, even though we were terrified and probably looking ridiculous! Favor ran screaming through the apartment door and shut it behind her, leaving McKenzie and me standing outside the apartment, continuing to laugh.

"I am so proud of you," I said, looking into McKenzie's big hazel eyes. "You have been such a big girl through all of this. I love you so much."

"I love you too, Mom. Thanks."

I gave her a hug. I didn't want to let go, and by the way she held me, I knew the feeling was mutual, so we held on a little while longer.

* * * * *

We walked into the apartment to find Mark and Favor setting up the memory game. McKenzie walked over to Favor and gave her a hug.

"I'm sorry," McKenzie said.

Favor hugged her sister as hard as her little arms could bear it. "Sorry, Kenzie," she said, and all was well—at least for now.

Mark looked up at me and smiled with relief that our girls were happy again. I brushed off his smile and went to my computer, turning my back on him.

"Everything okay?" Mark asked cautiously.

"No," I snapped back, "everything is not okay." I knew I was holding resentment against him, but I wasn't ready to let it go or deal with it. The wound was still fresh in my heart, and now I had just experienced my daughter's pain, and I was mad at him. "We'd rather be home right now, but that didn't happen," I said.

Mark sat wounded, unable to make things right and afraid things might only get worse. His heart was breaking. With tears burning his eyes and emotion taking over his ability to speak, he walked out of the apartment without a word.

"Where's Dad going?" McKenzie asked.

"Don't know," I responded.

"Is he okay?" McKenzie asked. "Should I go after him?"

"Nope," I said.

"Are you going to go after him?" she asked.

"No," I said.

The room was silent as McKenzie stared at me, beckoning me to go after him.

"He needs alone time right now," I said.

"I'm worried about Dad. He doesn't look good," she said.

"He'll be okay, McKenzie. He just needs to eat."

Mark had closed the apartment door behind him. He sat down on the steps and began to weep. He felt separated and alone. He needed a friend, and so he reached out to one of his best friends, David Estes, on FaceTime.

David looked down and saw Mark's call coming in. Until now they had only communicated through Facebook and text messages. Eager to talk to him and see him face-to-face, he answered the call, hoping to hear good news. But what he saw on the other side was a skeleton of the friend he had dropped off at the airport a few weeks ago. Staring back at him was a broken man. David could see Mark had been crying and was on the verge of breaking. His face was hollow, and he looked as if he was sick and had lost 30 pounds. The weight of sadness that hung onto him made David fear that the worst had happened.

"Hey friend," David said.

Mark struggled to smile and say something, but only managed a nod.

"How's it going?" David asked, knowing it could be a report he didn't want to hear.

Mark's lip began to quiver, "Not good," he said.

"I'm so sorry," David said. "Tell me what's going on."

Mark looked away and shook his head, fighting back the emotions that were pushing to get out. "I just can't do this anymore. I don't know how much more I can take." His exhaustion was apparent.

David had no words as he listened to his friend pour out the pain and remorse, which had clearly been beating him up for days.

"I should've just listened to her and gotten us out of Ethiopia when she was begging me to leave," Mark's voice began to quiver. "We wouldn't be in this mess...we'd be home right now. I should've listened to her. Because of what I decided to do, we could lose Favor. Because of me. I don't know how Missy is ever going to forgive me if that happens."

"I'm so sorry," David said. "I wish I could be there with you."

"What's going to happen if God doesn't work this out the way we are praying He will?" Mark asked. "She's never going to forgive me for not listening to her. It will be my fault if we lose our daughter. I just don't know how we can make it past this."

"I know you guys," David said. "You will work this out... no matter what happens."

"I don't know. If we lose Favor, I don't think she will ever trust me again. I'll lose my marriage..."

David wanted to bring comfort and peace to his hurting friend, "Mark, I don't have any answers. I wish I could promise you that God is going to answer your prayers exactly the way you want Him to, but I can't. Here's the thing I *can* promise you: God loves Favor more than you do. God has a bigger and better plan for Favor than you do, and if she gets left behind in Ethiopia, and you come home with your family, you will put your family back together and you will make it through this. God will find a way to be glorified in this, and He will save this child in spite of this horrible situation."

Mark listened quietly, but his anguish spoke volumes.

"In the meantime," David added, "I think some food and sleep would do your body good. This is not the time to worry about losing weight."

Mark tried to laugh. "Nice," he said sarcastically, "between the dogs barking all the time, and Islamic prayers going out over a loudspeaker at all hours, I'm not getting a whole lot of sleep."

"Yeah, I'd have a hard time sleeping with that too. How are the rest of you doing?" David asked.

"It's wearing on all of us," Mark said.

"You've got an awful lot of people praying for you guys," David said. "Why don't you let me pray for you now."

"Please," Mark said as he bowed his head.

"God," David started, "we thank You that You are with us. We thank You that You care about Favor more than Mark and Missy do, and that, however this turns out, You will receive glory for what is happening right now in this situation. I pray that You will strengthen Mark right now, that You will be his strength, and that You will be Missy's strength as they walk together in this battle. May Your bonds of peace hold them together. I pray this marriage will come out stronger than ever because You will do a miracle work in their lives and in their marriage."

David's words were penetrating Mark's heart and spirit. A weight was slowly lifting from his back.

"I'm reminded of the scripture that encourages us to stand," David said. "After you've done all you can. After you have girded yourself, and armed yourself, and you've fought with your spiritual weapons, there comes that time when all you can do is stand. When your arms are weary, and you can't swing the sword anymore. When you can think scripture, but your mouth is too tired to move, and you can't even speak it out of your mouth. What you can do is, in faith, set your face like flint and say, 'Here I stand!' Jesus, more than anything else, we ask, please give them the strength and the courage to stand. Stand against the corruption that they are facing. Stand against the enemy that is seeking to steal, kill, and destroy. Protect them, Lord, by Your mighty hand. We ask all this in Your precious name. Thank you, Jesus. Amen."

Mark dried the tears from his face. "Thank you!"

"Listen Brother," David reiterated, "I want to encourage you to start eating. Eat *something*...go get one of those barking dogs if you have to."

Mark tried to laugh.

"Kidding!" David said. "But seriously, you need your strength to be there for your family, and you not eating is not going to help you be the father and husband you need to be right now."

Mark agreed.

"In spite of how you might feel...man, I know you probably feel crushed and crumbling on the inside, but on the outside, you'd better stand up. You have to demonstrate "safe" to your family. They need that, and you're the one they're looking too right now. If ever you're going to be a decisive leader, it is now. Stand up, shake yourself off, and find your hope in the Lord."

"Thanks," Mark wearily said. "I love you, my friend."

Mark and David ended their phone call. Mark's spirit rose with new strength and hope that no matter the outcome, God was in control, and His love was enough.

* * * * *

Meanwhile, I sent a message to our prayer warriors, unaware that the very words I was writing were the words I needed most:

> This morning I woke up singing, "God I look to you." I realize that so many of you are in the same place we are, trusting God to give you vision beyond what you can see in the flesh.
>
> This morning God showed me a vision: He was standing before me with two paths. One was easier—it was getting out of Ethiopia last Thursday with Favor, undetected. We would

be home safe with our family, and still have a testimony that would glorify God. We would've been stronger for going through it, but left on that path were children that would never be united with their forever families and be adopted.

The other path was hard and rough, one that we would've never chosen. It put us face-to-face with our enemy and into a battle that could bring great loss. There was darkness and snakes on this path, and we couldn't see any end in sight. But, we knew God was there, and He would guide us through it. On this path, we had to lean on our Spirit and not our flesh, with just enough light for the next step. It would be the difference between being a foot soldier or being called out as a warrior.

There is something transforming in Mark and me—we are hearing a call to rise up in an area of life we never saw coming. There is an undeniable, righteous anger rising up to take back what the enemy has stolen and tried to destroy.

I know so many of you don't like the path that our nation is on, but I encourage you to dig deep and rise up to what God is doing in America through you. At times, we all have been on that harder path, but we are not alone, God IS with us! We need more time on our knees to learn how to see with spirit eyes and hear with spirit ears. God is doing something BIG, and I don't want to miss it because I'm too comfortable. Take any fear or anger and lay it at the Father's feet, pick up your sword and shield with a righteous anger, and fight to bring America back to God.

The hard path builds muscle and burns out the dross. In times like these, pressing into the Father is the only way to survival. Look around you. What does Jesus want to do through you? While we've been here, we have had the opportunity to pray for those with HIV and leprosy. I don't know if they'll get well. I'm just believing they will. Maybe they just needed someone to touch them and show them love. Every time you pray for someone and hold them up in prayer, you are building your spiritual muscle and planting good seed.

Thank you, again, for doing that for us. We pray you will all be bountifully blessed for how you have stood in the gap for us! We Love you!

My stubbornness blinded me to my own words about anger. I decided to post the picture of Favor in the gym that I'd taken the night before. As I did, I took a second look. A golden cloud in the room made the blue floors green, and right above Favor's head, there was a white form that appeared to be part of a large wing. Looking more closely, I could see several white shadows that appeared in the background. I didn't see any of these things when I took the picture. Did my camera catch Heaven coming down on us? I choose to believe it did, and grabbed onto another wondrous sign that God was with us.

Heaven coming down on beautiful picture of freedom—Favor running in The Academy gym.

CHAPTER 23
MAKING A PATH

"I understood why His heart aches for the orphans...how He yearns for them to feel loved unconditionally. To feel valued. I understood why He instructs us, as His adopted children, to go and help the orphan. We were once like them. I could hear His heartbeat— it was almost deafening."

—Missy Maxwell Worton

It was Sunday night in Addis Ababa, and the streets were relatively calm as Dave drove us through the city to attend the Reinhard Bonnke meeting. Bonnke is known for his crusades—some drawing more than 150,000 attendees in a single night—throughout the continent of Africa. Bonnke, on his ministry website, reports that as a young man, God placed upon his heart the vision of "the continent of Africa, being washed in the precious Blood of Jesus."[1] So many of our friends were excited that we would be in Ethiopia to experience Bonnke, and some of them believed it was one of the reasons why we were detained. I wasn't sure if that was the case, but I had to admit, God's timing was impeccable. He had lined it up perfectly for Mark and me to attend, and we had learned not to believe in coincidences.

As we approached, we could see crowds walking toward the large field that would hold the first Bonnke meeting in more than 20 years for the Ethiopian people. The cow pasture was known for having a stronghold of witchcraft over it. Witches had supposedly put curses on the land, but that didn't stop Bonnke from taking back the land for God's glory.

Dave drove through the special entrance for cars. Most people were on foot, some walking miles to get here. We pulled past the guard and went through a section called "the homeless city." The rooms were made out of anything they could find that had been discarded—sheets of metal, wood, or cardboard. As we drove by, we looked through the walls that barely stood to shelter those inside. I'd seen such levels of poverty in pictures, but not up close. The rotting smells and hopeless looks on their faces made it personal. I rolled down my window as we passed them, and I could hear jubilant music playing as we rounded the corner to see a pasture covered with thousands of beautiful, dancing Ethiopians! My spirit leapt. I couldn't wait to be in the midst of it.

Dave parked and started walking us through the crowds of people to find Pochi. Everyone we passed smiled back—full of so much life and love. What a noticeable difference from what we had been experiencing on our drives to court. I looked around—there were no chairs, no concession stands. All they had was a large, dry, cow pasture, set with a stage, a huge sound system, large projector screens, and a few lights so you could see where you were walking. In every direction I looked, I saw people worshipping God with pure abandon. Nobody was complaining about how loud the music was, or about sitting on the hard ground. They had come with one hope—to see Heaven come to Earth.

Mark and I did our best to avoid the cow patties and large cracks in the ground as we followed closely behind Dave. I was shocked that with all those people, we quickly found Pochi and some women from her church about halfway down the field. The praise music continued to ring out over the land, and there was no sign of anything but the glory of God in the place.

Mark and I listened as Bonnke passionately shared a simple message about God's love and how the name of Jesus is not spoken in Hell because it brings life and hope. Hell has no hope nor life. We immediately recognized his interpreter as one of the Covenant Church pastors we had enjoyed lunch with in the beautiful high rise several days ago. When Bonnke wrapped up his message and made a call for those who wanted to know Jesus, people from every direction started making their way toward the stage. That night, thousands gave their lives to a living and loving God. We watched miracles happen before our eyes: a lame man walked, huge tumors disappeared, a young girl's leg grew out healthy and whole. At one point, a wheelchair was thrown onto the stage. The man who used to be lame and confined to it had run home to show his family what God had done. We knew it was real. I had never seen so many miracles at one time; the experience was life-changing, and it renewed my belief that my God was a big and powerful God! He was a healer! He could do whatever He chose to do for those who believed on Him. God's Spirit was alive and moving in Ethiopia.

The Ethiopian praise music started to play again, and everyone around us started dancing in praise and thanksgiving. I understood why David danced before the Lord and why the Israelites danced after crossing the Red Sea—that's what joy does to you. Mark and I needed to be in this atmosphere. We were going up against our own giant and facing our own impassable sea. We felt God's restorative power come upon us, and we were filled with faith at the mighty wonders we had seen. How could we doubt that He had a miracle waiting for us? And so, we danced!

Mark and I at the Reinhard Bonnke meeting with more than 100,000 beautiful Ethiopians!

* * * * *

Before we left, I took a few pictures of the people dancing around me. They had such expressions of joy and gladness on their faces, and I wanted to remember this moment. I checked the picture before we left, and realized that I had caught what looked like fire coming down on people's heads, with hundreds of angels filling the sky above us. I took another picture. Maybe my camera was messing up. The same thing happened again, except more angels were visible in the photos. My camera was working just fine.

We were all filled with excitement as we drove back to the compound, but as we rounded the corner, we saw white plastic sheets covering bodies alongside the highway. It looked like white body bags lined up. We noticed people sleeping on the median in the middle of the highway, inches from the cars that drove by. It took my breath away.

"Oh my gosh," I said, "are these people all homeless?"

"Yes," Dave said.

"Are they families," I asked, "or just strangers curled up together?"

"Some are families," Dave said, "but most do not know each other. They sleep next to a stranger to keep warm at night. This is the only way to survive."

"What about the ones who are sleeping in the middle of the highway?" I asked.

"They are afraid someone will steal from them," he said. "This is how they protect themselves."

"They're inches from cars hitting them!" I said in disbelief.

"What are they afraid people will steal?" Mark asked.

"Anything," he said, "their shoes, jacket, food."

"Does the government help at all?" Mark asked.

"There are too many," Dave said. "85 percent are in poverty. Where do you start?"

The drive was quiet the rest of the way back to our apartment. I knew poverty was a big problem in Ethiopia, but the reality that people would snuggle up to strangers, covered by a plastic sheet on a urine-soaked sidewalk, wrecked me. I wondered how this horrific problem could even be solved. The image in my mind from the sight I had seen was vast... too many people to count, too many to forget.

After our long drive, we pulled up to the gate of The Academy. I took a picture of the charismatic church, built next to the high wall of The Academy. I looked at the picture. I had taken a section of the dark, unlighted area above this little miracle-believing church, but what I saw was more angels than I could count filling the skies. They came across like large and small orbs in the picture. Maybe I knew they were already there. After all, the light shines the brightest... in the midst of darkness.

The more I learned about this little church nestled next to The Academy, the more I wanted to experience it. Radical Islam had moved in all around their community; yet, they stood, loved, and worshiped, opening their doors every Friday to anyone who would come for healing. Instead of running, they stayed and served their community. They prayed for anyone, regardless of their beliefs, and God's love and power healed them. They simply loved the people around them, and much like Covenant Church that we had attended with Pochi on a few occasions, this little church knew how to bring down Heaven in worship.

* * * * *

When we arrived back at Jody and Pat's home to pick up the girls, we found out that the girls had left to go back to the apartment more than an hour ago. Jody tried to get them to stay until we got back, but they had their minds made up. It surprised us, but we figured that McKenzie babysat all the time, and Jody said they would be safe anywhere on the compound.

On their walk back to the apartment, the girls' imaginations took over. One of the armed guards spotted them and started walking briskly to catch up. The girls thought he was coming after them so they screamed and ran to the apartment, shoving the chair against the door. I'm sure the guard got a good laugh, but the girls were a little freaked out.

We hurried up to the apartment and banged on the door, but nobody answered.

"It's Mom and Dad," I said through the door.

McKenzie opened the door with big eyes, and gave me a huge hug.

"Please don't leave us alone again," McKenzie pleaded.

"We didn't leave you alone," Mark said. "We left you with some friends. You should've gone back there."

"I couldn't get Favor out the door to go back," McKenzie said. "She thought the guard was a bad guy coming after us, but I could hear him laughing when Favor said something in Amharic and took off running. I only ran because I knew I'd be in trouble if I lost her."

"He was probably wondering what two little girls were doing out in the dark alone," Mark said. "I'm glad to hear she knows to run if someone is chasing her."

"Oh, she definitely knows how to run. She's a fast little thing," McKenzie said.

Favor shot McKenzie a look.

"I'm sorry," I said. "We were just trying to keep you safe."

"Mom," McKenzie said, "you do know she doesn't understand a word you're saying?"

"She can feel it," I answered.

I put the girls to bed and snuggled up to them. Favor could understand little at this point, but she knew that I cared and loved her. As I lay between them, my mind went back to all the homeless people we saw. They weren't lazy—they were poor, and some of them were sick. I felt that so many of them, if given an opportunity to make money, would take it. There were no handouts or welfare. *How could we possibly make a difference?* My mind kept trying to figure out ways to fix this huge problem, until I fell asleep.

* * * * *

We woke up to "Blessed be the name of the Lord" blasting over the intercom. It was Monday morning, and the school was welcoming the students back from the weekend. We rushed down to the little coffee shop on campus to get our morning coffee—the best coffee I'd ever tasted, and each cup was just pennies to enjoy.

"Mom, did I tell you about the ugly huge cat we saw last night?" McKenzie said.

"What cat?" I said.

"It was huge, little ears and a big bushy tail. We tried to catch it, but it ran up to the attic."

Mark and I looked at each other.

"Do me a favor," Mark said, "if you see that cat, stay away from it! That doesn't sound like a cat."

"Hey, it's the Wortons! Having your morning coffee and... popcorn?" Jody said as she walked up.

"Breakfast of champions!" I said.

"How'd it go last night?" Jody asked.

"Heaven got a little fuller," I said.

"That's awesome," Jody said. "So, the girls were good when you got home?"

"Yes, but I think they got a little frightened by the security." I answered.

McKenzie looked up from her popcorn, "Hey, he had a gun," she said.

"These guys are great," Jody replied. "They're here to protect you."

I was so thankful to have a safe hideaway. I knew Jody and Pat would do anything to help us out, and I knew that at some point I would have to talk to them about another really big favor I might have to ask of them, but now was not the right time.

* * * * *

That afternoon, Pochi and Pastor picked us up to visit Covenant Orphanage in Holeta. When we arrived, the children ran out to greet us. They were all so happy, especially to see Favor and McKenzie.

They asked why we had not left for America yet. I watched as Favor's countenance changed. She looked down and walked away from all of us standing there.

"Favor," I called out. She turned and looked at me with a face that told me she was hurting. "Favor, come to me, sweetie." I held my arms out, and she ran to me and slowly put her arms around my shoulders. "We are not leaving you here." She looked in my eyes. "You are going back with us tonight. You are my little girl." Favor's eyes never left mine, and although I knew she didn't understand all the words I

Mark, Missy, McKenzie and Favor visiting the children at Covenant Orphanage in Holeta.

said, she knew I wasn't going to leave her. She smiled and gave me a hug before rushing away to join the others.

"So," Pochi said, "how are you feeling about the court and what you've seen?"

After the last court date, our confidence had been rocked, and we saw a fight before us with unbalanced scales.

"I don't know," I said, "I thought they would let us go once they saw that Adeferese didn't show up for his court hearing."

"Of course not," Pochi said. "This will take time. They have to hear his side, but don't worry, they will find nothing."

"All it took was a lie to stop us. What stops them from lying again?" I asked.

"Nothing does," Pochi said. "You have a smart and good judge. You have to believe she will find the truth." Mark and I sat silent. "You look worried, Mark."

"I am," Mark said sharply. I could feel Pochi pull back. "It didn't go well at our last court hearing. We could feel a change in the judge toward us. It's not a done deal that we'll be able to keep Favor."

Pochi said, "I know, it did not go well, but it's not just..."

"I know," Mark interrupted her. "Pochi, you used us, knowing we could lose her. It's kind of hard not to take that personally when we're the ones who get to feel the pain."

"We did not use you," Pochi stressed.

"Pochi," I asked, "why didn't you encourage us to leave that Thursday?"

"I didn't think you would have trouble leaving," she said. "You had everything, her passport, visa. Why would I think they would stop you?"

"Because you told us they could stop us," I answered. "But by then, it was too late for us to do anything about it."

For the next few moments we sat in an awkward silence. The only thing we could hear was the children playing in the yard. Pochi searched for words, while Mark and I sat in our reoccurring pain. She would start to say something, then hesitate and take a deep breath. "I know this has been difficult," she said. "I feel your pain, I see your pain, but I know this is God's will for a higher call. When I was a young girl, my father would take me on walks on this long road, in the forest nearby our home. It had tall trees and many bushes on both sides. I remember one day when we were walking he asked me, 'How do you think this road got here?' I did not know, because in my life it had always been. Then he explained how it used to be only a forest when his grandfather was young, but as time went on, they needed a path. So, many men came with their sharp tools and cut a path that became this road. Men cleared the trees and rocks away so it would be easier for those who would travel this way. It was hard work, but they knew it would be a blessing to others when it was finished. Some of them never got to use that road—they died before seeing it completed, but they worked on it anyway. 'Now,' my father said, 'we walk on this path, and we don't ask ourselves who did this so our way could be made easier or better. We just see a path, but someone made that path for us.' I will never forget my father telling me this."

Mark and I listened.

"You are making a path," Pochi said, pointing to us. "All you see are the trees and rocks in the way and how hard it is, but I see you making a path for others to walk through with ease. It is true, you might not get to walk the path. Most will probably never know the pain you went through to clear it, but God will."

I appreciated what Pochi was saying, but it wasn't a warm, tingly feeling that I felt, but exhaustion. I knew Pochi was trying to tell us that although it may not turn out the way we'd hope, it was going to help others in the long run.

The children came running into the living room and took every available seat around us. They brightened up the room and pulled us back into the moment. A flu bug was going around, and I could hear the sniffles and coughs as the Pastor began their chapel time. Pastor and Pochi had chapel for the kids at the orphanage every Monday evening.

We sat as the children worshiped God in their native language, clapping their hands, and lifting their voices. Then the Pastor shared a short sermon about how the Israelites were in an impossible situation—all hope had gone—but God made a way and they crossed the Red Sea. They escaped from those trying to hurt them. Nothing was impossible for God. He will surely make a way for us like He did for the Israelites. The children held on to every word as if it was life and death for them. I thought perhaps Pastor had fashioned his lesson for Mark and me, as a way to encourage us that God was for us.

We began to pray for each other, I could hear a sweet little voice next to me crying out. I opened my eyes and saw one of the most precious sights I could ask for: a room full of fatherless children crying out to their Heavenly Father. Favor's eyes were closed, and her head was lifted to the heavens, petitioning the Father with her whole heart. Her voice cried out His name as she would barely take a breath between her requests. I knew He heard her because I could feel His presence near us. I could feel the heartbeat of God for them. The love and passion that He had for each one of them was so incomprehensible and immeasurable. I understood why His heart aches for the orphans, and I experienced, in some measure, how He yearns for them to feel loved unconditionally. To feel valued. I understood why He instructs us, as His adopted children, to go and help the orphan. We were once like them. I could hear His heartbeat—it was almost deafening.

* * * * *

On the way home, Pochi began to tell us some of the things Adeferese had been saying about us to others. "He told me that he cannot understand why you care so much for this child," Pochi said. "He wants you to walk away from this. He is telling people that he will draw this out and drain all your money, or threaten you with jail. He thinks this will cause you to run back to America. I told him you will not run away, and he laughed."

I sat in the back seat, holding Favor in my arms. It really didn't matter what this man had said—I was not going to let his words determine my mindset. I wasn't going to let go of this little girl in my arms. I was holding on to the promise that victory was ours from the moment that we set foot in Ethiopia. I was fighting for her—no matter what he tried to do.

"He has told me that we must get her away from you, that you cannot leave with that 'kid,' or he and I will be in big trouble," Pochi said. "He asked me, 'Why did you come?' He wanted you to stay home and pick another child, and he is so mad that you did not listen to him. He says, 'What is so special about this child? Why must they have this one? There are a million more out there.'"

"Wait," I said, "did you say that he wanted us to pick another child? Does he think we pick kids like they are pets or commodities? He really doesn't get it, does he?" I thought back to the first time I came to Ethiopia, when Pochi had shared how the official at Debre Birhan had said that no one would care about these four little orphans and nobody would miss them. He and Adeferese were drinking the same Kool-Aid, but they were wrong. People do care, and people will rise up to help the orphans.

"Oh my goodness," Pochi continued like she had some fresh news. "He is very panicked that he doesn't know where you are hiding. He has people looking and asking where you are. I had a person call me and ask where you were hiding. I knew they were friends with him so I just said that I didn't know. We are telling no one. They are confused at how you just disappeared. 'They know no one in Ethiopia...how does this happen?' they asked."

"Why wasn't he at the court hearing last Thursday?" Mark asked.

"I don't know," Pochi said. "I found out that he was up in Debre Birhan, meeting with the regional officials today. It was his first time there. He has never even visited our orphanage. He's trying to prove that she was never in our orphanage."

"There are pictures of her at the orphanage and witnesses that saw her there," I said.

"They have nothing," Pochi reassured us. "He says he has the proof in an official envelope with a seal on it from the official so they can present it to the judge on Friday."

I took a deep breath. I had to believe in the promises God had given me.

"The president of the courts, MOWA, and the Embassy have all pulled away and are waiting to see what happens at your court hearing on Friday, before they decide to get involved any further."

Our hearts hit the floor. I could feel hopelessness push into my mind as she continued to talk. "Adeferese has someone at the Embassy that is standing with him, and I think he has gotten them on his side. They say he is in the right, and they all know Adeferese will get his way. They don't understand why you are giving up so much to fight for one little girl. They think you are crazy."

"Great! Any good news?" I asked sarcastically.

Pochi laughed, "Yes! God is on the throne."

I looked out the window. The mountains seemed to be disappearing in the darkness that was overtaking the day. My heart hurt, again—a little deeper tonight for some reason. Maybe it was all the negative news coming like arrows. I felt alone, abandoned by people who were supposed to help us. *How did it get this bad?*

"Emebet and the foster nurse are coming to support you on Friday," Pochi said. "They are both so mad at the official and Adeferese. The official told them that he would have them thrown in prison if they do not do what he tells them to do. They don't care, they are so mad at the way he and Adeferese are harassing them constantly."

"Will it be dangerous for them to be there?" I asked.

"They've done nothing wrong," Pochi said. "Why would it be?"

The conversation continued the rest of the way home, but my mind had gone elsewhere. I was fighting a personal battle. I had defaulted to being angry at Mark again for not leaving. I started silently crying to myself. *Why was I going around this mountain again?* I knew God had a greater plan, but in my weakness, I was angry at the situation. Maybe I was just tired and hungry.

* * * * *

We got back to the apartment, and I went downstairs to heat up the leftover Shiro, a traditional Ethiopian food primarily made from powdered chickpeas, for the girls. The old microwave in the teacher's lounge started with a turn of a handle—I hadn't seen one of those in years. As I stood waiting for the food while the loud fan churned, I saw something move in my peripheral vision...coming right toward me.

I turned and looked.

There, 10 feet in front of me, was a creature I had never seen. We both stopped in our tracks, looking right at each other. My mind started taking over with unheard comments: *What an ugly cat! Look at those small, beat up ears, look at that poor thing! It's huge! Look at that tail, it's so fluffy...Wait, that's not a cat. I bet that's the mongoose. Okay, I'm not going to move, and maybe he won't notice me. Nice mongoose...I hope he's a nice mongoose. Please don't attack me and give me some disease that will eat my brain.*

The mongoose quickly looked away from my gaze, but stood completely still—like he was saying, *Maybe she won't notice me if I look the other way and don't move.*

In one of the oddest minutes of my life, we both stood motionless until a loud, obnoxious *Ding!* announced the food was ready. At that point I screamed, and the mongoose bolted out the way he came. I rushed upstairs with the Shiro burning my hands.

"I think I just met the cat you were chasing last night," I said, out of breath as I entered the apartment. "That ugly cat is no cat. It's the mongoose!"

"You ran into the mongoose?" Mark asked excitedly. "Where?"

"Downstairs."

"Is it still down there?" he asked.

"No, and don't try to find it," I yelled to McKenzie, already with one foot out the door.

"Really?" McKenzie said. "Please?"

"No way," I said. "Come and have some Shiro before Favor eats it all, and I'll tell you about it."

As we sat around the table talking about the mongoose, I realized that this was an adventure that we needed to grasp with both hands. It wasn't every day that you could say you ran into a mongoose in the hallway while heating up some Shiro. It seemed crazy, but we all had the best night together. Joy had come in the most unusual way.

CHAPTER 24
LETTING GO

"Some of us think holding on makes us strong, but sometimes it is letting go."

—Herman Hesse, author, Noble Prize in Literature, 1946

The call to prayer pierced through our much-needed rest at 4 a.m. With no mute button, I found myself awake and annoyed that a person with tonal pitch wasn't a prerequisite for leading the call to prayer over a bullhorn. I started replaying the conversation that we had with Pochi the night before. *How could anyone expect us to turn our back on a child—especially after we had met her?* She knew we came to give her a family and call her daughter. We loved Favor! Before she was born, she was destined to be part of our family, and although no one wants to see a child go through such great loss, we knew her destiny was tied to us. God already knew how He would use this little girl to inspire so many to rise up and pray for the orphans.

Today was going to be a great day. Julie was coming to take Mark, the girls, and me up to the mountain that held some of Ethiopia's greatest historical treasures. I couldn't wait to get out of the city and breathe in the mountain air.

The views were gorgeous as we drove up the mountains. They would crest and then level off for a few miles. Snuggled in between were the most beautiful valleys and farmland. The land we looked over was alive with growth. The air was thin but pure and clean as we reached the top. I forgot where I was as we walked through the church cut out of the rock, and then through the First Chapel of Addis Ababa, where the Ark of the Covenant is said to have been kept at one time. My mind raced back to all the things I had read about the journey of the Ark, and how Prince Menelik I was said to have been King Solomon and the Queen of Sheba's loved son who journeyed to Ethiopia. No one will ever know if he had taken the real Ark or the copy that Solomon had made for him.[2]

We went to the palace of the first King and Queen Menelik II of Addis Ababa. We got to see the monks, and then there was a crazy woman who kept glaring at us and growling. I dared Mark to go pray for her, but he didn't want to get attacked. So, he prayed from a safe distance.

We walked around, looking at all the magnificent history before us, when I saw a little red cross hanging around some of the children's necks. It was the same cross that a beautiful woman had given our son Shewit when he lived on the streets after his mother and father had died.

"Where do they get those crosses?" I asked.

"The church gives them to the children in the city," the guide said.

"Do they go to the northern cities in the Tigray region?" I asked.

"They are from this area," he answered. "I don't think so."

"My son had one given to him on the streets of a city in the Tigray region," I said. "The woman just appeared to him and told him not to worry because God had a wonderful plan for him. He treasures it."

The guide gave me a quizzical look. "I only know of nuns giving these," he said.

Seeing the red crosses made me miss my little guy back home. I could almost see the moment that a stranger saw a precious gift in Shewit. He was probably hungry and almost at his end. This beautiful woman, who had given my future son a cross with a message that God had a wonderful plan for him, also gave him hope. She might have been a missionary. She might have been a nun or an angel, but I believe that cross helped him survive until help could come. I wanted to give my son a hug and share the moment with him—but we were worlds apart.

On our journey back to The Academy, I had the driver pull over so I could take a breath and look out over the city below us. Something about being on the mountain made me feel like I could think and see more clearly. Mark and the others came out to stand with me.

"You doing okay?" Mark asked.

"I think so," I said.

"What's going through you mind," he asked.

"Loaded question," I said, and turned to look at the woman walking past us. She had a very large, heavy bundle of sticks on her back. Her load was as big as she was, and she did it every day for pennies. I pulled out my camera and asked if I could take her picture. She nodded yes as she put her hand out for money. I quickly gave her a few birr and snapped a picture as she smiled. I stood and watched as she disappeared down the mountain road. There was something about this picture of a person carrying a heavy load that resonated with me.

"That was funny how she asked for money," Mark said.

"Yeah," I said, "very resourceful. I wish we could've taken that load off her back and given her a ride down the hill."

We didn't say much for the next few minutes. We just breathed in the splendor before us. We had climbed our mountain, and I refused to carry my load back down it. I mentally

A woman carrying a heavy load down the mountain for the equivalent of a few pennies.

saw myself laying down the "what ifs," the score sheet that had more cons than pros, and the anger. I thought about the book *Pilgrim's Progress*, and the main character Christian, who carried the heavy loads of life called "burden" on his back like an overstuffed gym bag—until he laid his burden down at the Cross. Like him, I was no longer going to carry an unnecessary load when I knew God had already made a way. We had done all we could do, and God would carry it the rest of the way. It was time to lay it down.

* * * * *

We got back to The Academy as school was letting out for the day. I rushed up to start dinner, and to check my emails and messages. As I was reading some of the comments on our Facebook posts, I noticed Mark wipe a tear away as he was reading his emails. He got up and went into our room, shutting the door behind him. I knew he was hurting. *Lord, please give Mark peace. Wrap your arms around him,* I prayed to myself.

You need to wrap your arms around him. Forgive him, I heard in my Spirit. I sat there at a crossroad. The truth be told, I wasn't ready to forgive him. I didn't want to let go of me being right and him being wrong. I still had a lot to lose, and I was mad that he hadn't listened to me. I could feel the war going on inside my mind. Then I thought about those poor women with the heavy loads walking down the mountain. Their backs bent forward from the weight of the dead branches they carried. What a miserable existence, but here I was, carrying my unforgiveness like it was my burden to bear—it was my own load of dead branches.

My stomach started to get nervous, like it always does when I know I need to change or accept a truth I don't like. Nobody likes to be in the wrong. About that time, Mark walked out of the room and sat down. He looked up and gave me a weak smile.

"Are you okay?" I asked. He couldn't answer me. His lip started quivering and I could see that he had been touched by something he had received. "Did something happen?"

He sat there, unable to speak as he shrugged his shoulders and nodded yes. "Can you at least tell me?" I asked. He took a deep breath and got his composure before trying to communicate what was stirring his heart so deeply.

"I was just reading an email Pastor Ray had sent me," he struggled to say.

I got up from my chair and walked over to him. "Do you mind if I read it?" I asked.

Mark handed me his phone.

As I began to read, a window was opened to the personal struggles my husband had been going through. By our Pastor's response, I knew Mark had reached out to him to receive the forgiveness he had not seen from me. I scrolled down and kept reading, I had to see what Mark had written to Pastor Ray. As I read Mark's words, my heart began to melt. The ice began to chip away, and I could feel freedom from the hold of resentment welling up inside of me. His heart spilled out the pain of losing the trust of a wife he loved and putting her and his girls in danger. He laid all the blame on himself, humbling himself to his pastor. Something in me changed as I read. I knew he had said the same words to me, but seeing it written to someone else broke the chains of bitterness. I had no other choice but to forgive, and in one moment, I did. I let go of anything he had done or I thought he had done. I was no longer allowing anger and blame to keep me from freely and fully loving my husband. We were stronger together than we were apart. The enemy knew that, but he underestimated love.

I looked up at Mark. His eyes had never left mine. Without a word, he saw love and forgiveness. He smiled and began to weep as I walked over and sat on his lap and wrapped my arms around his neck.

"I love you," I whispered, "and I forgive you, completely."

"I know," he said through tears, "I could see it in your eyes. I love you so much."

We kissed for the first time since being stopped at immigration.

"Ooh," Favor said, "Mom, Dad, yucky."

"Get a room," McKenzie said as she laughed. "No, really, my eyes are burning from this gross display of PDA!"

"I love your momma," Mark said to the girls.

"Yeah," McKenzie said, "we kinda got that."

"I love you," I said to Mark. "You're an amazing man."

Forgiveness leads to rest, and that night we both had the best sleep we had since arriving in Ethiopia.

* * * * *

The following day, we were picked up by Dave and Pochi to meet with Mesfin and some key people who had new information on our case. We pulled around to the back of the Delphin Hotel and made our way into the marble-encased lobby. The waitress brought us all a cup of coffee, and Mark and I listened as they spoke to each other in Amharic. We were becoming experts at reading emotions, and the conversation that was taking place before us didn't look good.

Mark finally spoke up, "Is there something we need to know concerning our case?"

They all stopped and looked at us. For a moment there was silence, then Pochi started to tell us what was going on.

"We believe that Adeferese has gotten to the judge," Pochi said, then sighed deeply. Mark and I felt a cold chill grab our bodies. "He was up in Debre Birhan, rallying people to his side against you and the orphanage."

"Why do you think he has gotten to the judge?" Mark asked.

"There is talk that she isn't going to let you leave the country," Pochi said.

Tears began to well up in my eyes, and I could feel the room start to spin. I didn't want to entertain the thoughts battling in my mind, but they were overwhelming me. I found myself wanting to give up and run.

Pochi and Pastor did their best to encourage us on the way back to The Academy, but it was clear we were all down about the turn of events.

"This is the dream Daniel had," Pochi said from the front seat. "Do you remember the dream about the four children and the python that was trying to destroy them?"

"Yes," I said.

"This is it, and the snake is the enemy," Pochi said. "He will not win. He will not destroy these children."

Mark reached across the back seat and grabbed my hand. I looked up and felt peace looking in his eyes. I was so glad that he was mine, and, if we had to go through this, at least we were going through it together.

We arrived back at The Academy just in time for Tea Time. It was something we looked forward to every afternoon with the staff. I saw Jody and knew I'd better talk to her before our court date on Friday.

"Jody," I said, "can I talk to you about something before Friday?"

Jody was full of so much joy and personality. She quickly took me aside so we had a little privacy.

"It's about the girls," I said. "We don't know what will happen on Friday, and it looks like more are against us than for us." Jody gave me a pout. "I don't know what Adeferese is going to say, and if he lies about us again..." I paused. I didn't want to speak anything negative, but I needed to make sure my girls were going to be safe. "He has already falsely accused us of things that could put us in prison, but if anything happens to us, I need you to get McKenzie back to Nashville with her Grandma Worton and brothers."

"What?" Jody said.

"I'll give you everything you'll need to get her home," I said.

Jody listened. At that point she knew that I was very serious about what I was asking of her.

"Then I need you to make sure the Aunt or Pochi get Favor back," I said. "They can decide what's best for her. I just want to make sure the girls are safe and back with people who love them."

"What are you talking about?" Jody asked. "You are going to win this court hearing and all of you will be going home together."

"I believe that," I said, "but I also know that Adeferese has power, and I want to make sure I've got a plan for the girls if something does happen."

"You got it," Jody said. "I'll make sure they are safe, but I'm still believing for the best."

"Thank you," I said as I gave her a hug. Inside, my heart was broken, and the thought that I would have to activate the plan for the girls crushed me.

News of things happening at home continued to wear us down. When it rains, it pours, and our upstairs bathroom had a leak that was pouring into our kitchen below. On top of that, our furnace had gone out in the middle of the night. Grandma and the boys had awakened to a freezing home, and Matt, our oldest child, had been home from school for two days, diagnosed with strep.

Mark's mind went straight to the bank account, but before he could allow himself to worry about it, Grandma let us know it was financially taken care of. Grandma was standing strong through it all. She was a grandma, babysitter, nurse, prayer warrior, and now, a subcontractor for home repairs.

I put the girls to bed and sat down to send our prayer warriors an update:

> Mark and I are getting ready to turn in for the night. We have come to the place where we know Favor was God's daughter before she was ever ours. We gave her to the Lord because that is the safest place she can be. She has such a light that shines out of her and we know her Heavenly Father will not leave her an orphan. We know He has gone before us and has already won this battle. If you find yourself up between 4:30 a.m.–7:30 a.m. on Friday, whisper a prayer for us. We'll be in court. God is probably waking you up for war! Pray that Favor's aunt, the orphanage coordinator, Mesfin, and we arrive safely to finish this case. The victory is the Lord's! The enemy has attacked us from every angle, even at home. Ben Wilson, my cousin, said, "that speaks of an enemy that is confused, panicked, and using up all his resources..." He knows he's defeated! McKenzie and Favor have taken a Sharpie to their skin, writing "Jesus is with us" on their wrist. A reminder that when Jesus is with us...who can be against us?
>
> We yearn to hear the words, "You are cleared to take your daughter home."

> Thank you for taking this journey with us. For holding us up in prayer at all hours of the day and night. We have felt your prayers in more ways than you can imagine. You are crying out for those who have no voice, those set for destruction in these hours. Your reward is great in the Kingdom of God!
>
> We love and thank you, mighty warriors and our brothers and sisters in Christ.

As I was typing the last few words, I heard Mark bang his head on the slanted ceiling over our bed. He groaned and grabbed his head. I quickly finished my update and hit the send button, as Mark pulled his hand from his head—it was covered in blood.

CHAPTER 25
FACING THE GIANT

"When the enemy attacks on every side,
that speaks of an enemy that is
confused, panicked, and using up all his resources..."

—Ben Wilson, cousin and prayer warrior

I ran to the kitchen to start boiling water and grab a towel. "Girls, help me with Daddy," I said as I ran past them.

They jumped up and ran to Mark's side, "Daddy, what happened?" McKenzie asked.

Mark sat on the bed, holding his head as blood ran down the side of his face.

"Daddy wasn't thinking," he sighed, annoyed at himself.

I returned with a towel and wiped away the blood, but it didn't take long before his head was covered with blood again from the deep gash on the top of his head. The last thing either one of us wanted was take a trip to the hospital. The girls helped me walk him to the kitchen and put him in a chair so we could get a better look. I had McKenzie apply pressure to the wound while I got the boiling water started and pulled some antibiotics from my bag.

Favor watched and held her daddy's arm. He had his three girls taking care of him.

Ten minutes had passed and the bleeding wasn't slowing down.

"We need to pray for Dad," I said.

"Okay," McKenzie said. "You first." I looked at her for a moment.

"Father," I said, "please stop the bleeding and heal this wound. I pray he doesn't need stitches. In Jesus' name."

"Um," McKenzie started, "Jesus, please help my dad not to go to the hospital, because that would be really, really bad."

"Jesus, Jesus, Jesus," Favor kept saying under her breath over and over.

I waited for a moment then slowly pulled the towel back. The bleeding had stopped. Blood was starting to clot up. "Oh, thank you, Jesus," I said in relief. I put the antibiotic cream on Mark's wound and gave him an Advil for the pain.

"He needs a Band-Aid," McKenzie said.

"That's a great idea," I said. "You have any ideas what we can use?"

McKenzie looked around the kitchen, then the bathroom. "I'm looking," she said. She went into our room and a few seconds later emerged with an eye pad cover we had received from Ethiopian Airlines. I put a cotton pad on the wound and McKenzie put the eye pad over it, pulling the elastic band tightly under Mark's chin. He was a sight, but at least we avoided a trip to the E.R.

* * * * *

Friday arrived, and Mark and I woke up with our nerves high because today, we would finally meet our accuser face-to-face. We didn't know how we would feel when that moment came, but we wanted to finish well. I looked in the mirror as I was getting ready. "I promise to hold up my part by not believing the lies of the enemy," I said. "And Jesus, I'm trusting You and Your word that we will have a victory today."

I could hear Mark playing a song in the other room that had encouraged us many times in this journey. It was God's perfect timing, and I felt like He was saying, *I got this,* through Rick Pino's song, "Abba."

As we walked to the front gate to meet Dave, I could hear the little miracle-believing church outside The Academy worshiping. It was loud and amazing. They were having their Friday healing service, and people were packed in like sardines. There was standing room only, with people flowing out into the street around the building. I wanted to go in, if only for a few minutes before our battle, but Mark thought he'd never get me out. So, instead, I sat outside and listened, letting the sounds that filled the air around us bring us strength and peace. I could feel a difference in the atmosphere as I sat there.

I didn't want to leave when Dave picked us up. I slowly crawled into the back seat of Pochi's Toyota. It was cozy, having the girls in the back with me. I felt an uneasiness about bringing them, but we had been told to bring Favor in case the judge had any questions for her. Driving through the crowded streets of Mercato was a new experience for McKenzie, and as usual, we were stopped in traffic. I had never seen it this busy—it was Friday, and the Muslims were filling the streets to pray around the mosques that seemed to be at every mile. The day of the week caused a bigger than usual traffic jam.

Suddenly, I noticed something was happening across the street to my right. We could hear yelling and someone screaming out in pain. Two strong young men appeared from behind a car, and they were dragging something out into the traffic. I watched, thinking it was probably a dog that had stolen some food, but then my heart jumped. What I saw was horrific—the two young men were dragging an old man! He covered his face and winced from the blows and kicks that came from his tormentors. He was dressed in rags and looked as if he hadn't had a bath in weeks. The men threw him into the street and stepped back, yelling at him as he struggled to get up. Dirt and oil stuck to his skin as he labored to get out of the street and to safety.

Out of nowhere, we heard a car slamming on its brakes.

We held our breath.

The car came to a stop inches away from the man. The old man looked up to the heavens, paused, then began to move his hands. The driver waited patiently in his car as the old man used the front bumper to get up and limp back into the crowd. We all watched, stunned by what had happened.

"Oh," McKenzie said, "why would they beat an old man like that? That was mean."

Dave shook his head, unable to find the words to answer her.

"Mom?" She looked at me.

"I don't know why," I said.

Traffic started to move, and soon we were driving toward the courthouse again. Dave dropped Mark and me off 30 minutes early. Then, he took the girls to a safe location nearby to wait, in case they wanted Favor to testify.

Mark and I stood patiently before the locked door to the court. I remembered the first time we had come to this building in August. We had Favor with us, dressed in her *"Pick me"* shirt and sparkly pink boots. She was so happy that she couldn't sit still. We were in awe at the gift God had blessed us with. Now, three months later, we were fighting to keep her.

I looked over at a woman who had come to the curb in front of the court. She was bent over and carried an infant in a wrap that went around the front of her body. A little girl who looked to be about three years old followed her, holding on to the hem of her mother's skirt. The woman found a pole, placed her back to it, and slowly slid down to a seated position next to the road. She didn't look at anyone. I wondered if she knew that the families lining up were here to adopt and if she picked that spot on purpose. The little girl crawled into her arms next to the younger sibling. She looked at her mother and put her hand to her mouth as if to say, *Do you have food?* The mother responded by shaking her head, no. The little girl looked up toward me, eyes filled with disappointment and need, as she leaned her head against her mother's chest.

I opened my purse and started digging for anything to give her. I found one small bag of crackers. "I'll be right back," I told Mark. I walked over to the woman with the little girl, kneeled in front of her, and handed her the crackers. The woman looked at me and smiled, taking the crackers from my hand.

I walked back to Mark's side and looked up to see Emebet walking down the street toward us. I couldn't believe, that under all the threats she had received, she braved coming out to speak up for us. It showed me how much she loved Favor. I rushed to give her a hug and thank her for being here. We tried to catch up over the next few minutes, but the language barrier made it hard, so I pulled out my camera and showed her what we had done since we saw her last. Her expressions of joy as she saw Favor's big smile in each photo were priceless.

"She is so happy," Emebet said.

"Yes," I responded. "She knows she is well-loved by us and you."

"Yes," Emebet said. "I'm happy she has you."

"You helped that happen," I said. "Thank you!"

Emebet grabbed her heart as a sign of being touched and then reached out to give me a hug. "Thank you so much," she said. As we stood there with locked arms, we couldn't say much else. We knew that we needed each other, and we knew we were thankful for each other. Our connection was a little girl who we both loved dearly.

The waiting room to the judge's chambers was full of excited and nervous adoptive families. Along with Mesfin, DJ and the foster mother came in and greeted us with hugs. It was humbling to think that in addition to Mesfin's legal service to us, that DJ and the foster mother would testify for us, if called upon. We found a few available seats and waited, knowing we would probably be the last called. We looked around and saw no one from EAI yet. After 45 minutes, I was getting anxious as the crowd started thinning.

"What if Adeferese doesn't come again?" I asked Mesfin.

"He will be here," Mesfin said. "He will be here. Don't worry."

"We can't be delayed another two weeks," I said.

"You won't be," Mesfin whispered.

I sat back and started to pray as Mark and Mesfin discussed our family back home in Tennessee. I was too nervous to talk. I knew it all came down to today and my stomach was doing somersaults.

Jamila from EAI walked in with EAI's lawyer and looked around. She spotted all of us, then glanced at the lawyer. From the expressions on their faces, we knew that they weren't happy to see DJ and the foster mother with us in the waiting area. I watched as they walked over and took a seat. Still no Adeferese. I wondered what he was up to, coming this late to an appointed court hearing.

Something didn't feel right. I could sense a danger. I wasn't sure if it was our appointment to meet face-to-face with our accuser, or an unseen attack from someone or something else. Was it possible that false evidence was going to be presented against us? My mind began to swirl with what it could be, then I heard a whisper in my ear. *Pray!* I knew that voice. I didn't have to look around, it came straight from my spirit. I started praying. I felt a suffocation—a struggle going on inside of me.

Jesus, I prayed, *I don't know what is happening, but I'm asking you for protection right now. I'm asking you to guard us. Don't let a false word be brought against us. Please don't let any plan of the enemy succeed.* I kept praying as the war continued. I was surrounded by people, yet no one knew the battle inside, and tears came to my eyes.

* * * * *

The girls were getting restless in Dave's car, parked a few blocks away from the courthouse. Favor jumped into the front seat and started teasing Dave, who was quietly watching and praying.

"Favor," McKenzie said, "don't bother Mr. Dave." Favor ignored her older sister. "Favor, stop bothering him." Favor, keeping with the little sister title, kept on playing with Dave, trying to get him to respond.

"Favor," Dave said in Amharic, "please go back with your sister."

Favor was tired of sitting in the car. It had been almost an hour since they had parked, and it was getting stuffy in the back seat. Favor tried to grab Dave's glasses. Dave calmly blocked her. Then Favor reached down and grabbed one of his shoes from under the gas pedal on the floor. Favor dangled it behind her, then in front of her, teasing Dave and making a game of it.

"Favor," Dave said, "I need my shoe back. Please give me my shoe."

She held the shoe behind her a second too long and McKenzie grabbed it from the back seat. Favor screamed with glee—she had her sister in the game now.

"Mr. Dave said he needs his shoe," McKenzie said, and started to hand it back to him. Favor lunged at the shoe with both hands and grabbed it as Dave took it into his hands.

"Snap," the thong broke from the base of the shoe.

"Oh," Dave said in frustration, "no, no, no." He calmly took his broken sandal from Favor and looked at it.

"Favor!" McKenzie said. "You broke it! That wasn't nice."

Favor knew she was in trouble and jumped in the back seat, burying her head in the corner.

Dave turned around to her, "Favor," he said, "I am not mad at you...Favor?"

Favor didn't look up.

"Can you fix them?" McKenzie asked.

"No," Dave said. "They are done. They are very cheap, for camping." Dave was leaving for a men's camping retreat immediately after he had taken us all back to The Academy. This had left him with no shoes.

"Do you have time to buy another pair this afternoon?" McKenzie asked.

"No," Dave replied.

"I'm sorry," McKenzie said. "Maybe they have some in one of those shops." She pointed across the street to a group of shops. Dave looked around. Across the four lane street was a clothing shop and he could see some sandals hanging on a rack at the entry.

"I will be right back," Dave told McKenzie.

"Wait," McKenzie said in shock, "you're leaving us?"

"I will lock the doors," Dave said. "Do not open them for anybody. I will be right there," he said, pointing to the shop where he had seen the sandals. "You can see me from here. You will be safe. I won't take my eyes off of you."

"Don't leave us," McKenzie pleaded.

"You will be okay," he said. "You can watch me. Nothing will happen." Dave locked the doors and started across the street toward the shop.

As if on cue, a white van pulled in behind the girls.

McKenzie, unaware, watched Dave cross the street and look at the rack of shoes. Three men jumped out of the van and walked toward the car.

Favor looked up and out the back window. Without a word, she scrambled to the floor and covered herself from head to toe with her scarves and jacket.

"What are you doing?" McKenzie blurted out, still unaware of the men.

McKenzie felt someone at the car's right-hand door. She looked up and saw a man standing next to the car, facing her. Her heart started pounding. McKenzie looked toward Dave. He was looking the other way.

Then suddenly, a man stepped in front of her view and pressed up to the left back door.

McKenzie desperately tried to look around him toward Dave. She opened her mouth to yell, but nothing would come out.

* * * * *

"Adeferese is here," Mark whispered in my ear.

I looked up. There he was, standing in the doorway with a man I had yet to see. He glanced over the crowd, then walked toward the area by the window, taking the farthest seat from us. He started a conversation with a gentlemen who seemed to know him well. I watched as he glanced out the window while the man would glance toward us. I wanted to wave at him as if to say, *Yeah, we're the ones he's talking about!*

"That man is married to the attorney who is representing the other family that went back to America without their child," Mesfin whispered to us, as he shook his head in disbelief. "They obviously know each other well. They have told that family that there is no hope to get their child. They think you are crazy for staying."

"There's no hope if their attorney is friends with Adeferese," Mark said.

I breathed a sigh of relief. Now it was clear why we hadn't felt right about going with that attorney. Again, God had stepped in for us and provided the attorney we needed.

"Mark Wortons," the secretary's voice announced.

Mark gave my hand a squeeze and we walked in together, taking our regular seats to the right of the judge. Emebet, DJ, and the foster mother stayed seated in the waiting area.

The judge looked up and gave me a quick smile. She was dressed in a striped top, with her hair neatly pulled back in a tight ponytail. I glanced around the courtroom. Everything looked the same, except for two extra court clerks seated to the judge's left.

Adeferese walked in behind his attorney, with Jamila walking behind him. They took their place beside Mesfin, facing the judge.

* * * * *

Three men were now surrounding the car that McKenzie and Favor were in. McKenzie's heart was pounding as she pulled the scarf on her shoulders over her head and slumped down in the back seat. One of the men tried to open the door, but it was locked. McKenzie tried to catch a glimpse of Dave again, praying he would turn around.

Dave chose a pair of sandals off the rack and handed his money to the woman at the counter. He turned to glance toward the car. His heart leapt with alarm when he saw the men circling the car. Without delay, he started running across the four lane street toward the girls, waving his hands in the air and yelling at the top of his voice for help. People near the area heard him and started surrounding the three men trying to get to the girls. Dodging the cars as he ran across the four lanes, Dave kept yelling for help. More people came.

The men were being enveloped by the crowd and getting pushed away from the car by the complete strangers surrounding them. The men shoved their way out and ran to jump into the white van and sped away, almost slamming into Dave as they peeled out.

"Thank you," Dave said. "Thank you for your help." The people watched as Dave unlocked the car door and ducked his head in to check on the girls. "Are you okay?"

McKenzie uncovered her face and looked up at Dave with tears in her eyes. She was so happy to see him. "You shouldn't have left us!" McKenzie cried out.

"I am so sorry! I was wrong," Dave said as he looked at McKenzie, petitioning her forgiveness.

"What just happened?" she asked. "Why were those men trying to get us?"

Dave shook his head and crawled into the front seat, locking the door behind him. "Where is Favor?" he asked.

"She's on the floorboard, covered up," McKenzie said. Favor hadn't moved since seeing the men come toward the car.

"Favor, are you okay?" Dave asked. "You are safe. You can come out of hiding."

Favor didn't move.

"Who were those men?" McKenzie asked.

"I don't know who they were," he said, "but they are gone now."

McKenzie was shaking. "Where is my mom and dad?" she asked.

"They should be back by now."

"They are still in court," Dave answered.

"That really scared me," McKenzie whispered.

"I am so sorry," Dave remorsefully said, "I won't leave again. Never again." It was clear that he was also shaken by what had happened. He was their bodyguard, and he was there to protect them. He knew this was a battle, but now he knew at what lengths the enemy was willing to go. "I am so sorry. Thank you, Jesus, for protecting the girls."

McKenzie couldn't stop the tears as she looked out the window at the people on the sidewalk. She wanted to go home where she felt safe, where she understood what people were saying, and where she understood the world around her. She wanted this nightmare to be over. She wanted to be in the arms of her mom and dad. She longed to feel safe again.

* * * * *

Adeferese stood in the courtroom with his chest held high and his eyes on the judge. She glanced up at him and said a few words in Amharic, then swore him in. Adeferese then pulled a sealed envelope out from his breast pocket.

Mesfin's eyes followed the envelope as it was presented to the judge. She made a statement to the clerk and opened the envelope to begin reading.

I turned and looked at our accuser—the giant standing between us and the freedom of our daughter. He stood so proud and pretentious, watching the judge as she read. *Why was he fighting so hard against us when all we wanted to do was give this child a home and a family?* He turned and glared at me, but instead of looking away, I locked eyes with him. I could feel the hatred he had for me spilling out. He had nothing but disdain as he flashed me a piercing stare behind his glasses. I knew he would like nothing more than to see us disappear. *Why did this man hate us so much?* There was no obvious reason for his actions, and I realized he was just a man being used by the real enemy. I looked at him, but not in anger or hate. I felt pain—not mine, but his. Then it happened...I felt a wash of love come over me for this man with such hostile loathing toward us, and before I could reason why, I found myself praying that God would draw him with love from head to toe. I prayed that he would be freed from the torment that had grabbed his soul, and I prayed that he would someday know the love of God as I did. I was astonished. All I had inside was love for this man, despite what he had done.

I smiled at him.

He narrowed his eyes and spun his neck to look in the opposite direction.

Dumbfounded, I sat there. *What had just happened? Where did that kind of love come from?* I knew it was God. He had been transforming my heart in this journey, but the depth of His transformation took me by surprise in that moment. I didn't need this man to like me or be respectable to me. I knew what God thought and He loved us both, and I was good with that.

"This paper from Debre Birhan says that she should be placed in foster care," the judge said. "Is this your only evidence?"

"It is all we need," Adeferese said. "The child was in foster care."

"Your Honor," Mesfin calmly spoke up, "the paper says she *should* be placed in foster care, but never said she *was* placed in foster care. One sheet says she should be put into foster care, the other says she should be placed in the orphanage for adoption by a family. They are signed by the same official. The one I have was signed three days after the one handed to you by Adeferese. Three days after this official signed that paper, he signed the paper I hold in my hand, which says she should be placed in the orphanage to be adopted."

As the judge listened to Mesfin and Adeferese disputing the two sheets of paper, I remembered the day I first heard that Favor was going to be put into foster care and would never be allowed to be adopted. I remembered how I ran to Cindy's home and stood in faith that God would take care of her, and He did. I remembered how all of us fasted and prayed for three days that the official would change his mind and allow Favor and the other three children to go back into the orphanage. I remembered how the official had then called Pochi into his office after those three days and miraculously signed the very paper Mesfin held in his hands. I remembered how Pochi picked up that piece of paper from the floor, after the official had thrown it at her, telling her to get out of his office. God had already done all that we had asked of Him. It all came down to a piece of paper. Was that one piece of paper enough to convince the judge? If so, we had won the battle the moment it was signed, months ago.

"Bring in the foster mother," the judge demanded.

The foster mother walked in and stood until the judge had sworn her in. I could see she was nervous; her hands were wiggling around as she held them in front of her body. Adeferese stared at her, but she never looked his way. We knew that she had been warned not to come and testify by the Debre Birhan official, but she was unmoved, waiting to tell her story and answer any questions asked.

"Tell me where do you work." The judge said.

"I work at the orphanage where this child comes from," she responded.

"Are you her foster mother as well?" The judge asked.

"I was told that I would only have to foster her until the adoptive family came to pick her up," she said.

"So," the judge said, "you were not planning to keep her as a foster child?"

"No, your Honor. That was never the plan. She already had a family working to adopt her."

"Did you receive payment for fostering this child?" The judge asked.

"I never received money for fostering," she said, confused by the question.

"Who paid for the expenses of this child then?" The judge asked.

"The orphanage took care of all the child's expenses," she answered.

"The orphanage?" The judge clarified.

"Yes," she said. "The child was always under the care of the orphanage. The government foster program never paid anything toward any of the four children. It was the orphanage seeing their needs were met—their food and clothing."

"Did you ever see Adeferese at the orphanage?" The judge asked.

The foster mother looked at Adeferese and then back to the judge. "No," she said with resolve.

The judge pierced her lips and took a deep breath. Her eyebrows lifted as she looked with disapproval at Adeferese. He swallowed hard. She held her gaze, waiting for him to speak.

Adeferese pointed at the paper he had brought her from the official in Debre Birhan. "You have the evidence in front of you that she was under foster care," Adeferese said. This set off a blaze of verbal whiplash from the judge, not only toward Adeferese, but at times toward Mesfin. Papers were flying and voices were getting louder and more passionate, except for Mesfin, who remained calm to the end.

"Your Honor," Mesfin softly spoke, "I believe you can see that this agency did not do their part for this adoptive family, nor did they do right by the child. Their job is to make sure the child is safe and in good care. He clearly did not check on any of these children and is now trying to save his reputation by accusing my clients of wrongdoing. He would rather give this child to a nonexistent foster care instead of a good family. He is proving that he has no interest in what is best for the child—only in his reputation."

"I do want the best for the child," Adeferese yelled out, "but I do not want my agency or my name damaged in the process!"

The judge cocked her head at his statement. He had said too much. Without a comment, the judge reached for her calendar and started looking for a date.

Adeferese began to say something, then abruptly stopped. The judge was done, and we could sense the chill in the courtroom.

"I will make my ruling sometime in the next two weeks," the judge said.

Our hearts sank. We looked at Mesfin for help.

"Your Honor," Mesfin quickly said.

The judge looked up, annoyed with the interruption.

"Your Honor, look at this man," he said, pointing toward Mark. Mark didn't have a clue what he was saying, although, he knew he was suddenly the center of conversation in the room. "This man is clearly exhausted. He has worn the same clothes for weeks now. They both miss and need to get back to their other children in America. Can we please have a ruling at a closer date? For the sake of this man?"

Everyone in the courtroom laughed, except Mark and me, who hadn't a clue what had just been said.

The judge looked at Mark, and for a moment, I saw pity in her eyes. "I will see you this coming Monday. I will write up my ruling over the weekend."

"Is Monday good for you?" Mesfin looked at us with triumph.

"Yes," I said. "That would be fine." Mark was silent. It was like the wind was out of his sails. I knew he was still hearing that we would be in Ethiopia for two more weeks, "Mark, she's going to give us a ruling this coming Monday."

"Really?" Mark asked in a daze. He looked toward the judge, "Thank you. Thank you."

The judge gave Mark a faint smile and wrote it down in her books.

Before we stood from our seats, Adeferese had left without a word. I turned and thanked the foster mother for coming and testifying for us. She began to go off on how disappointed she was that the judge didn't hand a verdict down and be finished with it all.

"Why wouldn't the judge tell you today?" The foster mother asked. "There is no question that Favor should be with you and they've done wrong. Something is not right. I think they got to her!"

I walked beside her in silence. I believed in our judge.

As we walked out the door, Emebet joined in on the conversation with the foster mom. They both were disappointed about the verdict not being handed down, and discussed among themselves what must've happened. My attention was quickly drawn to Mesfin as he grabbed Mark and pulled him into the hallway. I could tell something was transpiring.

"All I'm saying," Mesfin whispered to Mark, "is that I feel very positive about your case."

"Did the judge say something to make you feel this way?" Mark asked.

"Adeferese presented a very weak case," Mesfin stated. "She was not happy that she waited so long for a piece of paper that proved nothing. I feel very positive, but we'll have to wait until Monday to see which way she decides. She is a strong judge, and she will decide well. I hope nobody gets to her and tries to convince her otherwise."

"Do you think she would allow that?" Mark asked.

"No," Mesfin said. "I just know that they will try. She is strong. She will do what is right. I believe I made a strong case."

Mark listened. His mind was trying to grasp everything Mesfin was saying, but his body was tired and he was emotionally spent.

"The whole reason they say they are not letting you have Favor is that she is in a foster care program," Mesfin continued, "but they have no proof that the foster care exists or has done anything for her care. The orphanage is the only one taking care of her. The orphanage has paid for everything."

* * * * *

The street was full as we walked out of the courtroom. Mark noticed Adeferese talking on the phone near one of the courtroom offices that faced the street. He didn't look happy as he paced back and forth, speaking in an irritated tone.

"Wonder what that conversation is about?" I asked.

"I don't know," Mark said. "He doesn't look happy about something." We both watched him as unobtrusively as we could, until he looked up. We looked away for a moment, only to look back and see that he had disappeared.

"He is not happy with today," Mesfin said with a smile. "That is a good sign. I am confident we have a strong case. You can have a good weekend, knowing you did all you could, and you did it right." At that, Mesfin gave us a hug and walked up the sidewalk toward his car. Mark called Dave and found out they were parked up the street from where we stood, so we began to walk in that direction. McKenzie was the first one out of the car. She ran to us and quickly grabbed me for a long hug.

"I'm so glad you're done!" McKenzie said. "It took forever!"

"Mommy!" Favor yelled as she threw her arms around my waist. It felt good to have them both in my arms again.

"Now you know why we left you at The Academy those other times," I said to McKenzie. "Was it a long day?" Neither girl answered me, and I noticed that McKenzie didn't seem like herself. "You okay?"

"Yeah," she said, then looked away.

My eyes searched for hers. "You sure?" I asked.

"Yeah, why wouldn't I be?" She gave me a big smile and another hug. "I just missed you."

"I missed you!" I said, squeezing them both in my arms.

"The girls are very happy to see Mama." I turned around to see the foster mother standing behind me with Emebet and Dave. "Favor, come give me a hug," the foster mom said, holding her hands out to Favor. Favor went to give her a hug and a kiss on both cheeks. "You look so pretty!" Favor gave a timid smile and looked at me.

"She is a pretty girl," I said. "I need to get a picture of you with Favor." I reached in to get my camera and snapped some pictures of Favor with Emebet, Dave, and the foster mom.

Emebet, Dave, and Favor's foster mother with Favor after court on Friday.

"You are the strong one," the foster mother said. "He's weak."

"What?" I asked, thoroughly confused at what she was talking about.

She pointed toward Mark, who was wiping away tears from his eyes.

"See," she said, "he is crying. You are strong." She had an interesting but very flawed perspective. I knew my husband was not weak. Worn out and a little sensitive at the moment—but not weak.

"What's going on?" I asked Mark, hoping it was something I could handle hearing.

Mark was standing next to DJ, who had been one of our mightiest prayer warriors. Mark couldn't answer me as he fought back tears and pointed to DJ.

"I was telling Mark that I had a dream last night," DJ said. "The judge was handing you papers." He was fighting to hold back tears himself. "She was saying to you, 'You can take your daughter and go home.'"

Mark's eyes watered up again and the tears started to flow. The load of the past three-and-a-half weeks had taken their toll, and his emotions were raw. The desire of our hearts was to hear those words. DJ's dream was a confirmation of what we knew in our spirits to be true.

"Thank you, DJ. I believe it will happen," I said.

"God is a good God!" DJ said, "He will help you have victory. Favor will go home with you. This, I believe!"

"Yes," I proclaimed as I raised my arm in victory.

"Yes," the foster mother said, pointing her finger at me, "You are a fighter. See? Strong!"

I turned back around and looked at Mark. I knew she was trying to build me up as a woman, and I appreciated her tenacity, but if she only knew how far from the truth her statement was. Mark was the strongest man I knew, and as tears ran down his cheeks, I saw the man I fell in love with. The tears were proof of his strength—they moved me and confirmed what I already knew about his tender heart. He was with me, a warrior for the orphan, and for his family. I couldn't love him any more than I did right at that moment.

We said our goodbyes and thanked everyone for coming before we got into the car. I had barely gotten the girls in the back seat when I noticed two men approaching Mark. One, in his 30s, was a nice looking man who was guiding the older man by the hand. The older man stumbled with his stick, trying to avoid tripping on the curb. His eyes were completely white and we knew he was blind. He put his hands out, begging for money as the younger man asked for our help. I found a few birr and placed it in the man's hand, but Mark stopped him.

In an instant, Mark put his hand on the man's eyes and prayed that Jesus would heal him and for his eyes to be opened. "Be healed in Jesus' name!" Mark said. Everyone stood still. "In Jesus' name, be healed," Mark repeated.

The old man looked up and smiled at Mark as the younger man started pulling him away from where we stood. We could tell that he was not pleased that Mark had just put his hand on the older man, but as we got in the car, both men stopped and looked back at Mark. The younger man was now smiling as his old friend gave Mark a huge, toothless smile. His eyes were no longer white as before.

"Did you see that?" I asked Mark.

"Yeah," Mark answered, and watched as the men walked away from us.

"Wow," I said, "What got into you, oh Mighty Man of God?"

"I just thought, here's a blind man...the Bible says to lay hands on him and believe, so, I did."

Mark crawled in the front seat of the car, and Dave started to drive us back to The Academy as usual—but somewhere on the streets of Addis Ababa, I believe that an old man who once was blind, now sees.

Chapter 26

Be Still and Wait

"...Therefore take up the whole armor of God, that you may be able to withstand in the evil day, and having done all, to stand firm."

—Ephesians 6:13, ESV

The trip back to The Academy was quiet and long. Mark looked down and saw a new pair of thong sandals.

"New sandals," Mark said nonchalantly.

Dave didn't look down, but kept his eyes straight ahead. Mark thought nothing of it as he continued to watch the crowds that filled the streets in Addis Ababa.

The girls held me close as we drove. I loved having them near me.

"You see what you've missed?" I asked, "This is what we do every time we've had to go to court and leave you."

"I'll take The Academy any day," McKenzie said. "I hated today."

"I'm sorry," I said, "I know it was a huge bore to you."

McKenzie pulled back and looked at me. I could see she was about to say something, then she looked around, shook her head and placed it on my shoulder, drawing close to my side. I kissed her on the forehead and leaned into her. I knew my little girl, and something was bothering her, but I could sense that this wasn't the place to talk about it.

The streets were packed with people and cars as we approached The Academy, and Dave couldn't drive an inch. We could see the big black gate to The Academy within walking distance from where we were stuck.

"Why don't you let us out here and we can walk?" Mark suggested.

"It's so close, and there is no way you'll get across this road. It's packed." Mark could see Dave wasn't sure about his suggestion.

"I can take care of all these girls," Mark said, and puffed out his chest.

Dave smiled. He still looked uncomfortable with the idea, but he was running late with his plans, and he needed to get to the men's camp.

"Besides," Mark added, "Heaven help any man who tries to get close to my wife! She was raised with three older brothers, and she can take people out if they try anything."

At that, Dave laughed and nodded that he was okay with Mark's request. I had the girls cover their heads and gather their things, and we all jumped out of the car into a crowd of hurried strangers. I took the girls' hands in mine and held them tight as Mark grabbed McKenzie's hand. We pushed through the crowd until we stood in front of the welcoming black gate of The Academy. The security men greeted us and let us into our little home away from home.

Mark returned our day bags to the apartment and tried to check our emails, while I took the girls to the little snack shop on campus for some Injera bread with Shiro. Then I ordered some coffee and popcorn for Mark and me. Altogether, it only cost us 25 birr, which would be the equivalent of two American dollars. As we stood and waited for our order, several people approached us to ask how our court appearance went. They each seemed genuinely interested in every detail. It touched me that so many people on this campus were concerned and had been praying faithfully for us.

Mark joined us a few minutes later. The internet was down because of a fluke accident. It had been turned off when the computer guy came to shut down the dial-up service and activate the broadband connection. They had turned off the wrong one, so we couldn't contact our prayer warriors to tell them how our court date went. Later we would find out that God was in all the details, but for now, I knew they would be chomping at the bit to hear something, so we called Julie and asked if she could post something on our Facebook page to thank them for their ongoing prayers. Julie was happy to help out.

McKenzie and Favor enjoying their daily Shiro with Injera bread at the coffee house at The Academy.

That night we joined the school in the gym for the loud and exciting championship boys volleyball game. McKenzie had made some signs to hold up to cheer for the boys from The Academy. It didn't take long before Favor grabbed them both and headed to the top bleacher to cheer with the other girls on campus. McKenzie laughed then joined in with Favor and the rowdy crowd. I don't think either girl has a shy bone in her body, and that cheering must've worked. The boys won the Championship.

McKenzie ran down to me with something exciting to share. "Mom," she squealed, "the girls that live on campus have asked me to join them at a sleepover tonight. Can I do it? Please?"

I paused. "Did they ask just you, or did they ask for you and Favor to spend the night?"

"Just me," McKenzie said. "Mom, please? They live in the same building, down the hallway. I won't be far from you."

It had been almost four weeks since McKenzie had spent time with her friends back home. I knew she was lonely for some girl time. It would be good for her and us.

"Okay," I said. "Be careful. I'll take care of your dad."

McKenzie let out a shriek and threw her arms around my neck saying, "Thank you, thank you, thank you! I am so excited they asked."

"Just be careful!" I said. "You aren't allowed to leave the campus, okay?"

"No," she said, "We're staying here. I'll drop in to get my PJs later." At that, she ran off to tell a group of girls waiting nearby. A group scream went out and everyone left in the gym turned to look.

"What was that about?" Mark asked.

"I'll tell you later," I said. I looked up at Favor jumping down the bleachers one row at a time. "You ready to go?" She quickly made her way down and grabbed my hand.

"What about Kenzie?" Mark asked, watching her run out the side door with a group of girls.

"She's having a sleepover with some of the girls that live on campus," I said.

"And, we're okay with that?" he asked. "Do you know these people?"

"Yes, I know these people. They've been praying for us, and I grocery shop with her mom. McKenzie's been through a lot. I'm okay with her having a night with girls. They live right down the hallway from our apartment. If she needs us, we're practically within an earshot. Are you okay with that?"

Mark gave me a sheepish look. "Just asking," he said. Then he made the sound of a cat hissing.

I started laughing. I guess I had come on a little strong with my sales pitch. I grabbed his hand and the three of us walked to our apartment for an evening together playing the memory game.

* * * * *

The phone woke us up Saturday morning with a call from McKenzie. Her friend's parents, Leann and Tom, had invited us down for some waffles. We were so excited to have anything resembling American food that we tripped over each other trying to get dressed and out the door.

After we gorged ourselves on gluten-filled waffles, Mark took off with Tom, and I stayed to have a long talk with Leann before we joined back up to watch a soccer game at the complex. I did my best to get into the game, but watching kids play soccer only stirred my emotions and made me miss my son Shewit. I sat there and embraced the fact that I was in the land of his birth—the land where he first learned the love of soccer. He was already one of the top players for our local travel team, and he has dreams of becoming a professional player.

I was extremely homesick, and I could barely stand being in Ethiopia for one more minute. I could feel that sick feeling run through my veins and my eyes heat up with tears. I wanted to see my boys, hold them, smell them, even if they smelled like dirty laundry or a boys locker room. I didn't care—my arms and heart ached for them. Then I had a sinking feeling. *What if this takes longer than we think? What if we're here for months?*

"Mark," I said, "do you think we'll win?"

Mark took a deep breath before he answered, "I don't know. I don't know what to expect. I feel like we have a strong case, and so does Mesfin."

"What if," I paused. "What if, for some reason, it's not over Monday and we have to stay longer?"

Mark looked down at the ground. He breathed out an audible sigh, as though the thought brought exhaustion to him.

"I don't know if I can stay any longer," I said. "I miss the boys too much."

"What are you saying?" Mark asked.

I didn't want to admit that I couldn't take anymore, but I could feel that I was at my end. "I've just come to a place that I just want to go home," I said. "No matter what. I don't have the energy to keep fighting."

"I don't believe you," Mark said. "You're tired and you just need some rest."

"No," I said, "I need my family to be together again. All of us. I want to hug my boys. I miss them so much." I could feel the tears building up in my eyes.

Mark looked up and squinted, the bright Ethiopian sun was beating down on us. "Favor is part of our family now," he said. "We can't leave her."

"What if they don't give us a choice?" I asked. "We've got three other kids to think about."

"I know," Mark whispered, "but, I don't believe God would bring us this far to lose like that. Where is that fighter I traveled here with to rescue her daughter from the bad guys? What's happened?"

I sat on the bench next to my husband. I was exhausted and couldn't think past that moment.

"We have to hold on to what God told us!" Mark said emphatically. "He said we would have victory, then He sent a prophet to our hotel to remind us that we will have victory."

"I do believe," I said. "I'm praying, believing, and I do have a peace that Favor will be allowed to come home with us. She will be ours." I paused. "I'm just not sure it will be Monday. What if it takes several more months?"

"Why would it?" Mark asked as if he couldn't believe his ears.

I didn't want to admit what I was thinking. I didn't want to give any room to the enemy. "It's just...every time we get our hopes up that we're going to go home, we get disappointed. There's always something else. I'm tired of waiting to take my daughter home."

Mark put his arm around me and pulled me close. "Me too," he said. "Me too," and he kissed my forehead. We sat in silence. There were no more words.

* * * * *

That night, I boiled some potatoes and served them with salt and butter. The girls loved smashing them up in their bowls. They quickly got filled up, then helped me with clean up.

"I'll be right back," Mark said as he walked out the door.

"Girls, get your PJs on and brush your teeth," I said. "We have church at Pastor's tomorrow."

"Yes!" Favor said with excitement. "Pochi?"

"Yes, Pochi's church."

"I love that church Mom," McKenzie said. "They have fun."

"They do! I can't wait to get in that atmosphere. I love it!" I said.

"You mean you love to worship," McKenzie said.

"I do," I said with a smile.

Mark walked in, carrying a black computer. "Tom let us borrow his computer. He has this gadget on it that allows us about 15 minutes of internet."

"Really?" I said. "I can send out a quick email to our friends and family. Catch them up."

"First, I'm going to book our flight back for Tuesday night." Mark said.

"All four of us?" McKenzie asked. Mark didn't say anything, and kept trying to get the connection up.

"All four of us?" she asked again.

"Honey," I asked, "Did you hear your daughter?"

Mark looked up at McKenzie then back at me, "All four of us," he said. Both girls screamed out with glee and started jumping around the room.

I smiled and gave him a big hug as he kept typing away.

"I believe," Mark said as he connected with our agent and booked four seats back to America for the coming Tuesday night.

"Me too," I said. Something about taking our words of faith and putting them into action pulled me out of the gloominess that had tried to depress me all day. Mark and I believed that we could go home on Tuesday, with no plan B, or C, for that matter. God gave us His promise: He had given us a victory. We had His word, and we shut the door on all other possibilities, because we served a God who could perform the impossible.

I quickly sent our prayer warriors a message to let them know how it went in court, and to give them the news that we had our flights booked for all four of us to return to the U.S. We had faith that all of us were coming home, and we had decided to start offering thanks to God for what we knew He had already done. Our flight was to arrive back in Nashville the night before Thanksgiving Day, and we were going to live out the rest of this journey in thanksgiving and praise!

* * * * *

The church was alive with worship when we walked onto the property. Pastor waved to us from a distance. "It is a good day!"

he exclaimed loudly. "God is good, my friends!" There was no better way to start living out the rest of our journey than at a faith-filled church, and we came expecting God to show up.

"Yes He is," Mark yelled back. We were greeted with smiles as we walked into the church building. It seemed to be vibrating with joy. We walked toward the front until we found a seat. In the middle of worship, a beautiful little girl, about five years old, walked across the aisle to McKenzie, putting some green seeds in the palm of her hand. McKenzie looked down and got a big smile on her face.

McKenzie replied, "Amasedganalo (Ah-meh-she-guh-NAH-loh)," which means thank you.

The little girl's eyes sparkled and opened up with surprise. She started speaking to McKenzie in Amharic, thinking she knew her language, but McKenzie stood there clueless, smiling and nodding her head in agreement. The little girl reached up and hugged her; then she scampered back to sit with her mother and an older brother.

"Mom," McKenzie asked, "What are these?"

I looked at the seeds in the palm of her hand, I'd never seen them.

"What do I do with them?" McKenzie asked.

The older brother waved to us and showed how to break them open and eat the seed inside. He was holding a branch full of the seed pods in his hand. It looked like a weed or something they picked on their way to church.

"Okay," McKenzie said, "should I eat one?"

"Let's try one," I said. "I don't think it's bad or their momma wouldn't let them eat it."

During the next few minutes, McKenzie and I tried to open the pod, a job far more complicated than a seven-year-old boy made it seem. We got one partially opened, and to our surprise, the seed shot out like a bullet over the audience, hitting a man three rows in front of us on the head. The man looked back, scratching his head. McKenzie ducked and I closed my eyes to worship. Now the challenge was on, we had to beat this seed pod. So we tried again, and this time, we kept the seed in our hands. I tried it first. It tasted like a mild piñon or pine nut seed like we have in America. I could see I had an audience waiting to see if I liked it, so I looked their way and gave a thumbs up. Then McKenzie tried a seed. The family was overjoyed that they had shared their treasure with us. It was one of the sweetest things to see them share the way they did—especially since we knew food was one of their most valued possessions.

After church, the attorney that was representing the orphanage in court swiftly made his way to Mark. He was vivacious and almost glowing with a huge smile.

"How are you and your wife feeling about your case?" he asked Mark.

"We feel good," Mark said. "We're just standing and believing."

The attorney, as if pausing for effect, stopped and smiled a knowing smile. "This has been so powerful to watch what God has done through your family. Your faith has inspired me to have more faith in God," he said.

He looked down at his shoes then up at Mark with a grin, "You make sure to call me before you leave," he said. "Okay?" At that, he hugged Mark and gave him a sturdy handshake before turning and walking toward Pochi.

"That's all you're going to tell me?" Mark yelled to him.

He turned and smiled.

Pochi and Pastor walked up to us. "We want to take you out to lunch," Pochi said. "Where would you like to go?"

"That's your call," Mark said.

"You liked the Italian restaurant overlooking Addis a lot," Pochi said. "Let's go to Topview."

* * * * *

At the restaurant, packed with people coming out to eat after church, we pulled two tables together under an umbrella on the patio. Pochi and Pastor were all smiles as we settled in for an Italian lunch on the mountain.

"So," I said, "What was your attorney so excited about today?

"He says that everyone is talking about this case. They are all very excited to see how it comes out. It amazes people in so many ways," Pochi said.

"Why is that?" Mark asked.

"You are going up against very powerful people for the sake of a little girl," Pochi said. "This makes people think about David and Goliath. God is the only way you could win this."

"God *is* the only way we can win," Mark agreed.

"Yes," Pochi agreed. "This is why it amazes people so much. They want you to win."

People wanted us to win. That statement profoundly moved us. Complete strangers were watching and waiting, alongside friends and family, to see how a little girl's future would unfold. It was a David-and-Goliath, a good-versus-evil tale.

"Have you heard anything about the official in Debre Birhan?" I asked.

"He is very angry," Pastor said, shaking his head.

Pochi started laughing and said, "He called the foster mother Friday night and harassed her for going and testifying for you. He called so late that it only made her mad, and she let him have it. Oh, she was angry at him."

Pastor made a comedic face, like he'd seen that anger flare up before.

"Can they do anything to her?" I asked.

"For what?" Pochi said. "She went in and told the truth. That's all. She told him that she went because it was the right thing to do."

Mark and I listened as Pochi continued to share all that had happened since our court date on Friday.

"She asked him, 'Why wouldn't you want me to testify, if I was only going to tell what was the truth? What was not the truth that I said?' He did not answer her." Pochi said.

"I think he needs to be a little scared of her. She's a strong one," I said as I looked toward Mark to see if he remembered Friday's statement.

"I'm weak," Mark said on cue.

"What?" Pochi asked, confused.

"Oh," Mark explained, "She had said I was weak on Friday, because she caught me crying over something DJ said to me. It didn't bother me."

"She is a very strong woman though, to stand up to an official like that. She's got some guts!" I said.

Pastor smiled and nodded his head in agreement.

"She cares about these children," Pochi said. "She has been with me a long time, and she does not like to see what they are doing to these children. She knows it is wrong. We all do."

"Well, we will forever be grateful that she kept Favor and these other kids out of the hands of the a foster care program," I said.

"How is Emebet?" I asked.

"They are calling to harass her too," Pochi said, "but she doesn't answer her phone."

"She's a strong one too," I said. Favor leaned up against me, ready to leave. "I wonder how strong this one will turn out."

Pochi looked at Favor getting into my lap. "She is a very strong little girl," Pochi said. "God has big plans for her—I'm sure of it." Favor sat in my lap as we enjoyed the rest of our time with Pochi and Pastor.

Feeling the breeze blow across the mountain top as the sun beat down on us, I felt—for the first time—that our battle could be coming to a close. We had done everything that we were asked to do, and I didn't want to miss what God was going to do next. So, having done all, we now stood and waited on God to do the rest.

CHAPTER 27
JUDGEMENT DAY

"He doesn't call the qualified,
He qualifies the called."

—Mark Batterson, author of *The Circle Maker*

I awakened with excruciating pain shooting through my body. My eyes could barely focus as I searched the pitch black room for any sign of light. I was freezing, but was covered with every blanket we had. I reached to find my phone, but it was nowhere to be found.

Then the pain shot through me again. I grabbed my stomach and cried out, praying God would take the pain away. *Was it food poisoning?* I couldn't believe how much pain I was in. I dropped to my knees from the bed and slowly made my way to a standing position. I stumbled in the dark until I felt my way to the bathroom door. In the quiet, and for a moment, I thought I was in the middle of a bad dream. I felt disoriented and I could feel myself losing consciousness. I turned to get Mark...I needed help. I took a step toward the bedroom and felt myself falling into blackness.

"Honey," I heard Mark's voice in the dark, "Honey, talk to me. Are you okay?" I could feel Mark's arms holding me up. He must've caught me before I hit the floor.

"I need help," I whispered. I had no strength in my body.

"What's going on?" Mark asked, "Do you need the bathroom or to go to bed?"

"I feel sick," I mumbled.

Mark walked me into the bathroom and put a towel around my shoulders. Although it was warm outside, I was shivering uncontrollably, feeling as if I would rather be dead than withstand this pain. All I could pray was, *Please take away this pain and please God, don't let that guy with the bad pitch start singing over the bullhorn.*

Somehow I awoke to find myself lying on the floor of that small bathroom with my head in the shower stall, throwing up. I'm sure I was a fabulous sight to behold as sounds of a dying cow filled our small apartment. I crawled back to my bed and fell asleep until Mark woke me at noon.

* * * * *

Mark had taken care of the girls all morning. I woke up refreshed and ready to face the day, like nothing had happened. It was hard to believe that just hours before, I felt like I was going to die on our bathroom floor.

I started singing an old song that I used to sing in church called "We Have Overcome." I couldn't get it out of my head, so I found it on YouTube. The girls started laughing when they saw me dancing and singing, declaring the words for our case. Favor giggled and started dancing alongside me as I tried to get Mark and McKenzie to drop their cool factor and join us.

An hour later, we all made our way down to the staff's area lounge for Tea Time—the best part of the day—with Ethiopian coffee, pastries, and our new friends from the campus. One by one, they made their way over to where we sat. Most of them just wanted to let us know that they were praying and believing that we would get good news. A few friends invited us to join them for Thanksgiving dinner if we happened to still be in Ethiopia, although they did apologize that it would be a Thanksgiving dinner without the turkey and pumpkin pie. All the things we had taken for granted back home hit the reality pavement of my mind. This is what the thousands of American missionaries give up all the time to bring Jesus to others in foreign lands. They give up not only the turkey and the pumpkin pies but also the luxuries and traditions that we don't think twice about in the States. My one month homesick stage was just a glimpse into what they do for years without complaint. I felt sad, not because I might not have turkey for Thanksgiving, but because I hadn't seen or recognized all that missionaries do for God's Kingdom and their many sacrifices—no matter how big or small.

Jody walked over to me with a small gift in her hand. Favor and McKenzie followed closely behind, watching my every reaction. "The girls and I made you a little something the other day," Jody said, handing me a small, woven brown bag. "I know today's a big day, and hopefully this will be a wonderful memory of this time and not a painful one, but we're all hoping you're going to get good news today. I debated whether to give it to you now or after you heard the verdict. Then I decided that it's all going to be good."

"Thank you, Jody." I said, "You've done so much. What would we have done if you hadn't been here? Seriously." I was touched as I took the bag in my hands and started to slowly reveal the treasure inside. I pulled out a silver I.D. bracelet with "I love Mom" etched on the front and "Ethiopia 2012" on the inside.

"Favor wrote the 'I love Mom' and McKenzie did the 'Ethiopia 2012' on the inside," Jody pointed out.

"I love it! It will be a wonderful memory, no matter what, because you made it for me. Thank you!" I turned to the girls and gave them a big hug. "I'll never forget Ethiopia 2012. It's been a life challenge and a life-changer. I don't want to miss what God wants to do with all this."

"That is for sure," Jody said, "and I'm sure you won't."

"I know I won't forget it," McKenzie said with an awkward smile, then turned and joined her new friends outside on the covered porch. I glanced at Jody with a knowing look and back towards McKenzie. I knew that behind her smile, there was a little girl who was hurting deeply and just wanted to be back home.

"I'm sorry," Jody said. "I can see this has been hard on her."

I nodded my head in agreement.

"My girls went through a very hard time of homesickness when we first got here," Jody continued. "They still have little bouts with it, but we didn't have all this other stress piled on that your family does. I know McKenzie will be okay. She's a strong girl."

"Thank you," I answered. "I know you all are transitioning too. I don't think McKenzie was expecting a trip quite like this. There's a part of me that wishes we hadn't brought her, but then another side that realizes, what would we have done without her?"

* * * * *

We arrived at court at 2:55 p.m., five minutes before our court appointment. Our stomachs were turning as we ran up the three flights of stairs and into the waiting area. Out of breath, we walked into a normally packed waiting room to find only Jamila and EAI's lawyer, discussing something that abruptly ended when they saw us. We took our seats and caught our breath. Mesfin hadn't arrived, so Mark texted him to see how far he was from us. Jamila and the lawyer walked out into the hallway. Mark and I sat alone.

"I don't see Adeferese," I said.

"Yeah," Mark replied. He was distracted by an email on his phone.

"What?" I asked and tried to look at what had grabbed his attention.

Mark quickly shut his phone off and took a deep breath.

"Who was that from?" I questioned.

"It's not important," he said.

I looked at him. There was tension all over his body. Maybe he was worried about the verdict.

"We're going to win this," I declared.

Mark looked at me with no expression. "I hope so," he said.

I didn't know what was up with my husband, but I was sure it had to do with the email. At that moment, Mark received a text from Mesfin. He was down the street, grabbing a bite to eat, and would be there soon.

"He'll be here soon?" I asked, "Does he remember what time we have our appointment?"

"Yes," Mark said, "he knows. He's coming."

I could feel the stress in every word Mark said.

Jamila and the lawyer walked in and took a seat not too far from us. I looked at them. This agency had caused so much trouble for us, but today I felt a shift. They weren't as confident and arrogant. Jamila glanced at us and managed a weak smile. Her eyes had softened toward us.

The young lady who calls us into the courtroom came out to let us know the judge was ready to see us. We asked for a few more minutes to give Mesfin time to make it there.

"What's going on?" I asked.

"We got a few emails this weekend," Mark said. "They were from EAI America and Adeferese."

"What did they say?" I asked, with a knot quickly forming near my throat.

Mark shook his head in a way I recognized, and the news wasn't good. "Adeferese obviously got to them, and now they refuse to help us in any way. They are saying we took illegal actions, and they didn't have all the information or the facts. I saw an attached email from Adeferese to them that was telling

EAI America that we were doing criminal actions, and our lawyer didn't understand how serious this was."

"So they're believing his lies," I said.

"His side of the story," Mark corrected me.

"No," I stood my ground. "He lied to them about us. You don't pass court and Embassy—and then go through a court process again to win a daughter that's already yours—and call that criminal action. What a pile of..." I was so angry that I wanted to scream.

"I know," Mark said. "That's why I haven't shown you the emails."

"When were the emails sent?" I asked.

"That's the funny thing," Mark said with a grin. "They were all sent on Friday after we finished court, right after our internet went down at The Academy."

"Well," I laughed, "obviously God didn't want us to get them. I bet He was behind that little fluke accident with the internet. He wanted us to have a quiet weekend, free from harassment."

"Yep," Mark laughed.

"Bummer that everyone had to suffer no internet this weekend!" I said. "Don't tell them it was us. Can I see the email?"

"It'll just make you mad," Mark said.

"That bad?" I asked.

"Every sentence Adeferese wrote to EAI America has misinformation in some way. It's bad." Mark was right—I didn't want or need to see it.

Mesfin walked into the waiting room with a big smile on his face and sat next to Mark. Mark pulled out his phone and showed him the email from EAI America and Adeferese.

"This is what we got in our email box a few minutes ago," Mark said as he handed his phone to Mesfin to read.

"They sent this today?" Mesfin looked up at Mark with a curious look.

"They sent it Friday after court," Mark clarified, "but we just got it today."

Mesfin finished reading the email and shook his head. "Lies to scare you," he said. "They know they have no case, so they try to scare you to hand over the child." Mesfin smiled with a grin that said it all then licked his bottom lip. "This tells me they are scared that you are going to win."

"Really?" Mark asked. "Because it sounds to me like they are trying to throw us in prison if we don't hand her over."

"The judge would tell you to hand her over if she thought she was in any danger," Mesfin said.

The young lady came out of the judge's room and saw that Mesfin had arrived. "The Mark Wortons," she said. We all stood up quickly and walked into the small room that held the mystery we all hoped would unfold in our favor. I greeted the young lady with a smile and looked around the courtroom. A young man sat at his laptop typing away. He paused long enough to glance up and give us a smile. The judge was looking over some paperwork on her desk before she looked up and greeted us with an expressionless, "Hello."

She took a breath and asked the attorneys to stand up for the reading of the verdict, which she held in her hands. Mesfin stood up in the back of the room, next to Jamila and EAI's lawyer.

She began reading in Amharic, and again we found our lives in the balance, not understanding a word that was being said about a decision that would forever leave a mark on us. As she read the three-page verdict, I reached for Mark's hand. We were both shaking from nerves. I closed my eyes to pray and find peace in this moment. From the depth of my spirit I heard, "Today, I will vindicate you." I instantly felt peace, and I knew the battle had been won.

* * * * *

I remembered the dream that a little orphan boy had dreamt three years earlier, about a python that had four children cornered, ready to steal, kill, and destroy their future. I could see the heel of Jesus coming down upon the python's head, and the sword of truth slicing through the body of this slithery, demonic spirit, letting it fall powerlessly to the ground. I saw Jesus standing victoriously, and I saw four children running to embrace their forever families.

* * * * *

I looked up to see the young court reporter smiling and nodding his head *yes* at us. I quickly shifted my eyes to where Mesfin was standing, listening as the judge continued to read the verdict. He was smiling from ear to ear. He looked at me and acknowledged his approval of what was being read. I turned to Mark and whispered in his ear, "We won, I think we won. Look at Mesfin." Mark quickly turned to see Mesfin looking at both of us with a smile.

As the judge wrapped up the verdict, the room suddenly erupted with celebration. Everyone was smiling and congratulating us before we even knew what had happened.

We sat stunned as Jamila and the EAI lawyer made their way to us with hands extended, "Congratulations," she said with a sincere smile. "We are very happy for you and your child."

"Thank you," Mark and I replied, still trying to grasp that the battle was over. Before we could say another word, they were gone.

"You won!" Mesfin declared. "You won!"

Mark and I looked at the judge to make sure everything we were hearing was true. Did she just declare us victorious? We watched as she closed the three-page handwritten verdict and looked up at us.

"You can take your daughter and go home," she said, smiling the biggest smile I had seen her reveal in our five meetings in this small courtroom. They were the very words DJ had dreamed about nights before, and they were the words we had waited to hear for what seemed like forever. *"Take your daughter and go home."* The sweetest words to our ears.

I looked at the judge, who had joy in her eyes! She looked as if a heavy burden had been taken off her shoulders. I knew I was looking in the face of a woman who sought to do the right thing. There was no doubt that she had been receiving heavy pressure about our case, and judging in our favor could not have been easy, but she had stood strong. We were thankful for the courage she showed.

"Thank you," I said in her native language.

"You're welcome," she said in English. "Your daughter is a very loved child."

"Yes, she is," I said. "We will take good care of her."

"Yes," she said. "I know you will."

"Thank you," I said one more time before Mark and I turned to leave the courtroom.

* * * * *

Mark looked at Mesfin and took a huge breath, "It's over," Mark said, and they both reached out to give each other a big hug. "Do we need anything to take to immigration to pick up her passport and visa?"

Mesfin paused before running back into the courtroom and reappearing a few seconds later. "They are going to take the verdict downstairs to have the lady type it out for you. You need to take it to immigration," Mesfin said. "It will only take a few minutes, maybe 15."

"Will that give us time to get to immigration?" Mark asked.

"Yes," Mesfin was thinking, "I think the immigration office closes at five this evening." He glanced at his watch. "It is just a little past three now."

* * * * *

Mark informed Dave that we had won the case, and we would be down in 15 minutes. After 45 minutes had passed, Mesfin started pacing the floor, sticking his head into the judge's office. Mark and I watched as the secretary walked past him to go down the stairs to where the verdict was being typed for us. A few minutes later, the elevator door opened and the secretary stepped out and motioned for Mesfin to come to her.

Mesfin talked with her, then slowly walked back to where Mark and I were sitting. "It looks like this lady has been bribed to type your verdict slowly," Mesfin whispered. "This lady is their transcriber and usually very fast. Today, not so much."

"Why would they do that?" I asked.

Mesfin shook his head in disbelief.

"Is it to keep us from getting to immigration today?" I asked. "We won. What on Earth could they do?"

"They sent someone down to replace her and get it done for you," Mesfin said. "It shouldn't take much longer now."

Mark and I continued to wait. We could see Dave and the girls parked on the street below us. Even though we had won, the enemy was still in a battle with us.

Mesfin walked us down to the first floor waiting area where our verdict was being typed out. The moment we entered, as if on script, everyone paused and looked up from their work to stare at us. Mesfin said something in Amharic and they all went back to work. After a few minutes, Mesfin asked Mark to bring his wallet. They were charging us for the copy they had typed, but at least it was done. I looked at my watch, it was 4:55—too late to make it to immigration. We would have to wait until they opened tomorrow morning.

With the copy of our victorious verdict in hand, we rushed out to see our girls, who had been waiting patiently with Dave. As we walked down the sidewalk toward their car, the back door opened and Favor stepped out. Her smile was effervescent as she ran toward us with open arms.

"America...we go now?" She squealed as she jumped into my arms, squeezing my neck in excitement.

"Yes," I said through tears. "America...all of us!" I put Favor down and she jumped into Mark's arms as he covered her face with kisses.

"My girl," he said. "My girl."

McKenzie rushed over to us and joined in the celebration. We were all so happy to be going home together.

McKenzie, Favor, and I celebrating the news that the long wait to go home is over!

"Yay!" McKenzie said. "What took you so long?"

"We had a secretary who acted like she'd never typed before," I said.

"What?" McKenzie said, confused. "I'm just happy it's over. Are we leaving tonight?"

"We have to get her passport and visa tomorrow, but then we'll fly out tomorrow night. We have to go home and pack!" I said.

"But first," Mark said, "We need to run out to the airport and see if we can pick up her passport and visa."

* * * * *

Dave drove us out to the airport. It was a quiet night, so we were able to park close to the entrance. The girls and I stayed in the car while Mark ran to the immigration office entrance and knocked on the door. The woman, who had shown us no compassion on the night we were stopped at the airport, opened the door. Mark recognized her and caught his breath before speaking.

"Hi," Mark said, "I was the person you stopped about three weeks ago with my family. You took my daughter's passport and visa."

"Yes," she said, "I remember you."

"Really?" Mark asked, hoping she wasn't being sarcastic.

"Of course," she responded.

"We just won our court case," Mark said.

"Congratulations!" she said with a smile.

"Thank you," Mark said, "I was wondering if I could pick up her passport and visa from you?"

"No," she responded, "not here. It was sent down to the main immigration office. Do you still have the pink receipt we gave you?"

"Yes," Mark said.

"Good. Make sure you get a letter from them that verifies her release to leave the country."

Not wanting to question why he needed a letter when he had a valid passport and visa, Mark said, "Thank you. We'll see you tomorrow."

"Good luck," she said with a smile.

* * * * *

That night we were greeted with congratulatory remarks everywhere we went at The Academy. They were thrilled at the news of our victory. Back in the States, my Facebook post was spreading the word fast that we had won:

> God has WON the battle and He has given us the VICTORY!! FAVOR is coming to America!!...It's going to be a Thanksgiving to remember. Thank you so much for all the prayers! All the glory goes to God!!

New and old friends alike were celebrating our victory as they saw our post. My brother Steve ran over to my parents' house to share the good news with my father, who wept to hear that his new granddaughter would be coming home to America. Donna, a precious friend from our church in Franklin was working at Panera Bread Company when she got the news. She yelled out with joy, and she told everyone standing in line and behind the counter how we had won the victory and could bring home our daughter. People then started clapping throughout the restaurant! Donna quickly called her husband Norm, who was traveling to a business appointment. Norm pulled his car over as he started weeping in thankfulness and praising God on the side of the road.

Mark decided to reach out to the vice-consul of the American Embassy and tell him about our victory. It was seven in the evening.

He answered on the second ring.

"Hi," Mark said, "this is Mark Worton."

"Hey Mark," the vice-consul responded.

"I wanted to call and let you know that we won our case today," Mark said. "We finally get to go home."

After a silent pause in the conversation, the vice-consul responded, "Oh...really?"

The vice-consul's response took Mark by surprise, as if it wasn't what he was expecting. He took a deep breath as he felt his heart come up to his throat.

"Yeah," Mark said, "we did."

"Well," the vice-consul said, "I need to check and see whether you'll need to come down to the Embassy and sign any additional documents before you go anywhere."

"Okay," Mark said, "let me know."

"I will call you tomorrow," the vice-consul said.

Mark hung up the phone. *God, can I at least get one win on this?* he asked. *I'm just asking for a pass. Do we have to battle out everything?*

His mind immediately went to the email he had received from EAI America with Adeferese's request for their help to stop us. He searched for any reason we would need to sign additional paperwork at the Embassy, and what should have been a night of celebration turned into another restless night of Mark playing out different scenarios in his head. *Could we have come this far and still be stopped?* As Mark wrestled with his concerns through the night, he prayed that God would make a way for us to get out safely and legally without any further delays or battles.

CHAPTER 28
SAYING GOODBYE

"We knew we had all been the audience for a great work of God."

—Missy Maxwell Worton

The next morning, lines of people were wrapped around the block, waiting to be seen by the immigration office. Some had camped out for days—possibly weeks. Others were now sitting under makeshift shelters to shield themselves from the intense heat of the sun. Hundreds of people were waiting as we pulled through the gate to the parking area. Two distinct lines of people pressed in toward the well-guarded gate: to the left was a line of women, and to our right were the men.

"I don't see where the end of the line is," I said.

"No wait," our driver said. "You are Americans. You go to front."

"Are you sure?" I asked. The last thing I wanted was to make a mob like this mad. He nodded his head that it would be okay.

I looked up at Mark, then around at all the people staring at us, waiting patiently for their turn. There had to be no less than 2,000 individuals trying to get in to see the immigration offices. I was nervous. I didn't want to walk past all of them and cut into the line. My heart started beating faster as Mark grabbed my hand and started walking toward the steps.

"We'll meet you back here," Mark told the driver.

"I will wait as long as it takes you," our driver replied.

I didn't want to let go of Mark's hand as we got closer to the entrance. I could feel people's eyes watching us. We had to separate when he walked through the men's entrance. I slowly walked over to the women's line and made a beeline to the entrance where a guard stood watch. I looked around—nobody seemed to be upset that I had cut in line.

The guard looked me over and directed me to go to a woman who was sitting in a chair. She was dressed in a burka from head to toe, and all I could see was her eyes. I gave her a nervous smile before she lifted my arms and started to give me a very intrusive pat down. I was then told to hand over my purse and all my belongings. I watched as the two women went through every pocket and studied everything I had brought. The main guard took my camera and phone. "We keep," she said. I must've given her a look of confusion because she gave me a smirk, "You finish, you come back and get."

"Do you have a claim form?" I asked. The woman looked at me. "How will you know those are mine when I come back?"

She turned to a young woman sitting behind her and mouthed off something in another language. The young woman quickly took out a tablet and wrote down a few words, ripped it from the sheet and handed it to me. I watched as they put my items in a drawer behind the guard. I had the uncomfortable feeling that I would never see my camera and phone again, as I was directed out of the security area and into a large courtyard.

I looked around for Mark, but he was nowhere to be found. I wasn't sure which building to go to or what to do next. So,

I stood there, hoping Mark would find me soon. After a few minutes, Mark emerged from a different direction than I had last seen him.

"What took you so long?" he asked me.

"I was busy getting my annual physical examination," I answered. "Where have you been?"

"I was finding out where we needed to go," Mark said, as he grabbed my hand and led me to a building on our left. We were directed to go to a small office at the far end of the building. We rushed to the room, only to find that the individuals who worked in it were not there and the door was locked. So, we waited.

After 30 minutes, a man walked in and took a seat at one of the desks. Mark approached him and handed him our pink claim form that the immigration officer had handed us the night that we were stopped at the airport. He took it from Mark's hand and looked it over before turning to glance over a long list on his desk.

"I need to go to the other desk to look for the passport," he said. We watched as he sat down and pulled out a large box full of manila envelopes filled with passports. One by one, he pulled the passports out, looking at the picture and name. Mark and I sat quietly as he methodically continued. After he had finished going through at least 60 to 100 passports, he walked back over to the list sitting upon his desk.

"I do not see where we received this passport from the airport," he said. "It must be at the airport or we did not receive it."

"No," Mark said. "It is not at the airport. I have already been out there, and they told me it was sent here over three weeks ago."

He walked back to the other desk and dumped out one of the manila envelopes, "I will look again," he said, and one by one, we watched as he went through the same stack he had just checked. After 15 minutes, he turned to us and said, "I am sorry, I cannot find the passport here. My colleague is not in today, but he will be back tomorrow. You can come back then."

"That is impossible," Mark said, "we fly out tonight."

The man looked at us and raised his shoulders like he didn't care.

"We have a flight out tonight," I said. "We need to find her passport."

"I am sorry," he said. "You will have to fly out tomorrow, you will not fly out today because you cannot travel without passport. He will be here tomorrow. I do not know where this passport has been taken."

"Where would be the logical place it would be taken?" Mark asked.

We both stared down the man for an answer. The man shifted uncomfortably in his seat. He knew that we weren't going anywhere without our daughter's passport, and most likely we would be camped out in his office, in his comfy chair, until we had it.

"Please, can you check with someone?" Mark pleaded. "We need your help."

"Let me check one place," he finally said. He picked up his phone and called another office in the building. When he hung up, he looked at us with relief.

"I believe they have your passport on the third floor," he said.

Mark and I thanked him, and we immediately ran up the marble steps to the third floor office. The room was at the end of a long, marble hallway. Tall windows lined the hallway to our right, opened wide, allowing the breeze to cool down the upper floor. To our left was a lone doorway to the office that held Favor's passport. Three women were working behind the desk in a large, one-room office, with curtains covering the back wall of windows. One of the women approached us.

"We're here to get our daughter's passport," Mark said, as he handed her the pink slip to claim it. She took the slip and looked at it, then walked over to an older woman sitting at the main desk and handed her the slip.

"Her name is Favor Mark Worton," Mark said.

"Oh," the woman said, "the Debre Birhan case." She looked up at us and gave us a smile, then went directly to a pile on a credenza in the back of the office. Mark and I looked at each other—*How did she know it was our case?* Everyone in the office stopped what they were doing and looked toward us. Each one gave us a gentle smile before continuing with their work.

On top of that credenza was Favor's passport and Visa.

"You have your court verdict for us?" she asked.

Mark quickly pulled out the three-page verdict and handed it to the woman holding Favor's passport. She looked it over, then handed it back to Mark.

"This needs to be read and verified," she said. "You must go to room #100. He will verify it for you and give you a stamp before I can give you this passport."

"Thank you," Mark said.

We left, and Mark had me sit outside of their office on an old bench while he ran down to have our paper verified. The breeze had a welcome calming effect on me as I sat alone in this cold but palatial hallway. I thanked God that there would be no more delays and that we would all be able to fly out as planned. God's peace continued to fill me. I knew the battle wasn't over, but I had faith that He would give us a complete victory in the end. I had learned to trust Him with my whole heart, and that alone created the greatest peace I'd known in my lifetime.

Outside, I could hear a great crowd gathering. I went to the window and watched hundreds be directed to a section of the courtyard, single file. Most of the women were covered in burkas. I didn't know where they were from or why each one was here, but I knew God loved each one of them. I stood amazed that He could be looking out for all of them as well as taking care of us.

* * * * *

Mark found room #100, a large room with many desks and people. Mark walked to the man at the first desk and asked him to verify our court document. The man grabbed the document from Mark's hand and began the process of reading it. Halfway through reading, the man received a phone call. Mark watched as the man started to become very anxious, glancing up at Mark and back down at our court document.

Mark didn't know who was on the other end of that phone call, but in his mind, he could only assume it was Adeferese. Knowing that there were people out there who would and could stop us at any moment, Mark started praying that this wasn't another blockade put up to delay us from taking our daughter home.

The man peered at Mark through his glasses and took a deep breath as he hung up the phone and quickly continued reading to the end. He suddenly opened his desk drawer, pulling out his official stamp, stamped the document, and ran out the door, leaving Mark standing in his office holding the verified document.

It had been an hour, but we walked back through the door and presented the head woman at the desk our stamped and approved verdict. She looked it over and handed us Favor's passport and visa. I held it tightly. This small, red booklet had come at such a high price, and now it was finally back in our hands.

"The officials from the airport told me that we need a letter from immigration saying that she is cleared to leave," Mark said.

"We sent it out yesterday," she said, matter-of-factly. "We've already done that—it's taken care of."

Mark and I stood silent for a second. We knew her words held no truth. How could they? We had just won our case and there was not enough time to have done such a thing.

"How could it be taken care of?" Mark asked. "We just won last night?"

"I promise—it is done," she said.

"Can we have a copy of that letter?" I asked, knowing there wasn't a chance.

"No," she quickly answered back. "There is no copy. They have it there."

"I was out at the airport last night," Mark said, "and they have no letter. Can you please type a letter up for us to take today? We fly out this evening."

We could tell she was getting weary of us. She took a deep breath and looked at the other women in the room, who avoided looking back.

"Wait one moment," she said, and walked past us and down the hall. Mark and I stood in the doorway, wondering what to do next. Within 10 minutes, she returned to take us to her boss's office. We waited outside his entrance near his secretary's desk. There were several people waiting in the designated seats for the opportunity to see this top official.

Another 30 minutes passed. Mark walked back to the woman who brought us there. "Can you please tell me why we are waiting at the head of immigration's office for a letter of release?" Mark asked as nicely as his stress filled-demeanor could manage.

The woman stood up and walked Mark back to where I was waiting. Nobody had gone in or come out of the head of immigration's office in 30 minutes. The woman walked into his office, then returned a few minutes later. "He will see you next," she said.

"Do we ask him for the letter?" Mark asked, slightly confused.

"He will take care of you," she said. "You will get what you need."

A young man came to the doorway of the head of immigration's office. "He will see you now," he said.

The woman walked in behind us as we entered a huge room clearly made for someone of great importance. The room was carpeted and had massive, elegant, gold curtains hanging on two of the walls. In front of us was the head of immigration's office. He looked up at us behind his oversized mahogany desk and pointed to the chairs in front of his desk.

"How can I help you?" He asked, leaning forward with his hands clasped together in front of him.

"We were told that we need a letter of release from immigration for our daughter to be able to leave Ethiopia," Mark said.

"Do you have her passport and visa with you?" he asked.

"Yes," Mark answered.

"Let me have it," he said as he put his hand forward.

My stomach turned as I reached into my purse and pulled out Favor's passport to hand to Mark. The head of immigration took it and opened it up to her information page.

"Oh," he said, "the Debre Birhan case!"

"Yes," Mark answered.

"This was a big case," he said. "Big victory for you, yes?" He stopped and took a moment to look up at us and smile.

"Yes," Mark said, "it was."

"Congratulations!" he said.

"Thank you," Mark and I said in unison.

He looked at the woman who had brought us to his office. The two spoke back and forth in Amharic for a few minutes and she walked out. He picked up the phone.

"I will take care of this for you," he said, as he waited for his phone call to be patched through to the head officer of immigration at the airport. After a long dialogue between the two men, he said, "Favor Mark Worton," several times. Then he started spelling it out, for the officer on the other end. Mark and I held our laughs back at the sight of this powerful man yelling louder and louder our daughter's legal name. He looked up at us in the middle of the conversation. "He says he remembers you, and no problem, he will let you pass tonight."

"No letter is needed?" Mark quickly confirmed.

"No letter is needed," the head of immigration reconfirmed. "My phone call is good enough."

He finished his conversation and hung up, shaking his head. "Okay," he said. "You are all good to take your daughter and go home. Any problems, you talk to the head immigration officer. He will tell them I called."

"Thank you so much," I said in Amharic.

He smiled and nodded his head at us in approval, "You're welcome! Have safe travels."

* * * * *

We left the immigration office with a promise and a call, but no letter. "Do you think the call will be enough?" I asked Mark.

"It'll have to be," Mark answered. "What more can we do? We were with the head immigration officer of Ethiopia."

We walked outside to the mob that was still waiting to get through the guard gate into the inner courts of immigration. I walked over and showed the woman who had taken my phone and camera the slip of paper to reclaim my things. It took a few minutes, but I was relieved when she found my items and brought them to me.

* * * * *

Our driver stood waiting at the exact place we left him almost three hours earlier. As we were driving out of the immigration compound, Mark's phone rang. The call was from the vice-consul from the U.S. Embassy. He was in a different frame of mind than the night before.

"Hey, Mark," he said, "I wanted to call and congratulate your family on the court win you had, and let you know I've checked everything out, and the paperwork you have is sufficient to give to customs when you get to America. There is nothing left for you to do but take that little girl home."

Mark was relieved to hear the vice-consul in such high spirits about our case. "That's great!" Mark said. "I appreciate all you've done to try to help us."

"Sorry, we couldn't do more, but I'm glad it all worked out for you," he said.

Mark hung up the phone with a relieved look. Our driver rushed us back to the compound, where we finished packing and started making our rounds saying goodbye to the new friends we had made at The Academy.

Mark walked down to the main office and asked how much we owed them for the apartment we had used for more than three weeks. He was astonished to find out that it came out to less than 14 U.S. dollars a day. The price fit in our budget, and it was a blessing we never saw coming.

Within an hour, Pastor and Pochi came to pick us up. As the men were loading our bags in the car, I looked around at this place we had called home during one of the hardest times of our lives. It had been a refuge in the midst of a storm. Every corner would be etched in my memory, from the flags of all the countries flying from the side of the gym, to the large tortoises roaming the grounds, and the white-breasted crows.

The last friends we said goodbye to at The Academy were Jody and Pat. God had so graciously blessed us through this couple. He brought us together through our first adoption more than three years earlier, and He made a way for us to hide out in their safe haven. God is never random. Things we do today affect us down the road. Nothing is wasted. We realized our obedience to adopt our son Shewit from Ethiopia was the very seed we were reaping from in this blessing. It was all in God's divine plan. We knew there would never be a way we could repay Jody and Pat in this lifetime, but we also knew we had a wonderful God who had stored up great riches for them in Heaven. The good seeds they planted in us during our storm would someday spring forth with great blessings for them.

Enjoying a night out with our dear friends Pat and Jody Hilt.

* * * * *

As we drove through Mercato one last time, I tried to grab every detail around me, from the smells of roasting coffee beans to raw sewage to the countless faces filled with hopelessness. In my heart, I knew that someday I would return to help this nation and these people, but my body longed to be home, and my soul longed for a time of healing and restoration.

Pastor pulled up to one of my favorite ethnic restaurants. Standing in the parking lot, we were welcomed by all the pastors from Covenant Church. We walked in together, sat and had great fellowship, thanked them for all they had done, giving God the glory for the great victory we had won. We could all feel an undeniable bond between us.

"I have never been as challenged in my faith as this has challenged me," Pochi said. "I wept before God, asking Him to do the impossible, like David against Goliath, and He has done it. I believe all four children will be released and will be adopted because of this victory."

"Yes," Pastor agreed.

We knew we had all been the audience for a great work of God. None of us—even for a moment—tried to take credit for what had happened. We had seen the impossible become possible by the work of God's hand.

After the Ethiopian restaurant, we were driven to a coffeehouse near the airport, where Emebet wanted to come and say goodbye one last time. We sat and enjoyed the freshly roasted and brewed Ethiopian coffee—definitely something we would miss—there was nothing like it back home. As we sat there enjoying one another's company, I found myself asking God to not let me miss anything. I wanted to leave strong.

A final coffee-shop goodbye with the pastors from Covenant Church—Favor, Missy, Dave, Minilik, Mark, McKenzie, and Pastor.

* * * * *

Favor ran up to me. She needed to visit the restroom, so off we went, Favor running ahead of me into the bathroom and ducking into a stall. I walked into the ladies bathroom and noticed a young Muslim woman crying at the sink. She glanced up at me then back down. *Jesus, please give me the words to say to this woman. Let me be the one to plant a seed in her life of your love and who you are,* I prayed.

"Are you okay?" I asked her. She turned around and glared at me.

Okay, not much love there, I thought, but I was determined to leave a seed so I tried again.

"Are you okay?" I asked again. "Can I pray for you?" At that, she turned back around and looked in my eyes. Her expression had changed slightly and now she looked a bit confused.

"Are you from the United States?" she asked.

"Yes, I am from the United States. Are you from Ethiopia?"

"Yes," she answered.

"You are Muslim?" I asked, although it was obvious because of the burka she was clothed in from head to toe.

She nodded, *yes.*

"Well, I'm a Christian, and I have a love for Muslims." I said it, and I meant it. I had no fear—no preconceived attitude. I really had love for this stranger standing across from me. I was applying the lesson I had learned from Todd White in the *Father of Lights* film. I had watched in admiration as he had loved on Muslims in Israel.

The shock on her face was enough to make me want to jump with joy. My spirit leapt. I could see that it was a statement she had never heard before, or expected to hear in her lifetime.

Favor ran out of the bathroom, with her head wrapped in a scarf as the Muslim women do, but Favor did it to cover her newly-shaved head. "Mom," she said looking up at me. "Wash hands?"

I smiled at her, "Yes, please."

The woman looked up at me and turned her head sideways, "Are you married to a Muslim man?" she asked.

"No," I responded.

"Are you married to an Ethiopian man?" she asked. I could tell she was trying to make sense of the sight before her. It reminded me of a bumper sticker we had on our van back in Tennessee that says, "Live a life that demands explanation." This was going to be fun.

"No," I said. "My husband and I adopted her. We are both Americans."

She shook her head as if she didn't understand. "Why would Americans want to adopt an orphan from Ethiopia?" she asked.

"Because we love her. The God we know loves her. He loves all of those He created, and we are supposed to do the same."

I looked at her eyes. She was listening and holding on to every word.

I continued, "Christians are taught to love, regardless of skin color, religion, or whether they are a man or woman. None of those things matter because that is how our God loves. We are supposed to be a reflection of Him."

Her eyes had softened, no longer glaring at me with the cold stare. "I have never heard this before," she said. "A Christian having love for a Muslim? This is new to me. I thought Christians hated Muslims."

"I'm sorry," I said. "I know some don't show much love, some might be afraid, but we are taught to love. I know God loves you. He sent Jesus to show His love for you."

"I have heard of Jesus," she said.

Favor finished washing her hands and dashed out of the bathroom.

"Favor," I yelled, "Stop!" She was running down the long hallway back to the coffee shop. I knew my time was up with this woman, but there was one more thing I wanted to say before I left.

"I better go after her," I said, "but I want you to know the God I serve values you very much, and He loves you more than you can imagine! God bless you!" I gave her a quick hug and ran after Favor.

"Thank you so much," she said. "Your words touch me."

I will never know if the seed I planted will ever bloom, but I know I serve a God that had me come face-to-face with this woman, in love. He had changed my heart to reach out in love to her rather than in judgement or fear. I saw a human who God loved first. His love shocks others, especially when it comes in a package they aren't expecting.

I didn't have to agree with her faith, or whether she was right or wrong. I loved her supernaturally because I saw her as God did. Loving her was a statement that I have a God greater than the hate that has come between us because of religion and fear. I loved her because my God is her Creator and He loved her first. I saw her with God's eyes, with His value of her. She was a soul who God yearned to show His love to—through me. If God, the great and mighty awesome Father I know, can love her, and I say that I have His Spirit living in me, then I should love like Him. It has everything to do with how big I was seeing my God! His love was supernaturally flowing through my DNA, and I wasn't about to stop it.

CHAPTER 29
THANKSGIVING AND JOY

"We had come to rescue a little girl and
give her a home and family,
but in reality, an Ethiopian church—its leaders and people—
reached out and rescued us."

—Missy Maxwell Worton

An excitement rushed through my body—it was time to go home. Mark had been watching the time closely, making sure we would get to the airport in plenty of time. Mark took Dave aside as we walked out of the coffee shop. "I know you made sacrifices by taking care of us these last three weeks," Mark said, "and you have never stopped praying for us through it all."

Dave smiled at Mark. Such a genuine kindness and humility radiated from Dave.

"I know you turned down work that you needed in order to take care of my family," Mark said. "I can never repay what you've done." Mark took off his watch. "I don't have any money right now, but I wanted to give you something to say thank you."

Dave looked down at the watch in Mark's hand. Everything he had done, he did from a heart of kindness and love. He never expected anything from us. "Please," Mark said, handing him the watch. Dave humbly took it from Mark's hand and embraced him.

"Thank you," Dave said. "You do not need to do this."

"Just take it and be blessed," Mark said.

"Your faith blesses me," Dave said. "It encourages me to believe."

"When we get home, Missy and I want to send back something to bless you and your family," Mark said. Dave silently shook his head—he had no words.

* * * * *

Mark looked up. Everyone who had joined us at the coffee shop, along with the rest of the pastors and several new friends from Covenant Church, Pochi, and Emebet, were waiting in their cars to see us off at the airport. As Dave and Mark walked across the road to get in our car, a white Land Rover drove toward them. It looked like the vice-consul from the U.S. Embassy. The closer the car got, Mark could see that it was the vice-consul. The vice-consul then stopped the car in the middle of the road to talk to Mark.

"Hey," Mark said. "Seven million people in one city and I happen to run into you. What are you doing here?"

"Just out," the vice-consul said. "But I'm glad I did run into you. Listen, again, I want to say how glad I am that everything worked out for your family."

"Thank you," Mark said.

"I'm sorry we couldn't do more to help you," the vice-consul said. "But we are really glad it turned out this way. You handled it right and you honored the legal system here. You did good."

"Thanks," Mark said. "So, we're good to go?"

"Absolutely!" the vice-consul said. "Just please, if you can, contact me when you get safely past immigration. I would like to catch up when things calm down for you and talk more about what happened to your family. We want to keep this from happening again."

"I'll fire off an email when we get through," Mark reassured him. Then as quickly as he came, they said goodbye and he disappeared down the street.

"The vice-consul?" I asked, as Mark jumped into the front seat.

"Yeah," Mark said. "That was strange."

"He just happened to be in the area?" I asked sarcastically. "Mark, nothing is by chance. What'd he say?"

"Just that he was sorry they couldn't have done more, but he was very happy for us."

As excited as I was, we still had to cross another hurdle: immigration. We had no signed letter from the head of immigration's office—just a promise that a call would be enough. The thought of possibly getting stopped again made both of our stomachs turn with nervousness as we drove up to the airport parking lot.

Our caravan of friends pulled in beside us and we all got out to say goodbye. Mesfin also pulled up with a smile, and I watched with joy as this giant of a man stepped out of a small, sporty vehicle and quickly walked to my husband's side. He had a grey scarf around his neck and looked like he had just come from work.

We only had a few minutes left before we would need to head into the airport. Mesfin took Mark aside as I continued to chat with the friends who had gathered. "I wanted to come see your family before you left," Mesfin said. "But also, if they allow, I would like to walk you through immigration to make sure you have no problems."

"Thank you," Mark said. "We'll take all the help we can get. You know, you have been a Godsend. We will never forget what you did for us."

Mesfin knew we were thankful for his wisdom and friendship. It touched him in a very deep place. He lifted his eyes and began to say something to Mark, then paused before he could continue. Two strong men stood awkwardly silent, on the brink of tears.

"You are such good people," Mesfin softly spoke. "I'm asking that you and your family do not look down on our country because of this. We want you to come back to our country; what happened to you—it's not normal."

"I know it's not normal," Mark reassured him. "We love Ethiopia and that will not change because of a few people."

"Please do not look down on Ethiopia," Mesfin said again. "People here love Americans, and we have come to love your family very much."

"Thank you, Brother," Mark said as he gave him a big hug.

"Thank you," Mesfin said. "I have learned so much watching your family fight for this child. I will never forget."

"We couldn't have done it without you," Mark smiled.

"This has stirred my heart," Mesfin shared, "I want to help the orphans more. This is important."

"It is," Mark said. "Speak for those that have no voice... even your name declares it!" Mark reminded Mesfin of what his full legal name meant: "Defender of the orphan and homeless." It was insight into his purpose.

"Yes," Mesfin said in agreement, "I will—I promise."

"I love you, Brother," Mark said. "Thank you, again."

* * * * *

I stood across from Emebet. She wanted to say so much as she searched for words to express how she was feeling. "I am so thankful you stayed," Emebet said. "Favor will be loved well."

"She already is," I said.

"Yes," she said, grinning. "Are you happy to get back to your other children?"

"Very happy! I miss them so much I can barely stand it."

"You love being a mom," she said. "This is good. Will you please send pictures as she grows up?"

"You will not miss anything important," I said. "I will keep you up on all her adventures." I looked at this fearless woman standing in front of me who risked everything to get her niece to America. I wished I could take her too. She needed a family to help her through those days she was sick and in the hospital battling for her life against a cruel disease. "Emebet, do you have a church family?"

She looked at me, her eyes told me she was thinking of how to respond to my question.

"Do you have people who can help you when you go to the hospital or get sick?" I asked. "Does anyone come and pray for you in the hospital?"

She shook her head no.

"You need to let others be there for you," I said. "You're always there for them. You need to be surrounded by people who love and care for you when you need help." Emebet nodded her head in agreement. "Have you ever been to Pastor's church?" I asked.

"No," she said.

"They would be a great group of people to stand beside you," I said. "They prayed as much as we did for Favor being released to go to America. All the miracles you saw happen for us, were done by a big God who loves to do the impossible for His children." Pochi walked up beside me and I put my arm in hers. "Pochi's church believes like we do. We believe in a God of miracles. It would be a good family for you."

"Yes," Emebet smiled.

"Yes," Pochi said. "We will find a way to get you there this Sunday." Pochi gave Emebet a hug and they began to talk in Amharic excitedly.

"Hey," Mark said as he grabbed my hand, "we need to start heading out."

I took a deep breath. Although I was happy to be going home, I knew it would be a while until I would see these friends again. Each of these individuals had come to our aid and been there for us, in countless hours of prayer and doing everything humanly possible to help us on the ground. We had come to rescue a little girl and give her a home and family, but in reality, an Ethiopian church—its leaders and people—reached out and rescued us.

Mark and I hugged each one, then we all prayed together before we walked to the security gate with Mesfin. When we got to the gate, the security guard told Mesfin that would be as far as he could come with us, so we said our goodbyes.

"I will wait right here until you call and tell me that you are on the other side," Mesfin told us. "I will not leave until I hear you are past immigration."

Mark had no words as he reached out and hugged Mesfin to say goodbye a final time. Mesfin turned and gave me a big hug. "Thank you," he said.

"Thank *you*, Mesfin," I said. "You bring your family to America and visit us next time." Mesfin stood there laughing as we walked away and through the doors of the security check.

Mesfin, Mark and Pastor saying goodbye at the Addis Ababa airport.

We quickly checked in and got our tickets before heading toward immigration. Mark and I were both nervous, and I could feel my shoulders tensing up the closer we got to the roped-off lines we had walked through over three weeks ago. There they were, almost the same group of immigration officers, watching us walk toward them. I felt Favor's hand squeeze me a little tighter. I pulled her to my side and reassured her that this was a good place this time. I felt her arms hug my waist and her face burrow into my side. They all kept staring at us as we made our way closer to a window. I couldn't take it—they knew us, and we knew them—let's just break the ice.

"Hi!" I said, as I waved at the group of officers watching our every move. "We're back." They all smiled and waved.

"Yes," the woman officer said. "We remember you! Good to see you back—with your little girl."

"Thank you," I said.

"Really," McKenzie whispered my way. "Mom, you're talking to the mean lady who stopped us last time."

"Yes," I whispered back as I was maintaining my smile. "But hopefully they won't stop us this time."

The woman directed us to the first immigration booth. Mark looked at me and grabbed my hand. "Let's hope this works," he said.

"I'm praying," I whispered.

An older immigration officer, who looked like he could be a serious candidate for a day off, was in the booth. He put his hand forward to grab our documents without even giving us a glance.

Mark decided to give him Favor's documentation first and get it over with. The officer looked at her passport and visa and cocked his head, then began to read the three-page court verdict. Mark glanced over at me, taking a deep breath. *Oh, dear Lord, please, not again.*

Out of nowhere, a tall woman hurriedly walked past us and opened the booth with a key, placing herself leaning over the officer.

"What are you doing?" she said, "They are fine, you do not need to read all of this."

The officer put his hand in her face, as if to say, *talk to the hand*, and he continued to read, not missing a beat.

We could all see that the hand in the face did not sit well, and I could see her neck stiffen up with a *no you didn't* look as she pushed his hand away. "You do not need to read all this," she said sternly. "They have clearance."

Mark and I looked at each other. It was evident that it didn't seem to be going smoothly for us, and the first thing that crossed our minds was that someone had gotten to this immigration officer. We could see movement coming toward us from the immigration office. We turned around to see the entire group of officers heading toward our booth. My heart started racing, *Oh, please God, not again!* Favor and McKenzie were both holding onto my waist. I could feel them shaking.

A smaller man ran over to our booth door, unlocked it, and began speaking in a very sharp tone, "They are fine to go. The head of immigration has called and has released them to go. Now do your job and stamp their passports."

The officer reading our verdict looked up at him, startled, but didn't move.

"Now!" the man said, clearly annoyed.

We turned around to find ourselves surrounded by the same group of officers who had been there the night we were stopped. The main woman put her hand on my back. I remembered the last time I saw her I secretly prayed that she wouldn't be able to sleep after not letting us leave with Favor. I know—it was not my best moment.

"You stayed and fought for your little girl," she said to me. My eyes filled with tears. I don't know if it was the relief I felt or the exhaustion.

"Yes," I answered, "I could never leave her."

"I am so happy for you and her," she said. "I could not sleep thinking about your family. We have all wondered what happened.

I have never seen such pain and tears come from a child in all the years I have been here." She looked down at Favor and raised her chin with her finger. "You go to America?" she said to Favor.

Favor's face lit up. "Yes," Favor said. "America today."

"Yes, today you go to America," the woman officer said, giving Favor a high-five.

The other officers began giving her high-fives and congratulating us on being able to take her home.

One of the tall officers leaned over and smiled at Favor, "Where do you think you are going?" he asked.

Favor's face was glowing with joy, "America, America, America!" She giggled and jumped up to slap his hand with pure, unadulterated happiness. The people who once caused Favor fear as they surrounded her at immigration before were now cheering her on and celebrating with her. *How life can change!* We walked out of the immigration checkpoint toward freedom as a crowd of immigration officers stood waving goodbye to us until we were out of sight. It felt like a scene straight out of *The Sound of Music* when the children were all heading to bed after performing for their father's party guest, waving goodbye. I almost started waving and singing, "Goodbye."

At the top of the escalator, we found Julie waiting for us. A look of relief came across her face as her arms reached out to welcome us.

"You made it!" Julie said. "I can't tell you how happy I am to see you guys." The girls ran up to her like they hadn't seen her in weeks. Julie was finished with her time in Ethiopia and heading home for Thanksgiving. It seemed too good to be true that she would be on our flight back to America. It didn't take the girls long before they were asking to hang out with her—the grown-up they thought was cool. We let them trot off with Julie and find something to eat while Mark and I found some comfortable lounge chairs.

Mark immediately called Mesfin to let him know we had safely cleared immigration. Again, Mesfin pleaded with Mark to not think badly of Ethiopia because of what had happened. Mark reassured him that we loved Ethiopia, and that our feelings would never change. It was the land that had blessed us with two beautiful children to raise and love. Ethiopia would forever be a part of us.

* * * * *

As we boarded the Ethiopian Dreamliner, I found myself looking around, trying to remember everything that I was seeing and feeling in this moment. It was surreal. I had been waiting and dreaming of this moment every day since we had been turned away three-and-a-half weeks ago. I thought, *God please don't let me miss a thing. Help me not to waste a moment or miss a lesson you were trying to teach me in this. Whatever this trial was about, may I grasp it, learn from it, and make the change that I need to make in me.*

We settled in for the 16-hour flight home. I didn't realize how exhausted I was as I sat and stared blankly at the movie playing in front of me. I was either too tired or too excited to be going home—regardless of what the reason was—I wasn't getting any sleep on this flight.

Halfway across the Atlantic Ocean, all the screens suddenly went black and the entire cabin lost electricity. I looked at Mark, who had a very troubled look on his face. The first thought in Mark's mind was, *Adeferese!* We both had been told that the uniqueness of this plane was the lithium-ion batteries it used and how it was powered, but we could still hear the hum of the engines. We looked around us. If people were awake, they were looking around for answers with very panicked and concerned looks on their faces.

We didn't know why the plane suddenly lost all electrical power, but we did trust that God was in complete control of our destiny. He had just shown us His faithfulness, and He had been our defender and protector through the worst of times. Fear no longer had a hold on me, and this once white-knuckle flyer was unfazed by what was happening around me. I knew God had a future for me, whether it was on Earth or in Heaven. I had just been through Hell, and I left my fears there. I was as free as the precious new daughter sleeping next to me—and my new freedom felt wonderful.

I looked at Mark and shrugged my shoulders, "God did not bring us this far to drop us in the middle of the Atlantic Ocean."

"You're right," Mark sighed and smiled. We both fell asleep for the remainder of the flight.

A little less than six weeks later, we would find out that the entire fleet of Boeing 787 Dreamliners, including the one we were on, was grounded after U.S. regulators said they were not safe to fly until a fire risk linked to the aircraft's lithium-ion batteries had been resolved.[1]

* * * * *

We landed safely at Dulles Airport in Washington, D.C., the day before Thanksgiving, on November 22, 2012. It was 7:50 a.m. when we walked out of customs and saw our friends David and Kathleen Estes with their boys waiting for us, gifts in hand. The joy of being back in America was overwhelming to my senses.

David drove us to their favorite breakfast place. Mark and I wanted to order everything on the menu. French toast, bacon, waffles—you name it, we were craving it.

David had posted a picture of us the moment we walked out of customs with the comment, "That just happened." The celebration was on, and many people who had so unselfishly been praying and believing for Favor saw the fruit of their labor. Answered prayer was walking in America, and it was being shared and celebrated like wildfire through the internet. It was staggering to see the amount of love and joy that was being poured out over this little girl. We couldn't hold back our tears of thankfulness as we continued to read comments throughout the day.

With our dear friends David and Kathleen and their boys, just after we landed in America.

After an amazing day of fellowship and rest with our friends, they dropped us off at the airport for our final flight home. I looked around at the people waiting to board our plane. One lady glanced up at me and then to Favor and gave us a gentle smile. Others had their faces buried in technology, checking their smartphones.

"None of these people have any idea what God just brought us through," I said to Mark. "They have no clue what an awesome victory God just gave us just to be sitting here."

Mark looked up and around. "No, but we do."

"I see God so much bigger now, don't you? He can and will do the impossible. All we had to do is ask—and believe." I kept thinking aloud, "Trusting and obeying helped too. Not to mention all the people praying...we are blessed...and a little crazy."

Mark smiled a smile I knew so well, filled with wonder and acceptance, "And, that's why I love you so much."

* * * * *

My heart leapt as we landed at the Nashville airport. I looked down and saw Favor and McKenzie sound asleep. "Wake up girls! We're here."

McKenzie popped up and looked out the window. She was overcome with joy and started hugging the window with her cheek. "Nashville!" she said. "You're beautiful…beautiful! I can't wait to see my kitten—he's probably so big now."

"Start putting all your stuff in the bag," I instructed them. "We might have a few friends here to welcome you to America, Favor."

"Matt?" she asked, "Shewit? Grandma?"

"All of them will be there waiting to hug you!" I said.

"Do you think Grandma made some chocolate chip cookies for me?" McKenzie asked hopefully.

"I hope so," Mark said.

The excitement within us to see our boys was indescribable. Tears were welling up in my eyes as I walked toward the welcoming area at the end of the long terminal. We could see a large crowd of people were gathered before us, and the closer we got we could see friends' faces amidst the camera flashes. Our church family, soccer family, and so many of our friends and prayer warriors, who had spent countless hours on their knees praying for Favor's freedom, had gathered to welcome us home. Banners welcomed Favor, and friends and family held gifts for a little princess who finally got to come to America. The people who had been on our plane slowed down as they walked through the airport to see what the big celebration was about. Everyone was smiling from ear to ear or weeping with joy—we all knew the miracle it was to have her standing among us.

My eyes searched for Matt and Shewit. Then I saw Shewit with his soccer buddies, holding up a sign welcoming Favor. His face lit up when my eyes found his, and my arms reached out to hold my son as he dropped the sign he was holding and ran into my arms. It was so good to feel him in my embrace, just to hear his giggles in my ear. "Love you, Mom," he said.

"I love you so much!" I said, staring into his eyes. It felt like a dream, and I was making sure it was real. "I missed you so much, Shewit!" I didn't want to let go.

I looked up, hoping to find Matt, my 15-year-old son, in the crowd. I could feel him near me. As I kept searching for him, his smile was the first thing I could see, as he carefully pushed his way through those gathered to get to us. If I didn't know better, he looked like he'd grown two inches, and I couldn't

The entire family—together at last—Mark, Matt, Favor, me, Shewit, Grandma Worton, and McKenzie.

Jubilant homecoming party at the Nashville Airport!

wait to hold him in my arms. The moment I hugged him, I no longer could hold back the waterworks. My family was together. It was the best feeling in the world, and the tears that used to be bitter were now sweet with thankfulness and joy.

The next hour was filled with reunions, introductions, and pictures with friends and family. I wondered if this was how Heaven would feel.

Lori, our dear friend and one of our valiant prayer warriors, came up to Favor and me. "Favor comes to America!" Lori declared. "Somehow that's prophetic."

"I believe it is," I said, giving Lori a hug.

"Favor," Lori said, kneeling down to be eye-to-eye with her, "we've all been waiting to meet you." Favor smiled and nodded her head. "It's a pleasure to meet you, Favor Worton," Lori said.

As Lori and Favor were getting to know each other, I looked around at each one standing around us. It was Thanksgiving Eve, and we had more blessings than we could count. Each person had the fingerprint of God on them. They had been called to be a part of this testimony and a part in this victory that we were celebrating. Heaven had a reward for the many prayers they had offered up for the sake of a little orphaned girl—who no longer was an orphan.

* * * * *

It was a beautiful night as we drove from the airport to our home in Franklin, Tennessee. Grandma Worton pulled out a gallon-bag full of her homemade chocolate chip cookies to surprise McKenzie. They tasted like a piece of Heaven as we all devoured them.

"We're home, Favor!" McKenzie excitedly announced, as we drove up our driveway. Favor pressed her nose against the window to see the home she had only seen in pictures. She couldn't contain the giggles. When we stopped, she excitedly jumped out of the van and grabbed my hand.

We went up the garage stairs and opened the door that led into our kitchen and sunroom. Favor's eyes surveyed every inch, then she turned toward our great room.

"Welcome to your new home, Favor," I said.

Favor took a few steps into the two-story room, her eyes slowly moving across the great room to the dining room, into the foyer, and up the steps to the catwalk that led to the children's rooms upstairs. She took a breath and turned around to look at her new family—the people God had chosen for her. A smile came across her face and her eyes sparkled. She didn't need to say a word. We knew what she was feeling just by looking at her.

She was finally home.

A fun family portrait of the entire family in Ethiopian attire, taken within weeks of us bringing Favor home.

EPILOGUE

Highlights from the Worton Family after Ethiopia

Since we set foot in America, we have experienced joy, transition, healing, and growth—as we still do. Our first days were wonderfully exciting, filled with family, friends, news reporters, and production companies. Everyone wanted to meet this little girl who God had conquered giants for, and they wanted to hear more of our story that showed nothing is impossible with Him.

After the initial wave of excitement waned, we were left to transition a little girl from the cameras and memories to everyday life in America—a land of opportunity and even excess. Favor's senses were overwhelmed, and yet, at the same time, she wanted everything at the grocery store, the toy store, the movies, and everywhere else we took her in that first year or two. Although adoption has challenging moments—especially with older children who have experienced abandonment and abuse—it has been worth it to see her thrive and blossom.

Favor continues to be a shining light wherever she goes, spreading kindness and joy to those around her with her beautiful smile. She is a delight, a joy to her dad and me, and a loved little sister by her older siblings. She is also the extended family's favorite babysitter!

Like me, Favor has chosen to share her story. She has written a children's book, *Favor...Her Story,* about the years before she was adopted. The book is expected to be released shortly after *Don't Mess with This Mama.*

Favor currently thrives in academics and excels in playing soccer, basketball, and running long-distance races. She's becoming quite a speaker as well, sharing part of her story in a speech entitled, *"Freedom."* She's got just enough spunk and vitality to be a world changer, and she has decided that she wants to be a lawyer when she grows up, to help other children who are trapped in the same type of situation that she was. Favor wants to reverse the new laws in Ethiopia that prohibit foreign adoptions. Her desire is that orphans be allowed to be adopted into a forever family living in another country. She believes that being surrounded by a family who loves and believes in their children is the best way for anyone to heal and dream for a bright future.

McKenzie came home to her friends who were excited to hear all about her Ethiopian adventure. Missing four weeks of school didn't hurt her academically; she finished the year earning the "Outstanding Student of the Year Award." She and Favor are closer than ever, especially when it comes to shopping and grabbing a quick drink at the local coffee shop. She has been a great role model and loving sister to Favor. McKenzie continues to grow in her friendships and her zeal for loving every minute of each day with those she adores. She is thrilled to have graduated high school and is now working toward a Bachelors degree in Behavioral Physiology.

Mark had lost close to 20 pounds by the time we touched down in America because of the emotional strain in Ethiopia. Thankfully, within months he both gained a few pounds and was hired by a new company.

He continues to thrive collaborating with others, showing his strength as a builder of great sales teams and then reaching new heights with them. He is enjoying watching his kids play soccer or taking them on in Smash Bros. He's still the rock in this family and is happy to share our story of God's great victory to bring home Favor.

I, Missy, remember doing my best to glean everything from our experience from the moment we got home. It felt surreal that it had even happened. I struggled with the idea of writing a book about our experience for years, but in the end, I realized that our story was about what God had done—not about us. This book is His story. I am honored to share it, and I hope it encourages others in their faith. It describes the God-given courage that comes when you choose love over fear. It depicts how greatly God values the pleas of His children. It also reveals that God may not always deliver us from tough situations but He is always good. Looking back on what God did still renders me humbled and speechless years later.

My day-to-day life currently is full of joy being mom to four busy teenagers. You can find me on the soccer field most weekends cheering on Shewit or Favor, getting a manicure and coffee with McKenzie, developing an animated TV show, or talking politics with Matt. I continue to develop and write TV and film scripts, but I have found a new joy in being an author. I work hand-in-hand with several causes to help human trafficking survivors, as well as orphans.

The Continuing Journey for a Few of Our Friends in Ethiopia

Pochi kept working on behalf of the other three children she often mentioned to us, and within the following year after we took home Favor, they were released from the foster care system. Our case opened the door and paved a way for the adoptive families to return to Ethiopia, to win their adoption cases in court, and to finally take those precious children home. Favor and the three others were the four children in Daniel's dream.

Also, not too long after we won our case to take Favor home, Covenant Orphanage was exonerated in court from the false charges brought against the orphanage by Adeferese and EAI in Ethiopia.

Pochi still works with Covenant Orphanage, using every ounce of energy she has to make a difference for orphans, the homeless, the elderly, and the needy. To date, Covenant Orphanage has set up two children's homes in different regions of Ethiopia to take care of orphans from newborn through 15. The organization plans are to continue to expand and meet the needs of as many orphans as possible, as it facilitates adoptions within Ethiopia. The orphanage has also set up a child sponsorship program and a family empowerment program to help needy families.

Mesfin lives with his wife and three children in Ethiopia. He continues to successfully practice law in the region where he provides legal advice on civil, family, and commercial matters. He says he remembers the strong and unshakeable faith he saw, and the determination shown to take Favor home and give her a good life. The Debre Birhan case Mesfin said, "was not a mere professional exercise; it was an emotional and spiritual battle. The result was overwhelmingly good because of God." He keeps in touch with the Worton family and hopes to visit America soon with his family.

Emebet is attending a local school in Ethiopia and plans to pursue a career in marketing. I keep her up to date on Favor's life, sending pictures and keeping her informed on Favor's milestones and exciting adventures. She is healthy and vibrant and attends Covenant Church when she can.

Adeferese has not tried to contact either Pochi or the Wortons since he lost the case discussed in this book (known as the Debre Birhan case) concerning Favor and Covenant Orphanage.

Regional officials—As of the first printing of this book, the individuals involved with our story at the Debre Birhan regional office are no longer in positions of influence.

Other News about Adoption in Ethiopia

Ethiopian Adoption International (EAI)—On March 12, 2014, the parent organization, delivered a press release stating "...extremely large financial challenges over the last few years...,"[1] (necessitated its closure). The agency is now closed in Ethiopia, as well as America. In their time as an active adoption agency, they facilitated hundreds of adoptions. I have no doubt that when they began they were exemplary in their practice, and because of them, many children were successfully placed with a loving forever family. We know that the wonderful people who started this company acted in love and kindness for each orphan. In the past, they did so many things right, and our story will never take that away from the organization's legacy. Sadly, they never asked about our side of the story, or try to reconcile what they had done. So, what they used to be and what they were with us showed that they had lost sight of what was important—the truth, the individual child and the family.

The Ethiopian government suspended all out-of-country adoptions as of April 21, 2017, but was being urged by foreign diplomats to allow continued processing of cases that were in progress prior to the April 21, 2017 suspension.[2]

As of the writing of this book, Ethiopia's parliament has passed a law banning the adoption of children by foreigners amid concerns that they could suffer identity crisis and psychological problems, in addition to abuse and neglect abroad. The parliament said Ethiopia should take care of its own children. Lawmakers now say orphans and other vulnerable children should be cared for under locally available support mechanisms in order to protect them.

The Ethiopian government is encouraging local adoptions. Ethiopians are responding to the need and are adopting more than ever before. However, with so many orphans in the country, all efforts are barely making a dent in the need to place the children with loving families.

Three main reasons for the decline in adoption, based on the US State Department's view, include: adoptive parents failing to send post-adoption reports to the children's country of origin; the incidences of adopted children being re-homed; and unethical practices by adoption agencies.

Many orphaned children, though, are being helped by children's homes (like Covenant Orphanage) that provide shelter, food, and an education.

HOW YOU CAN HELP—A CALL TO ACTION

Thank you, for taking time to read our story. We pray that it has built your courage to help someone else less fortunate. Many individuals, after hearing our story, are not ready to adopt, but they often ask how they can help with the orphan and/or the human traffic crisis. Although there are hundreds of incredible causes that you can choose from, we wanted to highlight the causes that we know through firsthand knowledge and personal experience. The important thing is to get involved and to make a difference in these precious lives. Taking action will change your life!

Support Orphans in Ethiopia

Covenant Ministry International—This ministry is directly linked to Covenant Orphanage, the orphanage that worked with us, prayed for us, and stood beside us. This orphanage is the one represented in the story of *Don't Mess with This Mama*.

Although adoption from Ethiopia is not possible at this time, the organization welcomes financial donations to care for children in two children's homes, to equip teachers, to provide meals, and to educate local families. You can also give repeatedly to a particular child through a child sponsorship program.

If you would like to learn more or be a part of what Covenant Ministry International is doing in Ethiopia, you can visit Covenantministryinternational.org.

Serve Orphans in Haiti

Hands And Feet Project—Haiti—Our son, Shewit, serves on mission trips with this ministry.

This Christ-centered organization provides family-style, residential care along with sustainable solutions and dignified jobs to fight against the poverty-driven child abandonment and child slavery cycle that fuels Haiti's orphan crisis.

You can help by sponsoring a child, donating, or serving on a mission trip. To learn more, visit Handsandfeetproject.org.

Care for Children in Ethiopia

Ordinary Heroes—We worked with Ordinary Heroes to adopt our son Shewit. Our friend Kelly Putty founded this organization. She is a warrior for the orphans in Ethiopia and the homeless in Nashville.

Ordinary Hero started to find families for orphans and eventually grew into much more. The organization has fed more than 30,000 meals to children in need in Ethiopia and sponsored 675 children providing monthly food supply, educational support, and medical access.

Ordinary Hero also provides income-generation programs for sponsored families to become self-sufficient, and they provide support for children aging out of orphanages to grant them further educational support and livelihood.

You can learn more about Ordinary Hero at Ordinaryhero.org.

Fight Human Trafficking

Rescue 1 Global—Serving communities around the world until they are free from slavery and human trafficking. Their mission statement reads: Creating a culture of change in communities through: 1.) Education, 2.) Equipping and Mobilizing communities to participate in Prevention, Rescue, and Restoration ministry, 3.) Partnering with Law Enforcement Agencies, Government Agencies and other Non-Government Organizations, and 4.) Opening a Grace Oasis Center in every community Rescue 1 Global serves.

You can learn more at Rescue1Global.org

Consider the Call to Adoption

We recognize that adoption isn't for everyone, but if you feel a tug on your heart and that undeniable desire that this is part of *your* story, we would love to encourage you to take a step into one of the greatest adventures you'll ever experience.

Where do you start? The first step is to pray. Then talk about this big decision with your family—it affects everyone. This new child is a forever addition. If your family is on board, talk to close friends whose advice and input you value. Most people will be absolutely thrilled for you. In the end, the decision is yours, so have confidence and peace going forward in this new path. Next, if you know people personally who have adopted, ask them about their experiences. We believe that most people will be glad to give you all the advice you need.

If you have a sense of where you might be called to adopt from, try to find an individual that has adopted from that same country. That person can give you the best insight on adoption agencies to work with in that country.

To quote Pochi, "God always chooses the family for each child." So relax and enjoy the journey.

AN INVITATION TO KNOW JESUS

In writing *Don't Mess with This Mama,* Mark and I came to the realization of how different our journey would have been without our faith in, and personal relationship with, Jesus Christ. So, if our story has touched your heart, and if you have a desire to know Jesus in a deeper way, then we would like to invite you to take a moment to begin a personal relationship with Him.

All you have to do is pray a simple prayer saying, "Jesus, I want to know You more. Forgive me for the wrongs I have done and help me live the life You created me for. I believe You were crucified and buried. God raised You from the dead, and I now ask You to reign in my life as Lord and Savior. Thank You for Your love and forgiveness. Thank You for valuing me and giving me hope and a future."

Romans 10:9 says that if we declare with our mouths that Jesus is Lord and believe in our hearts that God raised Him from the dead, we will be saved. Being saved means you will spend eternity in relationship with Jesus both on Earth and in Heaven. Knowing Him is a relationship that is more intimate than your closest friend. Knowing Jesus doesn't prevent challenges from happening in this life, but with Him, we find again and again that He gives us peace as He carries us through life's difficulties. We come out on the other side of struggles closer to Him and stronger than we ever thought possible.

If you said this prayer today, we are so happy to welcome you into the family of God. We'd like to encourage you to share your story with us at iamfindingfavor@gmail.com, to pick up a Bible, and to find a local biblically-based church that will help you thrive on this new path your life has taken.

With Love,
Mark and Missy

ACKNOWLEDGEMENTS

How do you begin to thank an army of individuals who stormed Heaven's gates on your behalf night and day? How do you express gratitude to those who gave their valuable time to battle on the spiritual front for your family? No words can adequately thank this group of individuals, and there is no way to know all the countless prayer warriors that hit their knees in prayer for our battle to bring home Favor. So, I'll do my best, and although I may leave out a few names, it is not intentional. Please know we were overwhelmed by your act of love in action. I pray that the seeds of prayer you sowed on behalf of a little girl and a family, as well as the love and encouragement you gave us, will be multiplied a hundredfold.

Next, to my family—this book wouldn't have been possible without you.

Mark, you are my steady rock and silent hero. You are one who says little, yet when you speak, the world listens because of the endless wisdom, authority, and strength you carry. You are that rare jewel that when people discover you, they know they have found a priceless treasure. I can't imagine anyone else I'd rather do life with. You are the one God generously placed in my life to walk out this incredible adventure called life. Whatever God has planned for the days and years ahead, I'm glad he chose you to be beside me.

Matt, McKenzie, and Shewit, your hearts encouraged us to take that first step for this adoption. It was your selfless love to help another child that set us on an adventure of a lifetime. Your dad and I believe in your dreams, and we can't wait to see what God does in and with your lives. We will always be there to cheer you on! You are each amazing in your own incredible ways, and we are so proud of you! We love you each so very much!

McKenzie, you were the bright spot during this battle. I am so thankful we had you in Ethiopia with us on our second trip back for this adoption. Your joy was contagious, your heart was so pure, and your kindness and goodness was a sweet fragrance to your dad's and my soul. We know this was a challenging time for you, but you pushed through and faced it with such bravery and love. You are my hero, and I know God has a great future awaiting you. We love you and are so proud of the young leader you already are now. Oh, the places you'll go, my little world changer!

Dad and Mom Maxwell, the memory of both of you will always live in my heart! You were the first ones to encourage me to love the orphan. You spurred me on to do all I could with my life to help those who had no voice and were in need of help. When we first returned from our journey in Ethiopia, you were the first to encourage me to write our story down. You were my biggest cheerleaders, always believing in what God could do through me. Even though you are no longer with us in body, I can feel you near, cheering me on from Heaven in that great cloud of witnesses. I love and miss you so!

Grandma Worton (Warrior G'ma), or should I say Wonder Woman? You held down the fort while we were battling giants in Ethiopia. Because you so unselfishly gave of your time to be there for us and take care of our boys, we were able to have peace knowing things at home were in good hands. Thank you for being our prayer warrior, caretaker, house-sitter, dog-sitter, cab driver, nurse, sub-contractor, and encourager! We love you and pray that you are blessed beyond measure for what you have sown into our life.

David and Kathleen Estes, to have best friends in your life is a true gift, but when they know how to pray, activate their church, and come to your rescue before you ever ask, those are lifetime friends that understand you without a word being spoken. We are truly blessed to not only call you friends, but family. David, you were there for Mark during one of the lowest points of his life. You were with him through his pain, and whether you knew it or not, you were an encouragement to him during those conversations. You guys are a very important part of our life. Mark and I are blessed to call you friends. We love you and thank God every day for you!

To our friends and prayer warriors who we affectionately called our ***Facebook Prayer Warriors***. No words can adequately thank this group of individuals for being there 24/7 for us. You were always quick to respond, to encourage, and to offer hope with the most perfect timing. You'll never know how much you held Mark and I up. Your words lifted us out of the darkness that tried to crush us. Your prayers gave us strength when we had none. Your encouragement gave us hope in the midst of hopelessness, and your love covered us with peace that confounded the enemy. Your unrelenting prayers coming before the Father were the spearhead that brought victory. Thank you to Kathy Worton (Warrior Grandma), and to Steve Maxwell, who kept the Silver City Prayer Warriors updated and informed. David and Cathy Maxwell, Paul Maxwell, Ben Wilson, who was a constant pillar of wisdom and guidance, Lyn Wilson, Pastor Ray and Elizabeth McCullum, Pastor Todd and Dana McCullum, David and Kathleen Estes, Jimmy, Tracy, and the Mihnovich Family, Bob and Sharon Perry, Chris Overstreet, and Dean and Tasha Ives, who activated so many prayer warriors throughout the nation. Our gratitude also goes out to Greg and Carol Ives, Todd and Deb Fleury, Pete and Diane Drake, Gillian Tucker, who activated

International House of Prayer in K.C., Angie DeBlieux-Bryan, Chris and Hannah Tiblier, Stu and Lisa Gray, Jon and Claudia Hartman, Chuck and Bobbi Hammett, Leisa Coburn, Dee Calvert, Mark and Debbie Morrison, Lori Jenkins, Bill and Connie Bennett, Scott and Donna Rolin, Valerie Lopez, Jim and Doris Johnson, Jim and Becky Oliver, Chris and Rebecca Hill, Kim and Ricky Wells, John Ford-Colley and Dana Colley, Norm and Donna Auffhammer, Marty Layton, Mark and Ashlie Freeman, Chuck and Cris Peters, Randy and Patti McCoy, Joey and Destiny LeTourneau, Kara Leach Ashbaugh, Sam and Kathi Katina, Paul and Kathy Visconte, Kelly Putty, Greatsthlandhs Australia, Vana Hughes Puckett, Crystal Archie, Melanie Wardlaw Rowe, Lona Heins, Mark and LeeAnn Rampulla, Shane and Heather Pass, Chris and Shannon Cottrell, David and Shannon Sexton, Shannon Saiz, Clay Williams, Sue Hedberg, Amy Rottero, Kristin Shaw, Doug and April Eshleman, Becky Rutland, Laurie Cordoza Moore, Lee and Bethanie Feliciano, Brook Bello, Joe Huntsman, Jennifer Johns, Sandy Culbertson and Wendy Colby Beserra.

To my editor, Loral from Cowriterpro Editorial Services, what a joy and blessing to work with you on my first book. Your work is exceptional. I could not have asked for someone with more insight and wisdom to guide me every step of the way into the completion of a work representing what my heart wanted to express in gratitude. You kept my voice throughout and drew out the music hidden within the words. Somehow, you were able to reach into my inadequacies in writing and express what my soul was feeling in each moment. Thank you for the excellence with which you approach the art of writing.

To Kayla from Selah Press, I have loved working with you on this book. Your enthusiasm and belief in *Don't Mess with This Mama,* has brought such reassurance and inspiration to move forward to completion. Thank you for all you did to make my first manuscript such a great and successful experience.

To Kary Oberbrunner and the Igniting Souls Tribe, your daily encouragement and excellence in preparing me as a new author for my first book release was above and beyond what I could've asked. Thankful God brought you into my path for such a time as this. I look forward to a long and successful relationship.

To my friend and editor Kathy Haskins, who had the overwhelming task of transitioning my first draft from a mountain of grammatical faux pas and spelling errors to a readable book. What a challenge, and you did it all while keeping the mother's heart with which it was written. It's hard to find the right words to adequately thank you for the enormous task you did for me. You are a precious and treasured friend, a gift from God, and an incredible editor. Love you!

Chris Overstreet, you'll never know how thankful we are for your words of encouragement at such a pivotal time in our life. You were the vessel God used to bring words of promise and encouragement straight from the Father to our ears. The moment you stepped off the elevator in Addis Ababa, it activated another level of faith needed for this divine mission. Thank you for your obedience and allowing God to use you in such a powerful and beautiful way.

To Pastor and the prayer warriors at Covenant Church: you and your church brought us in and surrounded us with prayer covering and support. You stood in the gap for us praying continuously, and you helped us to connect with those people who would provide wisdom and encouragement to us when we needed it most. We will never forget our Covenant Church family. We love you.

Pastor Ray McCollum, thank you for your love and insight during this time. Your words of encouragement and your dream that gave prophetic insight into what we were really facing built up our spiritual muscle in a time of weakness. It was that dream that changed Mark's outlook and his response that brought forgiveness to our relationship much sooner than either of us anticipated. Thank you for being a pastor and father figure to both Mark and me. You always had words of wisdom at the perfect time.

Clay Williams, thank you for your friendship and your encouragement to Mark during our time in Ethiopia. Your emails were filled with scripture and prayer, calling Mark up as a mighty warrior during one of his biggest battles ever. You carried his hurt for him, and you spent time listening and in counsel and prayer with him during your calls. We are so grateful for you.

To our family at Celebration Church Congregation, Pastors Ray and Elizabeth McCollum, and Todd and Dana McCollum, you activated the army of prayer warriors at our home church for our cause. We were so thankful to have a church family that prayed for us and reached out to us with poignant verses from the Bible and encouraging words of affirmation and support. You were there for us from the beginning until completion. We love you!

Dave (our driver and body guard), not only were you up every morning before the sun interceding for our case but also you sacrificed time from work to make sure we got safely to court dates and meetings that were part of our journey. Your quiet strength was always in the forefront, and you were a right arm to Mark every time you were with him. You never complained and always smiled. You brought a blanket of peace to our family, and we will eternally be grateful for all you did for us.

Pat and Jody Hilt, when we were in the darkest hour of our journey, you were the light that always shined the brightest. You brought hope into a hopeless situation and help to a family that had nowhere to go. You brought joy into our life every time we saw you, and you were shoulders to cry on when our days were the most difficult. To say “thank you” seems to fall short when compared to the gratitude we have. You were life savers, a sanctuary to weary souls, and the hands of Jesus to our family. Thank you with all our hearts!

Mesfin, you were a true Godsend during our time of greatest need. We will always be thankful that the Lord sent you to help us. You went above and beyond anything we could ask or hope for when you became our lawyer. I remember watching your long discussions with Mark not only about the case but also about family, relationships, and the Lord. You are a man of great character and wisdom, and for a pinnacle moment, you were our voice when we felt we didn't have one. You were a calm, stabilizing pillar that never wavered. We are so grateful for you, and we look forward to having you visit us in America with your family.

Pochi, where to start? We love you dearly. We love your heart for the orphan, as it is like nothing we have ever seen. If it was up to you, every orphan on Earth would be placed in a forever family who values and loves them. That is the heart of God. Thank you for seeing something in us before we saw it in ourselves. You defined us and called us up to be warriors for the orphans. You called out the strength in us when we didn't feel it. You made a way for us time and time again. If you couldn't complete a task, you arranged for someone who could. We were never without assistance—because you were there. Most of all, you surrounded us with people who would love and pray for us. Thank you for believing in us.

Pastor Bezabih, you were always ready to greet us with a smile, open arms, and a warm embrace. Having you near and always available was like having a father in the flesh. I remember watching you absorb Mark's pain the morning after we were stopped at immigration and continuing to encourage both of us throughout our time in Ethiopia. You reinforced that our struggle, though difficult, would be worth the pain we felt at that moment. When we remember you, we remember your joy—because it was that joy that gave us strength.

Emebet, you are one of the bravest women I know! If not for your unquenchable courage, Favor would have never seen America nor been part of our family. We will eternally be grateful for your fearless tenacity to make sure a little girl would grow up in a family who loved, valued, and cared for her as our own. We love you like family, and we are so thankful for everything you did without thought of retribution for Favor—all for the sake of freedom.

Covenant Orphanage Foster Mother, thank you for being the strong fearless woman you are! Thank you for keeping Favor in a safe place until we could come and bring her home to America. You did it out of the kindness of your heart and out of love for a little girl! We will always thank God for the sacrifice you made. Thank you!

DJ, you were one of our mightiest prayer warriors! Thank you for always greeting us with your warm encouraging smile. Your insight and wisdom brought peace to us (especially Mark) as we were just beginning our battle. I will always remember how you shared your dream of the judge handing us the verdict and saying, "You can take your daughter and go home." It inspired us to keep holding on just a little bit longer.

Julie Hedberg, when I look at all the miracles God provided for us in Ethiopia, you are definitely one of them. Thank you for loving on my girls and for being a source of joy and fun for them. You brought a sense of normalcy during a time of confusion and hardship.

Sue Hedberg, you were our angel at immigration! God's timing of having you available to us the night we faced uncertainty was a constant reminder to Mark and I that every detail had already been divinely planned and taken care of. Thank you for your help, prayers, and for your warrior spirit for all the orphans you've fought for through the years to be placed in a loving home. You are a light and a hero for the downtrodden.

Marla at ReachOne Travel, thank you so much for your guidance and support throughout our time in Ethiopia. You were on hand at all hours—day and night—to make sure we had flights available at a moment's notice. You were a Godsend.

Friends at Favor's shower, you gave selflessly to help the orphan and spoke over Favor with words of promise and blessings. Thank you for your words of encouragement and prayers during our time of waiting.

Our many friends at "The Academy," one of my favorite memories was going to the Tea Times you would have on campus. It gave us the joy of getting to know so many of you and your heart for Ethiopia. Thank you for the countless times you stopped and encouraged us every time you would see us. You unrelentingly lifted us up in prayer and encouraged us that what we were fighting for was right—and worth the scars. You welcomed us with open arms, gave us a family in the midst of a storm, and rejoiced with us in our victory. Thank you from the bottom of our hearts!

Tom and LeAnn, thank you for your prayers, hospitality, and making us feel at home in a distant land, and those awesome waffles! You'll never realize how your kindness brought such joy to our family.

TSC soccer family, we are especially thankful for the soccer moms and dads that stepped in to get Shewit to games and practices while we were in Ethiopia—Donna and Jim Whelan, Lisa and Eric Johnson, Amanda and John Agnitch, and Shannon and John Seibert. Your constant encouragement, selfless acts of kindness, and cheering our boy on while we were gone was so appreciated. I especially loved seeing the action shots you sent us of our boy smiling while doing what he does best. It gave me such joy and peace knowing he had a family back home.

To my friends, Tracy and Jimmy, Elle, and family, without your love and constant advocating for the orphans in Ethiopia and worldwide, I would have never had the two blessings I call my son and daughter. I will eternally be grateful for you forwarding a "waiting children" email that led us to Shewit, and later bringing Favor into our life. Without you, there would be no adventure to write about. You are God-given, dear, and beloved forever friends divinely placed to change the trajectory of our path in order to fulfill God's purpose in our lives. We thank you! We love you!

To the staff at Hilton Addis Ababa, thank you for your kindness, excellence, and attention to detail. You had our backs during a crucial time, and you provided a safe place and protection when we needed it. We will always know where to stay when we return to Addis Ababa!

To our friends, Kimberly and Alberto Rivera, thank you for allowing God to use your gifts to bring forth music that inspires, heals, builds faith, and opens eyes to see into another dimension. The sound you release exhorts us to rise above the noise in this world and see the unseen. Although I didn't know you at the time of our Ethiopian adventure, you have become one of our dearest and treasured friends. We love you!

To my sisters in Christ who constantly lifted me up in prayer, encouraged me, and reminded me of my identity in Christ and who I was created to be: you, my friends, believed in me when I struggled to finish this book in the midst of loss and pain. You believed there was an audience who needed this story of faith, and you never stopped telling me I could do it! Lisa Gray, Bobbi Hammett, Claudia Hartman, Adrienne Evans, Kathleen Estes, Kimberly Rivera, Monique Taylor, Christine Johnson, Joan Turley, Gretel Rowland, Kim Wells, Dana Colley, Dana McCullum, Joy Willard, Shannon Cottrell, Angie Deblieux, Rebecca Alonzo, Wendy Porcelli, Corina Pataki, Lona Fraser and the Heartprint Writers Group, thank you for continuing to believe in this book, and for encouraging me to keep writing the many times I felt like putting down the pen. I love each one of you so much!

To my powerhouse friend, Angie Deblieux, you were always doing all you could within your power to bring us home, whether that was contacting senators or news reporters. Thank you for believing in our story and encouraging me to write it so that others would learn of God's unfailing faithfulness in our impossible situation. You have been a cheerleader and constant advocate for *Don't Mess with This Mama*. Your guidance and wisdom is unparalleled. Thank you for being a friend to me and my family on our toughest days, for your prayers, and for your love. We love you!

Lori Jenkins, you went above and beyond what we could ask in a friend. You believed in the calling God had on our lives through this story. You did battle in the States for us contacting senators and congressmen, and battled on your knees crying out for our victory. You are a true and loyal friend. Thank you for all you did for us.

Jesus, thank You for the calling you entrusted us with. Thank You for Your saving grace and for meeting us again and again when we needed You most. There is no *Don't Mess with This Mama* without You. This is and has always been Your story. We pray You are glorified in it. We love You!

And finally, to those that are not listed by name, but who prayed for our circumstances—we thank you, for without your prayers joining in a single cause for the plight of a little girl named Favor, this victory would've never come to reality. We are positive that the mighty God we serve will reward you greatly for every moment you held our situation in prayer.

NOTES

Chapter 1

Rick Joyner, *The Final Quest*, MorningStar Publications, Incorporated, 2010.

1. Graham Cooke, message given at the 2015 Blue Moon Rising Prophetic Conference, Franklin, Tennessee, June 24–27, 2015, Larry Randolph Ministries, larryrandolph.com.

Chapter 2

C.S. Lewis, *Essay Collection: Faith, Christianity and the Church*, Harper Collins, 2002.

1. Bimal Kanta Nayak, Orphan Problems and Community Concern in Ethiopia, *International Journal of Management and Social Sciences Research (IJMSSR),* January 2014: 9.

Chapter 9

Christine Caine, *Undaunted: daring to do what God calls you to do*, Zondervan, Sep 11, 2012.

Chapter 10

Rick Joyner, *The Final Quest*, MorningStar Publications, Incorporated, 2010.

Chapter 11
Christine Caine, *Undaunted: daring to do what God calls you to do*, Zondervan, Sep 11, 2012.

Chapter 22
Thomas Hauser, *The Boxing Scene*, Temple University Press, Jan 28, 2009, 122.

Chapter 23
1. "A Life on Fire—The Legacy of A World Changer: Reinard Bonnke," Christ for All Nations, https://new.cfan.org/reinhard-bonnke/, accessed July 3, 2018.

Chapter 24
Hermann Hesse Quotes. BrainyQuote.com, BrainyMedia Inc, 2018. https://www.brainyquote.com/quotes/hermann_hesse_384604, accessed November 20, 2018.
1. Grant R. Jeffrey, *The New Temple and the Second Coming*, Waterbrook Press Colorado Springs, Co, 2007.

   Leo Roberts, "Travelling in the Highlands of Ethiopia, " *National Geographic*, (September. 1935): 297.

   "From B'nai B'rith Messenger," *National Geographic*, January 1935.

   "Where Is the Ark of the Covenant?" Bloomfield, 39.

Chapter 27
Mark Batterson, *The Circle Maker* (Zondervan, 2011).

Chapter 29
1. "FAA will review Boeing 787 design and production," *Federal Aviation Administration*, January 11, 2013.

"Dreamliner plane review ordered by US Regulators," *BBC News*, January 11, 2013, https://www.bbc.com/news/business-20988117, accessed November 20, 2018.

"Dreamliner: Boeing 787 planes grounded on safety fears," *BBC News*, January 17, 2013, https://www.bbc.com/news/business-21054089, accessed November 20, 2018.

"All Boeing Dreamliners Are Grounded Worldwide," *The Wall Street Journal*, https://www.wsj.com/articles/SB10001424127887323783704578246213461653662, accessed November 20, 2018.

Epilogue

1. "Adoption Advocates International in Port Angeles Shuts down," *Peninsula Daily News*, https://www.peninsuladailynews.com/news/adoption-advocates-international-in-port-angeles-shuts-down-2/, accessed May 1, 2019.

   Claudia Corigan D'Arcy, "Adoption Advocates International Shuts Down!" Musings of the Lame, March 14, 2014, accessed November 20, 2018. https://www.adoptionbirthmothers.com/adoption-advocates-international-shuts-down/.

2. Ethiopia bans foreign adoption, *BBC News*, https://www.bbc.com/news/world-africa-42635641, accessed November 20, 2018.

ABOUT THE AUTHOR

Missy Maxwell Worton, is an author, speaker, former actress/singer/dancer in a nationally faith-based Broadway-style musical company dealing with family and faith issues.

She writes across media, not only as an author but also as a film and television writer. She exudes joy in all she does, and she loves being in God's presence as a worshiper. Missy's church ministry involvements have included leading worship as well as being in children's and women's ministries.

Missy's greatest desire is to awaken women to the superpower they have within them as a daughter of a mighty and loving God. She encourages women to fearlessly and courageously pursue the greatness and dreams they were created for by empowering them to fulfill their unique destiny callings.

She believes women can be among the strongest voices for justice to impact, influence, and transform the culture around them. She equips them to better the lives of others by bringing lasting change through the power of love and kindness.

Missy speaks on courage, adoption, adoptive family transition, inspiring mamas to become even better equipped for their God-given role, and a host of other life issues. She is an advocate for the orphan, the unborn, enslaved and trafficked. She is a devoted wife, and deeply invested in the lives of her four children. She loves being a soccer mom and playing board games with her family, as well as exercising with her dog.

To learn more about Missy Maxwell Worton, please visit: missymaxwellworton.com.

Your journey with Missy and Mark doesn't have to end here – they would like to help you build a lasting legacy.

DON'T MESS *With This* MAMA

Risking It All to Rescue Our Daughter

A TRUE STORY

MISSY MAXWELL WORTON

FOREWORD BY CHRIS OVERSTREET

Start by getting a FREE GIFT a
missymaxwellworton.com

For Coaching/Training or to book Missy & Mark at your next event or continue your adventure with:

- Unstoppable Trainings
- Marriage Retreats
- International Events

ERIN MCCAFFREY PHOTOGRAPHY

Learn more at missymaxwellworton.com

Made in the USA
Las Vegas, NV
28 March 2021